Tim

Keep the balance

Regards

THE STRESS STRATEGISTS

Failure is an event, never a person.

—Dr. William D. Brown

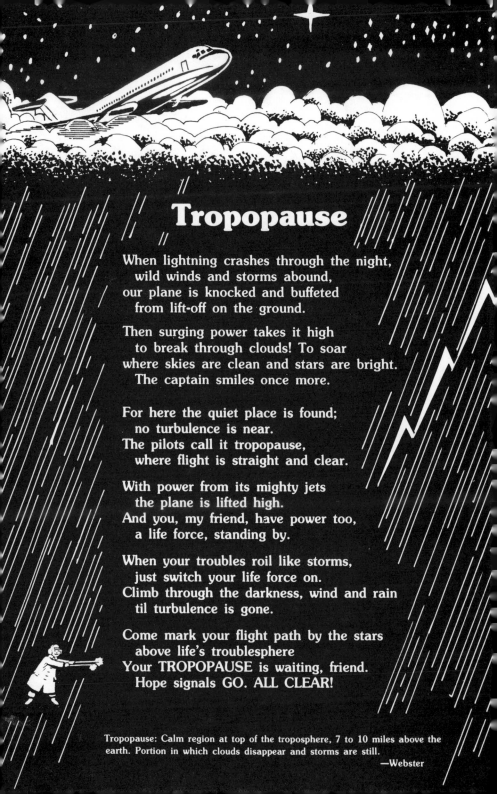

Tropopause

When lightning crashes through the night,
  wild winds and storms abound,
our plane is knocked and buffeted
  from lift-off on the ground.

Then surging power takes it high
  to break through clouds! To soar
where skies are clean and stars are bright.
  The captain smiles once more.

For here the quiet place is found;
  no turbulence is near.
The pilots call it tropopause,
  where flight is straight and clear.

With power from its mighty jets
  the plane is lifted high.
And you, my friend, have power too,
  a life force, standing by.

When your troubles roil like storms,
  just switch your life force on.
Climb through the darkness, wind and rain
  til turbulence is gone.

Come mark your flight path by the stars
  above life's troublesphere
Your TROPOPAUSE is waiting, friend.
  Hope signals GO. ALL CLEAR!

Tropopause: Calm region at top of the troposphere, 7 to 10 miles above the
earth. Portion in which clouds disappear and storms are still.

—Webster

*We dedicate this book
to the founder of the*
National Speakers Association

Cavett Robert
C.P.A.E., Chairman Emeritus

The Good Book tells us that "Perfect Love casts out fear." Since fear is the basis of stress, love must also conquer stress. **Cavett Robert** is known among the speakers of the world as their "Ambassador of Love."

He is the inspiration, the encouragement, the lighter of lights for speakers, who love him as wholeheartedly as do his international audiences.

COLONEL CHARLES WESLEY SCOTT
U.S. Army (Retired)
569 Chatham Trail
Jonesboro, Georgia 30236
(404) 471-7748

Colonel Charles Wesley Scott

After enlisting in the Army in 1949, Chuck Scott rose through all the enlisted and commissioned ranks from recruit to full colonel before his retirement in 1981 with almost 32 years active service. A highly-decorated combat infantry veteran, the Pentagon called him the best qualified Mideast specialist in the Army and their top expert on the Arab (Persian) Gulf region. In March 1985, after three weeks on the frontlines with the Iraqi Army, he wrote an eight part newspaper series on the Iran-Iraq war. To date he is the only journalist the Iraqis have permitted to visit the war front.

The Distinguished Service Medal, Silver Star and Bronze Star are among his more than two dozen military awards and decorations. His many civilian honors include: Southeast Father of the Year and the Nonfiction Author of the Year Award in 1984 by the Dixie Council of Authors and Journalists for his book "PIECES OF THE GAME." A summa cum laude graduate of St. Benedict's College, Chuck is a certified translator in three languages including Persian (Farsi).

Even after extensive combat duty and the incredibly stressful ordeal he endured during the 444 days he was held hostage in Iran, Chuck has emerged with his wry sense of humor intact. He is a politically savvy speaker who brings to the lecture circuit a spellbinding presence that has thrilled audiences on three continents.

Prologue
by Colonel Charles Wesley Scott

It was my month at Gethsemane. A month of torture, relentless interrogation, near starvation and haunting threats of a slow and agonizing death.

It was November 1979 and I was a pawn in the international chess game history would call the Iranian Hostage Crisis. My militant Islamic fundamentalist jailors believed I was a CIA operative, a spy. They were determined to legitimize their seizure of our Tehran Embassy by beating an espionage confession out of me.

Finally, in early December, the physical torture and the questioning ended, but the psychological torment continued: e.g., late one winter night, I was dragged from my prison cell and spread-eagled against a wall as a firing squad moved into position behind me. I heard the commands in Persian: "Get ready!" and, seconds later, "Take aim!"...and I heard live ammunition clicking into the chambers of their G-3 automatic rifles. I thought it was all over and I prayed that I would die quickly, denying my tormentors a final spectacle over which to gloat.

Over and over, for the longest half hour of my life, they repeated the first two commands of the firing squad sequence, but they never fired. Finally I was moved inside and strip-searched. The cruel drama had not been staged to murder me. It was a calculated act of raw terror, designed to break my will; to make me beg for my life.

Physical scars of my 444 days as a hostage remain, but, thankfully, there have been no emotional scars at all.

The Iranians got nothing from me, and when it was over, I had won the toughest battle of my life. It wasn't luck or courage that got me through, it was my method of harnessing harmful stress and making it work in a positive way. I describe this technique in my book "Pieces of the Game" and in my stress management and inspirational speeches. It involves mental self-management, physical exercise and setting realistic goals. This strategy works for me and it can work for you—even when the going is really tough.

Briefly, my goal-setting technique is based on the observation that when one is subjected to severe mental or physical pressure, one's willpower may become a "floating line." One loses perspective, rationalizes and may do or say things that would be unthinkable under normal conditions.

When the pressure is unbearable, goals become our guidestones, helping keep things in perspective by focusing our attention and commitment on the standards of conduct and performance we set for ourselves in them. Goals help us most when our flagging willpower tends to become a "floating line."

I know that if I hadn't used this technique during my long ordeal in Iran, eventually, my spirit would have been broken. Then I would have lost the only thing the Iranians never succeeded in taking away from me: my integrity and honor.

Nothing in life is to be feared.
It is only to be understood.

—Marie Curie

DR. NORMAN VINCENT PEALE
1025 Fifth Avenue
New York, New York, 10028

Dr. Norman Vincent Peale

Author of thirty-one books, of which THE POWER OF POSITIVE THINKING, one of the most successful books ever published, has been translated into forty languages, with a sale of over 15 million copies worldwide. The title has become part of the language. The latest book is his biography, THE TRUE JOY OF POSITIVE LIVING.

Dr. and Mrs. Peale are co-editors and publishers of the inspirational monthly magazine, GUIDEPOSTS, circulation of 4.6 million paid subscribers, with 15 million readers each month.

Messages by Dr. Peale are mailed to 850,000 people monthly from the Foundation for Christian Living, Pawling, New York. Over 31 million copies of his inspirational booklets are distributed yearly.

Awards: Presidential Medal of Freedom, presented by President Reagan at a White House ceremony, All Time Great Ohioan Award, Society for the Family of Man Joint Medallion to Ruth and Norman Peale, and 27 other awards.

Is heard daily on 442 radio stations in THE AMERICAN CHARACTER, sponsored by ITT Corporation, and a weekly radio series entitled POSITIVE THINKING WITH NORMAN VINCENT PEALE, heard coast to coast on powerful 50,000 watt stations.

Writes syndicated weekly newspaper column, POSITIVE THINKING, for leading dailies.

Two thirty-minute films featuring Dr. Peale, HOW TO BE A REAL SALESMAN and HOW TO RAISE YOUR BATTING AVERAGE IN SELLING are shown by many companies to their salesmen.

Has received 18 honorary doctoral degrees.

Introduction
by Dr. Norman Vincent Peale

I think the title "The Stress Strategists" by Dottie Walters is great. Dottie is always coming up with creative ideas to help all of us live better lives.

Certainly no one can be at his or her best until one becomes a stress strategist; until he or she becomes master of stress, using it creatively. Properly handled and directed, stress can produce energy. And that energy can be channeled to maximum effectiveness. All truly successful people are stress strategists in that they are controllers, masters and engineers of the energy factor which the Creator places in every human being.

One of the wisest physicians ever to practice the science of medicine was the famous Doctor Sir William Osler. He always advised his medical students of the quality of unperturbability. He said, "No quality ranks with unperturbability. It is the essential bodily virtue." And no doubt the Doctor would rate it highly as a mental virtue also, for he described unperturbability as "coolness and presence of mind under all circumstances, calmness amid the storm, clearness of judgement in moments of grave peril." And he added, "It is a blessing to you and a comfort to all who come in contact with you."

We usually think of stress as something bad that should be gotten rid of. On the contrary, stress means "emphasis upon" and therefore can be either good or bad depending upon our thoughts concerning it and our control of the emotions involved. Hence it is vitally important to be a stress strategist—one who uses beneficial force and emphasis to bring about good results.

Anyone who has the will and enthusiasm to stress courage, belief, faith, confidence and a sum total of good values, who emphasizes the best in life, is a stress strategist of the highest order.

I knew the famous American poet, the late

Edwin Markham, one of whose great lines was "At the heart of the cyclone tearing the sky is a place of central calm." He is wisely saying that the greatest force is generated out of a calm center. A person who maintains, at the center of life, an undisturbable calmness like "the peace of God that passeth all understanding" is at once a master and correct user of stress. He is a super stress strategist.

It is for this reason that we practice positive thinking for it is controlled, though up-beat in nature, and creatively utilizes stress as a positive asset.

To be under pressure is inescapable. Pressure takes place through all the world: war, siege, the worries of state. We all know people who grumble under these pressures, and complain. They are cowards. They lack splendor. But there is another sort of person who is under the same pressure, but does not complain. For it is the friction which polishes us. It is the pressure which refines and makes us noble.

—*St. Augustine*

DR. KEN DYCHTWALD
Dychtwald & Associates
1023 Amito Avenue
Berkeley, CA 94705
(415) 839-9311

xviii

Dr. Ken Dychtwald

Ken Dychtwald Ph.D. is a psychologist, gerontologist, lecturer, author and outspoken figure in the fields of human development, health promotion, stress-management and aging.

Presently, he is President of a consulting firm, Dychtwald & Associates, with offices in Berkeley, California and Washington, D.C.; was the Founding Director of the "Institute on Aging, Health and Work" of the Washington Business Group on Health; is the Director of the Bodymind Training Institute of Scandinavia; and serves as Senior Advisor for the Task Force on Aging Studies, El Camino Hospital.

In his capacity as an authority on aging, life planning, wellness/health promotion and stress-management, he has consulted with and/or conducted programs and seminars for a variety of corporations, health facilities and government agencies.

Dr. Dychtwald is also an adjunct instructor in psychology, gerentology and health related sciences at several colleges and universities, and frequently appears on television and radio shows throughout North America, the Merv Griffin Show, CBS Morning, A.M. Los Angeles, and A.M. San Francisco.

His publications include: BODYMIND *(translated into nine foreign languages),* Millennium: Glimpses Into the 21st Century *(translated into three foreign languages),* Stress-Management: Take Charge of Your Life, Wellness and Health Promotion for the Elderly, The Aging of America *(forthcoming), and more than one hundred articles in professional journals and popular magazines.*

Foreword

Managing Stress:
The 20th Century Challenge
by Ken Dychtwald, Ph.D.

America is experiencing a major epidemic today. Unlike epidemics of the past, it is not a disease transmitted by bacteria or viruses. This epidemic is an increase in diseases and problems related to stress, and it touches all our lives.

Stress: A Modern Epidemic

Why has America become so excessively stress-ridden? There seem to be three primary reasons. First, life in the Twentieth Century is extremely hectic. In the past 50 years we have entered the atomic age, the space age and the computer age; the global population has more than doubled; and the gross national product has quadrupled. We are constantly bombarded by new information and sensory input. Rapid change has become a way of life. We are told that 50 percent of all married couples get divorced, and that 80 percent of all divorced people remarry. The average American changes jobs every three years and moves every five. In sum, the pace and pressure of modern living have reached near-lethal proportions. We are no longer living in the "fast lane." It seems that we have moved into the "laser track."

Second, with the advent of urban civilization, we abruptly changed from being vigorous and active, to living an almost *sedentary lifestyle.* Humans once spent 10 to 15 hours a day in physical activity and labor. We now spend almost all of our time on mental activities that involve very little movement or exercise. Not only does our sedentary lifestyle deprive us of a healthful physical outlet for our stress, but it also makes our bodies and minds less fit to withstand its effect.

Third, despite the tremendous increase in the pace and pressure of living, *most people are ill equipped to cope effectively with mounting stress.* As never before in human history, we are constantly barraged with pollutants, noise, information, and rapid lifestyle change, and for the first time in human evolution, our physical, mental, and social support systems are just not hardy enough to withstand the pressures we impose on them.

The Stress-Response: An Ancient Mechanism for Survival

Technically speaking, *stress is a physiological condition of the body—a state of arousal and excitation in response to a perceived danger or threat.* We are all familiar with the physical signs and symptoms of the stress state. Think about how you felt the last time you had to swerve to avoid a collision while driving: your heart raced, your blood pressure rose, your senses intensified, your palms became sweaty, your muscles tensed, your stomach knotted and your attention narrowed.

This reaction, sometimes referred to as the *fight or flight response* is the result of a complex physiological chain reaction which occurs in your body in response to a threat. Our prehistoric ancestors, on encountering a dangerous animal in the wild, would have felt exactly the same response, as their bodies switched into a stress-induced "high gear" to deal with the emergency.

As the term implies, *the original purpose of the fight-or-flight response was to prepare the body to respond either by fighting the enemy, or by fleeing.* Whether the primitive hunter succeeded in killing the mountain lion, or in running away from it, the result was the same: once the threat was resolved, the body could relax, eventually returning to its normal baseline functioning.

As a primitive survival mechanism, the fight-or-flight response served our ancestors well as a means of mobilizing the body's defenses in times of emergency. Why, then, has stress become such a problem in modern life?

In the case of the primitive hunter, once the danger was dealt with by fighting or fleeing, the problem was resolved and the stress was relieved. However, if we look around us today, we will notice that *the options of* **fighting** *or* **fleeing** *are rarely appropriate in our modern world.* For example, if you have an argument with your boss, you may feel all the symptoms of stress—tense muscles, rapid heartbeat, rapid breathing—but you can't relieve your stress by striking out at him, nor would it do to run away. And so the level of anger, frustration or arousal persists in the absence of socially acceptable outlet, and at the end of the confrontation you still feel as if you want to fight or run away. The fight-or-flight response has now become an internalized feeling that you carry about with you, like a ticking bomb. It's as though you are now a *"stress response looking for a place to go off."*

If the fight-or-flight response is activated without

being used for its intended purpose, it can become a major source of distress. If it is fired off too often, or persists too long, the body remains in a state of continual alarm or mobilization, and the potent hormones released in the stress response can actually damage the body's vital organs, the nervous system and the immune mechanisms. Ironically, *it appears that the* **stress response,** *which was a vital survival mechanism for our remote ancestors,* **may in fact be killing us today.**

It is because of the day-to-day buildup of unrelieved stress in modern life that we are experiencing an epidemic of stress-related problems and diseases. In fact, *it is estimated that a huge 85 percent of the mental and physical ailments in America today are stress-related!* Many of the common minor disorders, such as headaches, tight muscles, constipation, high blood pressure, insomnia, ulcers, irritibility and chronic depression, which we often dismiss as "just a part of life," may actually be early warning signs of excessive stress. In fact, Stress may well be the single greatest deterrent today to health, long life and productivity.

Stress Can be Managed

However, Stress does not have to be a negative experience; in fact, well-managed stress can represent a valuable mechanism for transformation and growth.

The Chinese language contains a clue to the two sides of stress. *The Chinese character for "crisis" is composed of the symbols for "danger" and "opportunity."* While stress can be damaging, at the same time it can challenge us to grow. In the positive stress cycle, when we are confronted with stressors, we respond in a way that promotes growth, reinforces the development of effective coping mechanisms, and leads to even greater strength when we are confronted with new stressors.

In this volume, many of America's leading experts on high performance behavior share their tips, techniques and strategies for effective stress-management. From their collective wealth of experience and knowledge they challenge us to harness the power and energy of the stress in our lives—to use stress as a fuel for positive action, and remove it from being a barrier to the realization of our personal and professional goals and dreams.

They show us how the sense of elation and accomplishment that comes from dealing effectively with stress enhances our own self confidence and makes us even more capable of dealing with stressors in the future. In this way, the stress of modern life can ultimately become a source of challenge, richness of experience, and enhanced mental and physical vitality.

The *Stress* Strategists

C O N T E N T S

Peter Ueberroth tells how he staged a wildly successful magical Olympic Games amidst pressure... all people needed was a rallying point to give them reason to stand up and cheer for their country, their communities, themselves and share their great spirit with the peoples of the world.

LOU PEEL
Lou Peel Institute
P.O. Box 1684
Hutchinson, KS 67504-1684
Bus. (316) 662-1200 • Res. (316) 662-7154

Lou Peel

Lou Peel was on board the ill-fated TWA Flight #847, hijacked in Athens, Greece. Her husband, son Bob, and daughter-in-law Kristi were also on board, along with 149 other passengers and crew members. The date: June 14, 1985.

The plane had just taken off on a flight from Athens to Rome when it was hijacked. Its subsequent odyssey took it to Algiers twice and Beirut three times. Lou Peel was among the group released on the plane's first visit to Beirut.

Her daughter-in-law was released two days later. Lou's husband was released after three days and nights on board the plane. Lou Peel's son, Bobby, was one of the 39 hostages held until June 30, 1985.

From these events and stories, Lou Peel has put together an unforgettable chapter. There are lessons in this nightmare for all of us.

Lou Peel, a successful and dynamic business woman, is President of Lou Peel's Institute and Vice President of Peel's Beauty Supply Co. She is a well known radio and television personality, who specializes in helping thousands of people, both individually and in groups, work toward these goals.

Lou Peel is a respected member of the National Speakers Association, Toastmaster International, and International Platform Association. She has been awarded a Certificate of Merit for Distinguished Achievement in The World Who's Who of Women.

TWA Flight 847—HIJACKED
by Lou Peel

"Courage mounteth with occasion."
—Shakespeare

"Trans-World Airlines Flight 887—Cancelled." The numbers were posted in the Athens airport and a wave of disappointment swept over the four of us.

We were ending a beautiful seven-day cruise aboard a yacht owned by dear friends. The

Mediterranean had been lovely, but we were weary and anxious to return home. My husband, Bob, had fallen and injured his ribs during the cruise, and our son Bobby and his wife Kristi were anxious to return home to their three daughters.

TWA Flight 887—Cancelled. Disappointing to say the least. Bobby seated Kristi and me in the waiting area of the airport, and he and Bob rushed off to make other reservations for our return. It was June 14, 1985.

The Athens airport was a flurry of people— people hurrying to catch flights, standing in line for tickets, checking luggage and waiting to rearrange reservations. Kristi and I visited about our cruise and discussed the treasures we had purchased during our various shopping trips...prayer beads, gold coin charms, lovely dolls and cute tee shirts for her girls.

I heard my husband arguing with the female ticket agent. The time was 9:55 a.m. Bob and Bobby had arranged another flight on TWA 847, which should have left at 8:55 a.m. The TWA clerk said, "Hurry, the plane is about to leave. I can't give you assigned seats. You will just have to find seats on your own. Hurry."

We passed through the security check point. I thought it odd that the security men were several feet away drinking coffee. We were in such a hurry, I almost forgot my purse. I quickly grabbed it, and the TWA clerk rushed us across the field to the plane.

When we got aboard there were no seats together, so we scattered; two on one side of the plane and two on the other side. I managed to get a window seat and relaxed as I looked forward to watching the take-off and beautiful clouds. Maybe we could sit together after our arrival in Rome. The plane lifted and began to level out.

Terror in the Air

Suddenly, two men came running down the aisle from the back of the plane. I have never seen men run so quickly. I thought someone was hurt, sick in some way or had fainted and they were rushing to help. They were not tall men and were slight in build, between 18 and 20 years of age. They were dressed similar to airline stewards, in white shirts and black pants.

I heard the wheels click into position just as the speaker was turned on. Our head flight stewardess, Uli Derickson, announced, "Ladies and gentlemen... we have just been hijacked!" We were told to be very calm and very still because our lives were in danger.

One of the hijackers took over the microphone and in English demanded, "Put your head to your knees and fold your hands over your head...NOW!"

I thought at first I was dreaming. A very bad

dream. There was no hysteria, screaming or crying from the passengers. I heard the terrorists running back and forth. They were running so fast I couldn't see anything they were doing, plus we had to keep our heads down the whole time. I later learned a terrorist had pulled the pin on a hand grenade and that is why 153 people could do nothing.

The atmosphere in the plane was noisy—the terrorists shouted constantly. I really couldn't understand what they were saying because I was so scared.

Hunched over in what is now known as the "847 position" (head between knees, hands clasped behind the head), thoughts kept going through my mind about being safe and walking down steps of the TWA plane...seeing myself walk through the front door of my home. Prayers became a way of release. I remember saying the Lord's Prayer over and over in my mind..."Forgive those who trespass against us"...you cannot believe what enters the mind at that time.

They Demand Passports

The two men were moving all the people in first class to other seats. The hijackers were very loud, screaming at the passengers as they moved them to other seats. They demanded passports, which Uli began picking up, and asked who was military...who was with the government...to come forward. They demanded whoever had tape recorders to bring them forward. I had two in my suitcase, but it was in the luggage compartment.

A young man sitting across from me said he had one in his attache case in first class...he left. He had a flowered shirt on exactly like the murdered Navy diver wore in pictures I later saw. I don't know if he was the Navy man or not. I remember thinking what a nice looking young man he was, as we'd entered the plane earlier.

I heard no noise other than the sound of the hijackers running and shouting. The terrorists moved all the men to window seats and the women to aisle seats. But as we approached Lebanon, I was still sitting in a window seat.

After a brief time I heard the plane landing. The blind covering my window was only half-way down, and I turned my head and looked out at the barren ground. One of the terrorists screamed at me, "What are you doing?" At that moment, I looked into a shiny silver and gold gun he pointed at me. I nearly died. My head went back down, but before it did, I glanced at him. What a good looking young man I later thought...beautiful brown strong eyes... small well-kept beard.

Run for Your Life

Uli came next to me and said, "Come quick...leave

your purse... RUN! Run for your life! I slid down the emergency slide near the galley. The wind was blowing and it was hot...like a hot windy Kansas day. I could see the airport. My family didn't see me leave, as their heads were still down.

I heard a voice say to me, "RUN, RUN, NO.... You are going the wrong way!" It was confusing. I wanted to run away from those guys and they wanted me to run to them. I turned and ran the other way toward a pale cream-colored van with no windows. Black machine guns were everywhere. The men rushed me to the back of the van and opened the door.

I was the last one in, I think. As I sat down, I looked on the floor of the van and saw a huge stretcher, green in color. That was the most frightening thing to me—not knowing what would happen to us. The women in the van were crying, and I said, "Let's hold hands. It's going to be all right." Nineteen of us had been released in Beirut: two children and 17 women.

One soldier said we would not be hurt. Looking at all the machine guns around us, I wasn't too sure. We were taken in the van to the other side of the very small airport and ushered inside. Twenty machine guns and twenty hand guns were turned on us. I looked at the soldier who'd told me we would not be harmed and asked if I could go to the bathroom. When I found it, the doors were locked.

They gave us a drink of water and it tasted delicious. We were greeted by the head of the Beirut airport and were then escorted to the Mid-East Airline terminal where we boarded a plane.

Civilians on the plane asked all kinds of questions. Some hostages said we were on the plane three-and-a-half hours; others believed five hours. To me it seemed like an eternity. At one point the steward said something to me very quickly in English, but I couldn't understand what he said.

They served us orange juice and a very different type of raisin cake, but I couldn't touch it. I went to the back of the plane to the bathroom and saw the steward again. I asked him to write on a piece of paper what he'd said to me. He said very abruptly he didn't have time.

As I left the plane in Cyprus, to my surprise he handed me the note. It was later turned over to the FBI in St. Louis, Missouri. The message in the note remains a blur, but I will never forget the last word--"Piracy."

A Barrage of Questions

After our arrival in Cyprus, we were taken to a special airport room where we filled out many reports and were asked many, many questions. The debriefing and completion of forms took about two hours. The forms were necessary to get us in and out of the country, since the hijackers had taken our passports.

All of our clothes and cash had also been left behind on the plane. We in the first group of freed hostages did not have any jewelry taken from our bodies—we lost only what was left on the plane in our purses and luggage. But my family said after we left the plane, everyone had everything taken from them. Purses and carry-ons were dumped on the floor, and the hijackers took all jewelry and cash.

The American embassy in Cyprus took complete control of our situation. Our government immediately loaned each of us $200 in cash. All I wanted to buy was some shampoo, a comb and lipstick. We were given plastic bags to carry our money and small purchases in. These bags were a gift from a pharmaceutical company. We were all lovingly teased and called the "bag ladies."

I was the first one to talk to the press in Cyprus. I definitely feel Toastmasters' impromptu exercises are rewarding in many phases of life, and this was no exception. I had confidence in myself, and strong feelings that things would be all right with complete protection from the American embassy in Cyprus. The embassy officials were a fantastic team of men. They worked together and handled the press so the press wouldn't take advantage of the situation.

When I received a call in my room from U.S

newsman Dan Rather, I was in Paris, waiting for the safe return of my family. He wanted to tell me of his great concern for my family, and asked if I would explain what had happened prior to my release. I have no way of knowing if I was quoted.

Sixteen Harrowing Days

The chronological events are well known:

- June 14, 1985—TWA Flight 847 carrying 153 passengers and crew from Athens to Rome was hijacked by Shiite Moslem Lebanese. Its subsequent odyssey took it to Algiers (twice) and Beirut (three times). I was released June 14 in Beirut.
- June 15, 1985—One American was killed. He was Robert Stethem, 23 years old, a Navy frogman from Waldorf, Maryland.
- June 16, 1985—My daughter-in-law, Kristi Peel, was released in Algiers and joined me in Paris.
- June 17, 1985—My husband, Bob Peel, was released due to poor health (injuries received during the yacht trip). 37 passengers and three crew members remained aboard the ill-fated TWA 847 (all of them at this point were American men, including my son, Bobby). They were later taken from the plane in Beirut, with the exception of the three crewmen, and held in various homes throughout the city.

The terrorists demanded that Israel release

approximately 700 Shiite Lebanese prisoners who were arrested by the Israeli Army during its withdrawal from southern Lebanon , and were being held without charge in a prison in Israel.

• June 19, 1985—My husband joined us in Paris.

• June 30, 1985—My son Bobby was released along with 39 other hostages (including the crew).

The thought that went through my mind as I viewed my son entering the Red Cross car in Beirut, bound for Damascus was, "Thank God, he is safe." A friend had invited me over to watch via her satellite. Chills went over me and I gave my prayers of thanksgiving. There aren't words to express my feelings of gratitude for the safety of my family. We were only able to cope with our ordeal through constant prayer and positive thoughts.

I felt President Reagan did everything in his power to obtain the release of the hostages. There were many things working for us that were not obvious to anyone not directly involved. During the ordeal, I did not take any action to try to contact President Reagan. I had total confidence in our government and in our president.

I was very pleased when my son arrived (from Germany) in Washington, D.C. When we boarded the plane in Washington for Kansas and home, he asked for some paper. Then, sitting quietly, he wrote a letter to the captain of the plane we were on.

He wrote that he really appreciated the captain

more than ever before. After we landed, the captain greeted him saying, "Thank you for the letter, Bobby Peel. We appreciate having you home."

The Men's Ordeal

Bobby had lost 16 pounds. He told us that while the hostages were held on the plane, they were served dry bread and cheese. The first day they also received an orange, an omelet and a glass of water with ice. Then bottled water was passed around, with no glasses. This was the only food provided during their many flights.

Bobby said after the hostages were taken to different homes in Beirut, his diet consisted of pita bread, feta cheese and on occasion, cold chicken and rice from Mid-East Airlines. There were no plates or silverware used. The hostages drank bottled water or Pepsi (Coca Cola is not served in Lebanon, since the Israelis drink Coke).

Bobby said while in Lebanese homes, they were treated well overall. The worst part was the mental stress—living with the fear they might be held there for six months or a year. One of the guards brought his child to meet the hostages, and one of the guard's sisters offered to wash the Americans' clothes. One night when the food didn't show up, one of the guards went on top of the flat roof and cooked two chickens over charcoal.

When my son was on the Army plane to Germany, he was served veal parmesan in the form of a TV dinner. He said, "Mom, it was the best I ever tasted."

Bobby also lost feeling in three of his fingers as a result of the ordeal. The Army doctors in Germany said his fingers had gone numb from sitting in the "847 position" for so long that the knee exerted too much pressure on a nerve in his elbow. He is slowly regaining feeling in his fingers now. My son slept three days and nights when he returned home.

The Aftermath

For my husband, son and daughter-in-law Kristi... real rest is just now coming to us all. We were physically and mentally exhausted. We're getting back to normal slowly. We received our baggage only recently (mid-July). The locks on my husband's luggage had been cut out with a razor blade, and four pair of shoes and one camera had been taken.

My suitcase had been jumped on, leaving the exterior rippled. The contents looked like they had been stirred with an egg-beater. My white things were spotted with rust, and there were insects in everything. My two tape recorders were still in the suitcase, but one nightgown was taken.

We have been asked by TWA to submit a list of what was missing. They have worked to help us in every possible way and I am proud to say they are a fine company.

We've received two phone calls from hostages I became acquainted with in Cyprus. Bobby is in contact with and very close to some of the friends he made among the hostages during captivity, and he plans to attend the upcoming wedding of one of them.

What Can We Learn

Flying had been a real challenge to me in my early life. I used to prefer traveling by train (ha). Eventually I found it took too long to travel by train, and now I am way over a million-miler in planes. My thoughts remain that travel overseas is one of my biggest goals and dreams; going around the world is the greatest thing ever. Yes, I shall continue to travel.

If I were asked for tips on traveling abroad, I would list the following.

- Have your attorney prepare a current will.
- Insure the jewelry you wear.
- Carry travelers checks. Ours were all replaced by the bank. All our cash was taken. It is not insured unless specifically covered by an insurance company. Even then, it is sometimes not entirely covered.
- Carry only credit cards you will use on the trip.
- Don't carry your safe deposit box key, or other

unnecessary keys.

• Pack a wash-and-wear shirt or dress. I lived for fived days in the same dress and slept in a towel.

I do believe that to prevent hijackings, airport security should be strengthened, and all luggage checked prior to loading. Well-trained marshalls should be on each plane, but it would be very difficult if someone pulled the pin on a hand grenade.

A special note to Toastmasters of the world: Being asked to talk to reporters in Cyprus after the hijacking was a real Toastmasters test. It was a difficult occasion, but an opportunity nonetheless to practice what Table Topics teaches: how to speak on your feet without fear, anxiety or anxiousness for the moment.

After the trauma followed a strength I have never felt before. Still, the embassy people in Cyprus told reporters not to harass me or they would stop the interview immediately. I remember doing interviews with NBC, CBS, CNN. It was wild for a while, without rest.

Toastmasters International's training is the greatest way of learning to meet any situation in life! We must join as speakers to promote world peace and must not forget the seven hostages still held in Lebanon.

(Reprinted by permission of Toastmasters International and Lou Peel, author.)

WAYNE COTTON, CLU
Cotton Concepts Group Ltd.
202 Terrace Inn Office Plaza
4445 Calgary Trail
Edmonton, Alberta, Canada T6H 5R7
Toll Free 1-800-661-8899

Wayne Cotton, CLU

Wayne was raised on a farm in Western Canada. He entered the life insurance business at the age of 21. Wayne is a life and qualifying member of the Million Dollar Round Table.

He is past president of the Edmonton Life Underwriters Association and a former member of the National LUAC Board. He has lectured at many LUAC Education Schools across Canada.

Wayne and his staff run two companies in Edmonton, Alberta. Cotton Planning Services Ltd. specializes in insurance, estate planning, and retirement financial counseling.

Through Cotton Concept Group Ltd., Wayne is active in publishing and seminars. Thousands of life underwriters in twelve countries use the marketing presentations Wayne has developed.

Wayne's speaking topics include financial, retirement, and estate planning. Wayne speaks to life underwriters on financial planning, marketing, balanced growth, stress, and successful living, He has spoken at hundreds of sale congresses and insurance company conventions and has conducted seminars in 48 states in the USA, 9 provinces in Canada and 10 countries worldwide.

Wayne lives a very unique lifestyle. He commutes by air 500 miles to his office in Edmonton, Alberta, then returns to Kelowna, British Columbia for three days a week to enjoy the resort lifestyle of the fruit-growing Okanagan Valley.

2

The Stress of Success
by Wayne Cotton, CLU

"Problems Create Beneficial Rearrangements"
                —Wayne Cotton, CLU

Stress Crisis

Test pattern! My mind had gone "test pattern." I ran a two day meeting in a distant city, and I don't even remember being there.

Stress, fatigue, exhaustion, and burnout had

taken their toll over an extended period of time. The pressure had been extreme on my body and mind. I pushed myself to the very brink of human mental endurance. To this day, I have no recollection of being in that city.

Oh, I was there, alright. I have the receipts to prove it. But I wasn't really there. Scary? You bet. Especially when I realize how mentally blitzed I was. Did the others all around me know what a zombie I was? Perhaps they assumed I was overtired, or a little distant.

Stress is not just a figment of one's imagination. Stress is real. I thought I was invincible, that stress was a state of mind. Burnout was for weaklings. Nothing could be further from the truth.

When I look back, that period of my life seems like a bad dream. But it really happened. My daily diary tells the tale of many months that eventually became years. Had I listened to my own signals, or to those who cared, the bad dream might have never happened.

Learn from my experience. Don't repeat my mistakes. I became a workaholic who couldn't take vacations, and suffered eight stress related medical problems. As a slow learner I had to experience total financial ruin, personal and industry disgrace before beginning recovery.

Let me share the philosophy I have come to believe. You may learn from my painful experiences.

Career Success and the Other Side
of the Coin

I started in the life insurance business when I was 21. A farm boy, I soon became caught up in the thrill of success, the thrill I imagined I would get out of life when I eventually became a success.

I read dozens of books and took success courses. I listened to lots of cassette recordings, and all of the speakers who came to town. I watched the leaders in my industry and dreamed of when I would become one of those elite few. I knew business and financial success were golden keys to future happiness.

We are great believers in goals, attitudes, inspiration and success. Everywhere people scheme, dream, strive and drive to become bigger and better. For some, the dream is elusive. For others, it becomes an obsession.

Business or career success is important. But, remember, your career is only one side of the coin. Many of us behave as if career is the sole reason for living.

If we let it, obsession can run our lives. Some of us become a cog in a wheel of our own making. We are consumed by our jobs, industry, companies, or our success drives for money, power, or ego gratification... often at great personal cost. For others, the job is survival. A friend's father once stated, "We dig the ditch to earn the money to buy the food to get the strength to dig the ditch." We must be very careful not to get stuck in that rut.

There is much more to life than just career. On the other side of the coin is your personal life and well-being. Be concerned about stress removal, relaxation, personal interests, time-off, and vacations. To be truly successful, your goals must include your health and the relationships with those you love.

The Road to Success Is Paved with Potholes

We often experience setbacks—the potholes in the road—which can become internalized problems. Stress is often the result. We must have strategies for dealing with the stress of success. Then the considerations on the other side of the coin receive their fair share of attention.

One of the reasons for stress is our desire to succeed. Desire is not wrong; we should want to succeed. Success is important. The reasons for stress lie in our definition of success—we often measure the wrong things. This produces a success attitude based on money, power, possessions and ego gratification. These are only a part of success.

I saw a T-shirt one day. On it was printed, "Anybody can be a father...but it takes somebody special to be a Daddy." I thought, fantastic! They've finally made an award for something important!

We become so wrapped up in our search for achievement. Sometimes we're interested only in tangible rewards: a bigger trophy, nicer plaque, larger home, better office, more staff, higher volume of business, ego recognition, and financial reward. Nobody gives you a reward to being a good Daddy or Mommy, or a plaque for being a loving husband or wife. Nobody pats you on the head for being physically fit, or shakes your hand for managing stress well enough to live to age eighty. Nobody recognizes you for being a well-balanced satisfied, fulfilled human being. Only you can do that. It's an inside job!

I'm not saying you shouldn't be an achiever, or a leader. But, please remember to measure the personal cost at which you achieve that success.

We're a competitive people in many ways. Ego gratification, competition, and recognition are driving forces that sometimes push us blindly ahead. We look at the next guy and say, "If he can do it, I can," without stopping to think what it is that we are chasing. Is what the other person wants what you want? If so, fine—go for it! Maybe what you truly want isn't what the other person is doing at all. Understand what you really want for your slice of life. We take too many of those things on the other side of the coin for granted, until some of them are taken away.

The Fiasco

Let me tell you why I feel so strongly. By 1980 I became very involved in my career. I was twelve years into the game, and really going for it. I listened to the greats of our industry and knew I had to work hard to live up to their expectations. I went seven years without taking a vacation because I was too busy getting ahead. I took ten days off. But then I went another three years without taking anymore. That's ten days off in ten years! Long weekends were my opportunity to get caught up at the office. It was always just one more year until I had it together. One more staff member until it was all organized. One more market to develop, one more month, just one more. I was a totally involved workaholic at 34 years old. I couldn't quit! My work week consisted of early mornings daily and late nights three or four nights a week. I was in the office until 2 or 3 p.m. on Saturday. Then by 10 o'clock on Sunday morning, I had wound up this machine called Wayne Cotton, Workaholic, to do it all over again; agitated, pressured, miserable and grumpy. By Sunday afternoon, I had severe headaches. By Sunday evening I was back in the office again! I wasn't simply selling life insurance. I was totally consumed by my business.

In 1980, I blew a fuse. I was over-involved, trying too hard and had too many commitments. Managing three companies that all needed my attention at the same time, I had eleven members on my marketing and support staff. I was speaking more all the time and publishing several marketing presentations. I was president of a 700-member life underwriters association and founding president of a new 22-member study group. I was poorly organized, flailing out of control.

Life is a series of adjustments. My adjustment rate became a phenomenon all its own. My priorities were replaced by more urgent ones many times each day. I worked longer hours with fewer breaks in an attempt to keep up. Few of these urgent priorities had anything to do with my real job, my primary source of income, which was selling life insurance products to prospects and clients.

I pushed myself over the brink of human mental endurance in November. I ran that two-day meeting, but I don't remember being there. I was mentally blitzed, fatigued, couldn't think clearly, or make decisions effectively. I was totally burned out.

Continual pushing and striving create stress problems. I had a series of eight stress-related medical problems between 1977 and 1981. Nerves, stomach, blood pressure, head and back problems. Running, my favorite form of exercise, was impossible because of heavy muscle spasms in my back. Doctors told me I would be in a wheelchair within two years because of arthritis in my spine. My dream of skiing with my kids evaporated. I lived on pain-killers for a year and a half, just to keep walking. These were the effects of negative stress.

Meanwhile, I was still receiving plaques and trophies, letters and accolades for the wonderful job I was doing in our industry. I won an award for running the top Life Underwriters Association in the whole country. I got what I wanted: ego and industry recognition for being a super achiever. But my personal cost from all this was ridiculous.

Then Jim, a young friend of mine—an LUA board member, a CLU, a life member of the Million Dollar Round Table, a brilliant young man, age 31—died suddenly. Not from an accident. He had a heavy chest pain and drove himself to the hospital. The medical tests showed severe hardening of the arteries. The doctors waited until after the weekend to perform a double bypass, but they couldn't get Jim's heart going after the operation. He was stressed out. Dead at 31. A life of great human potential...gone! That's not unheard of. Check your local obituary column on the number of people who die in their 30's, 40's, and 50's. They don't all die in car accidents; stress problems definitely cause their fair share.

My cash flow deficit totaled $80,000 in 1979, backed up with more substantial losses in 1980. I was busy being a "future success," getting involved in all the new deals, I was trying to have all the latest, including incorporating new companies and developing new markets before the old ones were even close to being profitable.

The final straw came late in 1980. I zigged when I should have zagged in financing a new business deal and was backed into a corner I couldn't get out of. Years of stressing and straining felt like an accumulation of endless futile failure. My advisors told me to declare bankrupty. Friends told me to leave the business and get a regular job. I refused to consider either possibility. This could have been a period of heavy mental re-evaluation, but the heat was on! The sheriff was on my doorstep. We learned to know each other on a first name basis! Life was a series of adjustments. The tyranny of the urgent became my daily code.

I shut down my major business operations, then had to sell my home in order to readjust financially. There were so many liens against it that I had to put money in just so the creditors could take it away. We lost all the equity that we had built up. My cash flow was at a standstill, my office was gone, my staff disappeared. I had no real assets, owed a fortune, and had seven legal judgements against me. I fell asleep involuntarily out of sheer mental exhaustion, waking up with the "zooms" at 3 or 4 a.m. every morning. That's what happens when you wake in a panic—your mind zooms off in all directions in an anxiety attack that never seems to end. My blood pressure centered on 150/100; that meant about a twenty-year reduction in life expectancy for my age. The stress and pressure on my wife was huge. Our marriage eventually crumbled. My plans to be a super success, a hero in this business, hadn't included this. None of the "greats" talked about the personal cost of being successful.

Why am I telling you this? I want to share the outcome of this disaster with you. Out of every problem comes a solution that leaves you in a better position than you were in before. PROBLEMS CREATE BENEFICIAL REARRANGEMENTS.

Starting Over

So back to square one. I opened a new office and hired just one secretary. Sixteen major creditors and several minor ones were all on my case at once. I talked them into giving me more time by describing the total financial collapse that would occur if any one of them forced me into bankruptcy. The only thing I had left was my ability to earn income. I believed in the potential of that ability as long as I had peace of mind to work.

We bought a little 1,100 square foot condominium with a $500 down payment and a fat second mortgage due one year later. It was back to the basics; we started all over again.

Whenever you try to get results, you have to focus attention specifically on what you wish to accomplish. Prioritize, set up a simple game plan, and then follow through. I now had no choice but to do what I should have been doing all along.

I couldn't work harder. I had to work smarter. I slowed down, took time to rebuild, to rethink, to reevaluate the priorities. I didn't get to the office until 9:00, 9:30 or some days 10:00 a.m., but when there I wasn't panicking nearly as much. My pace seemed different, my problems smaller, my priorities clearer. I was ready to handle each day's key items.

My energy level started to rebuild. My blood pressure went down. I quit working evenings and weekends. The tension in my body started to subside. I was able to get off pain-killers. My back eventually returned to normal, my headaches and stomach problems went away. My attitude and strength improved as the rebuilding process took place. I felt the release of pressure and found myself laughing, smiling, enjoying. I spent more time with my kids and took time off. I even felt inspired to write poetry of my feelings, and eventually published a booklet of poems called *Reflections*.

What happened? Sales production climbed dramatically. Focusing produces results. My bottom line improved by six fugures that year. I paid off a truckload of liabilities. When our second mortgage came due on our condominium, I paid it off out of excess cash-flow from that month. My new major objective in life was to become worth nothing by the time I was forty. I was so far in the hole financially, I figured if I could get back to zero by age forty, I would be doing well!

Life Is For Excellence

Several years have now elapsed since the *fiasco,* the name I have given to that period of time. There has been a lot of change. My companies are thriving. I have built my staff back up to twelve. We are far more organized and productive. We focus on getting results. Times are good.

They say you have to go too far in order to know how far you can go. I went too far. I've enjoyed success and achievement since the fiasco, but I have a much better perspective than I did before. Many people do bigger and better things than me, but I love my lifestyle. I enjoy my flourishing companies and all of the 180 vacation days that I take every year.

We become competitive—pushing, aggressive, striving, driving human beings. We crank it out day-in and day-out thinking that the increase in position, power, net worth, or ego-reward is worth the effort. Achievement is important but at what personal cost? Life is for excellence, not just a temporary high from your career. Everyone must someday walk out of the spotlight. Those who lead a balanced existence achieve the most satisfying lives. The whole-person concept is important. Recognizing the value of the other side of the coin is vital to your future well-being. Here are my strategies for dealing with the stress of success.

Problem Solving Attitudes

Develop a proper attitude about problems. My mentor in this area is Dr. Norman Vincent Peale. When I was going through my darkest hours in the fiasco, I often read chapters from one of Dr. Peale's books. His attitude about accepting problems as a sign of life is incredible. He taught me to look for solutions rather than to get immersed in the negatives of the problem. Instead of becoming "unglued" at the onset of a setback, let us be thankful for the wisdom and insight we've been given.

We often allow ourselves to be overwhelmed by minor problems that are really only daily challenges. Recognizing the difference between the two helps to alleviate the stress. We must learn not to give a dollar's worth of energy to a five cent item. Because we don't each possess an accurate crystal ball, we will never know if a decision was perfect until after the fact. Learn to be approximately right. Make a decision, then move on.

Frank Sullivan, a past president of the Million Dollar Round Table, talked about the concept of mature simplicity. He said we go through three stages; wide eyed enthusiasm, complicated sophistication, then hopefully mature simplicity. This has been true in my circumstance. Complicated sophistication was one of the reasons for the "fiasco." We should try to be better than we are, but at fewer things. We complicate our lives to the point that we can't possibly achieve self-satisfation. We want to be number one at everything. Learn to develop a noncompetitive attitude. Be number one on your own terms, not everyone else's. Decide what is important to you; then eliminate non-essentials.

Develop Time-Freedom

When I moved to Kelowna, British Columbia, in western Canada, a friend said, "Wayne, two kinds of people move to Kelowna. One kind loves to fish. He hears about the excellent fishing. He is here for the lifestyle, but he can't afford a nice boat. The other kind moves here because he sees the opportunity in this valley. He sees tourism, industry, and business. He does well, working and developing money freedom. He buys a nice boat, but he has no time to use it!" Money and time freedom: both are important. We should strive to own the "nice boat," but also have time to use it.

This concept is particularly difficult, especially for young people climbing the success ladder. Put things into proper perspective. Regardless of how well we like our job or how much pressure it creates, it is still nothing more than a job. Some of us (myself included) tackle our jobs with insane missionary zeal. We stop only because of exhaustion and fatigue. We must remember why we are working. Love your work, but a job is just a job. Your career is just one component of your life. Don't forget the rest.

Develop time freedom so you can enjoy the fruits of your labour. This is one of the really significant lessons I have learned as a result of living through the setbacks I experienced.

Design an Annual Road Map

I color-code a full annual calendar on a single sheet of paper. My yellow days are days off or vacation time, 180 days each year. I learned the hard way that vacations are a must. If you don't take a holiday, God will give you one. He gave me a few I wasn't planning on! Not everyone can structure their time in the same way. I take regular long weekends as well as several weeks off each year. I am a sprinter, not a long distance runner.

Red days are industry commitments: speeches and seminars I conduct. At present I use120 days allocated for this purpose. This suits me fine: more commitments would take me away from my children and my lifestyle.

Green days are those days left over for the office. Green is for GO! When I work, I really go. On these days, I deal with the staff, see clients, and handle my heavy administration load. When on green, I work hard doing my job, and satisfying my workaholic tendencies.

Try to plan a whole year at one time. It will excite you to think about what you want to do with your time off, and will help you focus on priorities when you are working.

If you would like a blank copy of an annual road map for the current year, please write to my office.

Practice Stress Removal

I used to think that I was invincible—stress was a state of mind, burnout was for weaklings. Now, I know better. Stress is real. Excessive stress is damaging. The human body is a non-renewable natural resource. Stress is cumulative: it builds and grows. If you build negative stress up too high, you could blow a fuse.

I am still a very busy person with the number of things that I attempt to accomplish at once, but the pressure is not nearly as heavy as it was. Regular vacations, long weekends away from work and daily "mini-holidays" all help to remove stress. A mini-holiday is a short daily break or two that helps you back away from the heavy pace. I meditate or take a "power nap" at least once a day. Most office days I go to a health club to relax in a jaccuzzi. My favorite exercise is running, so I go for a three to five mile run several times a week. I seem to have more incentive for consistence in the summer when there isn't two feet of snow on the ground! But then, my skis work a lot better on the snow.

Go For a Less-Stressful Lifestyle

I dreamed for years of living in the beautiful fruit-growing Okanogan Valley at Kelowna, British Columbia, 500 miles away from my office in Edmonton, Alberta. Kelowna is a nice place to live and raise children, but I didn't want to work there. I kept postponing the decision to move. In 1982, a doctor discovered a tumor in my throat. There was a significant possibility of cancer. He operated right away, removing half my thyroid, and a three-inch-in-diameter tumor from the centre of my throat. The scare made me think that life is too short to defer what I really want to do. The morning of the operation, I decided that, if all was well, we were going to move to the Okanogan Valley. There was no cancer. Two weeks later we were living in Kelowna!

I kept my office in Edmonton where my base-market, staff and business operations are located. I commute to Edmonton by air for those weeks that are designated as work weeks. On work weeks, I catch a

Sunday evening flight out of Kelowna and head back to the office. My days in Edmonton are long and busy as I focus on getting my job done. On Thursday afternoon I catch a flight back to Kelowna to enjoy a long weekend living the lifestyle offered by the Okanogan environment. It's a great place to live with mountains, lakes, orchards, a small-town atmosphere, and it's 500 miles from the office! I don't have an office in Kelowna, nor do I sell insurance there. We are there to enjoy. Some say I'm semi-retired, others say I'm semi-retarded! I am doing my own thing, and I enjoy it. I won't commit to living the rest of my life in Kelowna. As my children get bigger, it may become important to live in a larger centre. For now, this lifestyle has helped me get rid of the high stress level that I once had and to learn there are a lot more important things in life than the office. My production has climbed dramatically since I cut my worktime way down. That's what happens when you focus for specific results.

Re-Dream Your Personal Dreams

What are the things you've dreamed about that you've put off to the side? I enjoy snow-skiing and the incredible exhilaration of standing on a mountain top looking at the beautiful world below. But I didn't go skiing for seventeen years. I was too involved, I couldn't afford the time.

Kelowna has several major ski hills within forty miles of town. I always wanted to go skiing with my children. When we moved to Kelowna I was ready!

I had one of the most unbelievable highs of my life the first time I went down the mountain with my kids, Tamara and Ben, skiing beside me. In 1984 I bought a ski chalet on our favorite mountain. We enjoy lots of days on the ski slopes during the six-month season. I love the challenge, the fun with the kids, and the inspiration of the world of snow. When I fly down the mountain, I am happy for the opportunity to enjoy my health and my kids.

Enjoy the Relationships With Those You Love

My marriage ended after eighteen years. Learn to live your relationships one day at a time. The future is now. Let me share a story to tell you about the importance of relationships with the people we love. This story is about a Dad and his little four-year-old daughter, Adina. One Sunday morning in the autumn, the Daddy and Adina got up early. They were sitting on the kitchen floor making some things out of play dough. They made a little man, a dog, a horse, and chicken. They were having a good time. The Daddy went downstairs to his den to do some reading. Adina followed and said, "Daddy, let's make something!"

"Okay, Adina. You figure out what you want to make, and we'll make it." She thought for a minute, then said, "Daddy, let's make a butterfly."

So they did. Her Daddy gave her a piece of card and told her, "You get your crayons and your scissors, and cut out some wings, and make a butterfly. Then you can color it."

She got busy, and she made a really neat butterfly. The Daddy helped her cut another card to make a little base so the butterfly would stand up by itself. They set the butterfly up on the Daddy's desk, and then they went out to enjoy the day with the Mommy and Adina's little sister. About 11 o'clock that night Adina woke up from her sleep and called her Daddy.

She said, "I got a headache, Daddy. I don't feel so good." the Daddy and Mommy checked, and the little girl was running a fever. They worked to bring it down, but the next morning she was still sick. Her Mommy and Daddy took her to see the doctor. Adina had spinal meningitis. It hit her hard. Five doctors worked on her all Monday night, but they couldn't save her. By six o'clock Tuesday morning she was gone. Life for her on this earth was over. Later that day, the Daddy went downstairs to his den to start making funeral arrangements for his little girl. He was tired, angry, frustrated, defeated. All the things he had worked so hard for had suddenly been whisked away. His efforts seemed so futile, the balance of life terribly fragile. That Daddy was empty. He'd been crying sobs all night, sharing with his wife the loss of their little girl. When he walked into his den, guess what he saw sitting on his desk. A butterfly! It was hers, a symbolic love gesture from that little sweetheart to her Daddy.

You may ask me, "How do you know that story so well?" Because, I am that Daddy. Adina was my little girl. She left so many things behind, like the lip imprints on the windows where she gave her Daddy window kisses goodbye every day when he went to work. It took a long time to wash those windows. She left paths of fingermarks in the sandbox that he built for her just a few weeks before. She left her brand new swing, gently blowing in the breeze. It was her fourth birthday gift. She left little plastercine animals lying on the kitchen counter. The most significant thing she left for me was her butterfly.

Why do I share this story? A butterfly is an important symbol of love, beauty, and growth of the evolvement that occurs in our relationships and our lives. A butterfly symbolizes the evolvement in our ability to love.

I've got a plaque in my office that says, "Life is for living, caring, hoping and sharing with the people that we love." Sometimes those lives are awfully short. I wear a butterfly ring on my little finger, a constant reminder of this important area of my life.

Grow, achieve and develop. Strive and drive. Be successful and get ahead. But don't ever forget the real reasons why you put in the time, the effort, the energy, and why you put up with the frustrations.

I hope you don't have to build up a whole bag full of experiences like I have in order to get your priority system in order. There's been a lot of pain for me, but I've learned, and grown through it. I hope you can grow from what I've experienced and learned. In your goals and aspirations, take time to consider personal cost. Develop strategies for dealing with stress. Get a handle on your real objectives. Let them be your guide to self-fulfillment. Perhaps my thoughts can help you envision a better tomorrow.

What Do I Want?

TO DREAM	*To always have a dream or two, a vision, a desire that pulls me forward to heights designed especially for my talents.*
TO ACHIEVE	*To want to be me, and to achieve in a way that allows me to be true to myself and the rest of my life.*
TO WORK	*To enjoy the thrill of accomplishment...the recognition from those who can learn from my example of good and bad.*

TO EXPERIENCE *To have the opportunity to do so many things that are ready and waiting to be done. To learn the thrill of new challenges and the rewards of a new experience.*

TO ENJOY *To be spontaneous in my actions —to do crazy things that others don't consider as being the way it has to be. To take the moment to have fun in all the ways that present themselves.*

TO LAUGH *To let go of fears, concerns, and daily trouble and to let loose in enjoyable fun that warms my soul and regenerates new enthusiasm.*

TO CRY *To never feel so restricted or so proud that I can't weep when happy or sad or hurt. To cry is to feel, to enjoy, and to love.*

TO LOVE *To let go and to love without the vulnerability and criticism of those who don't feel the need to do the same.*

TO BELIEVE *To have a deep belief that God put me here to fulfill a purpose and that I must be accountable to that reason for being here.*

Strength of mind is exercise, not rest.

—**Pope**

JERRY V. TEPLITZ, Ph.D.
Jerry Teplitz Enterprises
4317 Tillman Drive
Virginia Beach, VA 23462
(804) 498-1552

Jerry V. Teplitz, Ph.D.

Dr. Jerry V. Teplitz's background is as unique as the techniques and approaches he teaches. He is a graduate of Hunter College and Northwestern University School of Law. He practiced as an attorney for the Illinois Environmental Protection Agency.

At that point, Jerry's career took a dramatic change of direction. He studied and became a Master Teacher of Hatha Yoga. More recently, Jerry has received a Doctorate Degree in Wholistic Health Sciences from Columbia Pacific University.

Currently the President of his own consulting firm, Jerry conducts seminars in the areas of stress management, management effectiveness, and sales development. The list of Jerry's clients includes: IBM, Motorola, Holiday Inns, Young Presidents' Organization, and American Bankers Association.

Jerry has authored several books, including Managing Your Stress: How To Relax and Enjoy, *and* Build A Better You-Starting Now. *As a professional speaker, he has spoken to well over a quarter of a million people.*

Jerry has also been honored by his peers in the National Speakers Association by receiving the title of "Certified Speaking Professional" and has been selected as "Top Rated Speaker of 1984" by the International Platform Association.

Discovering My Strategies Really Work!
by Jerry V. Teplitz, Ph.D.

"As meditation, or the thoughts of love."
—Shakespeare

I've been teaching stress management techniques for 12 years to over 250,000 people. Since I personally practice what I teach, I've been able to experience how well these techniques have worked under most "normal" circumstances, as well as some unusual ones, too! Two years ago I was tested by a situation beyond what I had ever experienced before, and the techniques and I passed with flying colors.

I'm going to tell you my story first and then how to do the Stress Strategies that I used. My experience took place in March of 1984. I was scheduled to conduct several seminars internationally for the very first time. I was being sent to the Caracas, Venezuela, and Sao Paulo, Brazil Chapters of the Young Presidents' Organization. YPO's membership is composed of presidents of companies having a minimum of 50 employees and doing $5 million in business.

Since my high school Spanish was extremely rusty, I was armed with a dictionary of Spanish phrases, my passport, and my ticket. I thought I was ready for anything.

The flight to Caracas was uneventful. The program for the YPO Caracas Chapter was a one day seminar on "Managing Your Stress" given on Saturday. It was very well received by the participants. On Sunday morning, I was scheduled to fly to Rio de Janeiro to vacation for a day and a half before flying on to Sao Paulo, where my seminar was scheduled to begin at 9:00 a.m. Tuesday morning.

This was when things began to go haywire. My flight from Caracas to Rio connected through Bogota, Columbia, which is the equivalent of flying from New York to Chicago in order to get to Miami. This was both the only routing available and the only flight that entire day! I was scheduled to have a 2½ hour layover in Bogota.

The Caracas flight left one and a half hours late. When we finally landed in Bogota, I discovered that I had only 45 minutes until my next flight to reclaim all my luggage and go all the way through customs with it before I could go to the Avianca ticket counter to get the flight on to Rio.

By the time I cleared customs, it was only 10 minutes before flight time. I piled all my luggage onto my luggage cart and raced for the Avianca ticket counter. The agent looked at my ticket and her first words were that it was too late for me to make the flight. I must have looked really shocked and helpless because she then said, "Well, OK, I'll see what I can do."

She quickly checked my bags to Rio and then she personally escorted me from the ticket counter all the way to the departure gate. She even got my seat assignment from the gate agent (that never has happened flying in the United States). She then realized she had left my luggage claim checks at the ticket counter, so she even ran back to get them.

I Need A What?

I thought I was all set to go.

As I was about to board the plane the gate agent asked me for my ticket, my passport and my visa.

What visa? That's right, I had no visa! The gate agent absolutely refused to let me board the plane. All I could do was stare in disbelief as the plane departed...with my baggage safely aboard.

How could this have happened? When the seminar was originally arranged by YPO headquarters in New York, I had asked my YPO contact person to check on whether I needed a visa. She never got back to me about it (she had completely forgotten to inquire). Since this was my first international travel experience, I forgot to ask her again.

I found my ticket agent again, and asked her what I should do now. She said I would have to wait until Monday to get a visa from the Brazilian Embassy, and then take the next flight to Sao Paulo, Brazil which departed Monday night at 10:30 p.m. That was an all night flight and I would arrive in Sao Paulo on Tuesday morning at 9:30 a.m. My seminar was scheduled to start at 9:00 a.m.!

The Angels Arrive

I had no other choice. I would be stranded in Bogota for almost two days. I had no idea of where to stay, what to do, where to eat, or even what the currency rate was. On top of it all, I had no clothes. I was in a state of high, high anxiety, and I was close to tears.

As I wandered around the airport anxiously

trying to get my brain to function so I could figure out what to do next, I spotted an Information Booth. I went in and said, "Habla Ingles?" (Do you speak English?) to the people behind the counter. A woman being served at the counter turned around and said, "Yes, I do." It turned out she was originally from Bogota, but now lived in New York City. I suddenly felt as if I'd made contact with an angel from heaven.

She told the Information Booth people to make a reservation for me at one of the better hotels in Bogota. She helped me exchange my money for Columbian pesos. She told me what sights I should see, and she even told me how much to pay the cab driver. I left the airport for the hotel, feeling I had been rescued. In the taxi is where I used Stress Strategy #1, a deep breathing exercise, to calm myself down.

The woman receptionist at the hotel spoke English. Since I needed to talk to someone, I blurted out to her my predicament. She wound up volunteering to take me to the movies that night, to the Brazilian Embassy the next morning, and then sightseeing that afternoon before my plane departed. Another angel had descended upon me and her name was Nona!

I went up to my room. I was still very upset about what had happened, and I also was very anxious because I didn't know if I would be able to get a visa immediately on Monday, or if I would have to wait a day or two to get it, or if I would be able to contact the YPO people in Sao Paulo to let them know my new arrival plans, or if they could delay the starting time of my seminar in Sao Paulo. I knew I needed to do something to calm me down.

This was where I put into practice Stress Strategy #2 which was to meditate. Meditating was a way for me to rid myself of all the stress and anxiety I was feeling while re-energizing myself, too. When I finished I was feeling wonderfully better. I even had my appetite back, so I went downstairs to have some lunch.

It was off to the movies that night with Nona. Surprisingly, the film was in English with Spanish subtitles!

The Brazilian Connection— Telephone and Visas

First thing Monday morning, I tried to call my contact person in Brazil to let her know about my scheduled arrival at the Sao Paulo airport at 9:30 a.m. on the day of the seminar. The telephone number I had been given connected me with a Brazilian company. Their switchboard operator spoke broken English. She said that she had never heard of either YPO or the name of the person I was calling. She hung up.

At first, I panicked and had no idea who else to call, then I realized the Young Presidents' Organization is composed of presidents of companies. I called back, and asked to speak to the president. I was told that while he was not in, his secretary was, so the operator transferred me to her. Thank God she understood English, and she knew what I was talking about. She would have my contact person call me back in a few minutes.

When my contact person called, I explained the situation to her and suggested moving the starting time of the seminar to noon just in case the plane was late. She said a luncheon was scheduled. I said, "Let's forget the luncheon and just serve sandwiches." She reluctantly agreed. I hung up feeling relieved that the seminar was going to work.

Now, it was off to the Embassy in a taxi with Nona. There I was told I needed two passport photos, so we left in search of a photographer. After finding one and getting the photos, we returned to the Embassy. I filled out the visa application form, and in less than five minutes, I had my visa! All that hassle for a piece of paper that took less than five minutes to get! With the drama behind me (so I thought), we went sightseeing.

Later that afternoon, I met briefly with a YPO member in Bogota that the Sao Paulo people had contacted to offer me assistance. At 10:30 p.m., I boarded the flight to Sao Paulo which was scheduled to stop first in Rio. As soon as they closed the door to the plane, I moved quickly and was able to grab three empty seats across. I slept for three hours.

Almost Disaster!!

My baggage, which included all the materials for the seminar, had originally gone on the Sunday flight to Rio de Janeiro. I had asked the Bogota baggage personnel to wire Rio Baggage Claim and have my bags forwarded to Sao Paulo. He agreed but said that he didn't know whether the Rio personnel would cooperate. He suggested I check with Rio Baggage Claim when the plane landed Tuesday morning.

The Avianca DC10 landed on time in Rio. There was only 30 minutes until the plane left for Sao Paulo. I grabbed my passport, ticket, claim checks, and ran to baggage claim. I found a baggage agent who spoke some English. He looked in his records and found "NOTHING": no record of my bags having come in from Bogota; no record of Bogota's telex; and no record of my bags having gone to Sao Paulo!!

He kept searching through the records and still nothing! Meanwhile, time was running out. My plane was leaving for Sao Paulo, while my baggage and seminar materials were lost. I told the agent I would try and figure it out in Sao Paulo, and I went running for the plane.

As I was about to reach the gate, someone yelled to me to go downstairs to board the plane. I flew down the stairs and boarded a bus that took me out to a Boeing 737. Wait a minute, I had come in on a DC10, and now I was leaving on a 737. The planes had been changed without my knowing it! I suddenly realized that I had left my attache case (with all my seminar notes) and my shoulder bag on the DC10!

I immediately told the ramp agent. She radioed over to the DC10, but they couldn't find the bags. She said they couldn't hold the plane any longer, and that I would have to take the next plane if I wanted to look for my carry-on bags. I was horrified (and ready to cry). I had to be on this flight. It was then that she said the next plane was leaving in just a half hour.

Since it was crucial for me to have at least my seminar notes, I left the plane and raced back to baggage claim. There sat my attache case and shoulder bag. (Hooray)!!

They bussed me right over to the next plane, and it departed on time. I sat back and did my deep breathing exercise (Stress Strategy #1) to calm myself back down. The flight arrived in Sao Paulo at 10:00 a.m. After clearing customs, I easily found my YPO contact person, and we headed for the "lost and found." A miracle! My luggage, including the box containing all my seminar materials, was there. I was ecstatic!

We drove to the hotel where the seminar would be held. On the way, she informed me that the luncheon had not been cancelled, as we had earlier agreed. It seemed that the meeting room was being given to the organization without charge as part of the luncheon package. My "all-day" seminar would not start until after the noon luncheon, and South Americans being who they are, lunch did not actually start until 1:00 p.m.

During the hour I had before the supposed noon luncheon time, I knew I needed to raise my energy. Since I only had three hours of sleep and plenty of stress, I decided to revitalize myself by going to my room and meditating (Stress Strategy #2).

Finally at 2:00 p.m., my now abbreviated one-day seminar on "Managing Your Stress" began. Afterwards, I was gratified to discover that the participants really enjoyed the seminar and felt it had been a very beneficial experience.

My Discoveries

One could focus on the negative aspects of this trip, as there were plenty of those. However, for me, the real focus is seeing the positive aspects of the experience since I believe we can learn and grow from everything in life.

The most obvious lesson is the need to research

the entry requirements of the host country when one travels internationally.

An even more important lesson was that my own stress management techniques really do work! Despite my brief feelings of hopelessness and helplessness, I was quickly able to rebalance my emotional state many times.

Here are the two strategies that I used during my South American trip. Try them for yourself. I know they'll work for you, too!

STRESS STRATEGY #1: Deep Breathing

This deep breathing exercise is easy to do any time and any place—on a bus, in a train, in a cafeteria, before a business meeting, or taking an exam. For homemakers, it is a refreshing addition to morning breaks. You can even use it if you have had an unexpected argument with someone, and you need to calm yourself down. It's also good to reduce tension and to sharpen your concentration before the start of an athletic competition.

To do the deep breathing exercise just follow these instructions. (See Figure 1):

1. Sit upright with your spine straight but not rigid.
2. Close your eyes. (If you're in a situation where this would be uncomfortable or impractical, such as while driving a car, you can

keep them open.)

3. Exhale forcefully all the air from your lungs.
4. Inhale through your nose to a slow count of eight, filling first your stomach, 1...2...3... let it expand—then your chest, ...4...5... 6..., and finally your shoulder blade region ...7...8.
5. Exhale through your nose to a slow count of eight, emptying first your shoulder blades, 1...2...then your chest,...3...4...5..., and finally your stomach...6...7...8. You can imagine you are a balloon deflating slowly through a pinhole.
6. Repeat this process a total of three times. In very stressful situations you can do it five times.
7. To conclude, sit quietly with eyes closed for a minute or two. This is very important because this is when you will actually feel your body relaxing.

STRESS STRATEGY #2: Meditation

Meditation is a stress strategy technique that also has the power to alter your life in very dramatic and positive ways. Remember, by meditating several extra times, I was able to fly all night, conduct a seminar all afternoon, and go out for a late night dinner—without collapsing! If you've never done it before or don't know very much about meditation, just read and follow these instructions and you will be able to immediately meditate effectively.

The benefits of meditation are both physiological and psychological. The physiological benefits occur each time you meditate. Your heart rate will slow down, and your breath rate will slow down. All your vital signs will actually be at a lower level than during your deepest state of sleep. By meditating for 20 minutes, you will actually feel as if you have had six to eight hours of sleep. Meditation is also a way to beat jet lag because you are very quickly resetting your biological time clock.

The psychological benefits from meditating are that you will become more happy, more joyous, and more comfortable with yourself. Many of the problems in your daily life will simply disappear.

Do's and Don'ts

Here's a list of do's and don'ts to keep in mind while you're meditating.

1. Meditation needs to be done twice a day for 20 minutes each time period. In the morning, you can do it any time before you eat breakfast. In the late afternoon, you can do it anytime before dinner, or at least an hour after your meal. If your schedule does not permit you to meditate 20 minutes twice a

day, you can do it instead for several shorter periods during the day. So long as the total time is 40 minutes, you'll still receive all the benefits.

2. If you wear hard contact lenses you may wish to remove them.

3. If during the meditation, you find your mind wandering to other thoughts, do not become upset or angry. Simply let the thought go, and return to the meditation technique. Again, do not be angry with yourself regardless of how many thoughts you have, or what the thoughts are about since you cannot make your mind stop thinking thoughts. By not becoming upset you are actually meditating correctly.

4. If during the meditation you have an itch, or an irritation, correct it immediately.

5. If during your meditation you need to answer the phone or go to the door, you can; however, you'll need to continue meditating as soon as you can for an additional five minutes beyond your normal time.

6. Don't meditate just before bedtime as the technique may re-energize you and keep you awake.

7. The way to time your meditation period is to use a clock or watch. When you want to know the time, simply open up one eye to

briefly glance at the clock. Don't time your-self with an alarm clock as the sound can be too jolting.

8. Don't meditate right after eating.

9. If you fall asleep while you are meditating, that's perfectly all right as it's your body saying it needs a bit more rest. Simply meditate for another five minutes beyond your normal time.

10. When you've meditated for 20 minutes, simply stop doing the technique, keep your eyes closed, and sit comfortably for two minutes. During this two minute period you may gently move your arms or legs. This two minute period is allowing you to physiologi-cally return to your normal heart and breath rate.

Getting Ready

Sit comfortably in a chair, or against a wall on the floor. If you sit in a chair, your feet should be flat on the floor. If you are wearing glasses, take them off. If you have tight clothing on, loosen it.

Do this gentle stretching exercise to relax and straighten your spine:

1. Raise your arms straight up over your head and stretch toward the ceiling.

2. Stretch your arms and neck up, and hold for

several seconds.

3. Twist your body from the waist to the left, hold for several seconds, and then to the right, hold for several seconds.
4. Rotate back to the center, stretch up one last time and then lower your arms slowly.

The Technique

The meditation technique you are about to learn is called "Hong Saw." It requires you to repeat the words "Hong Saw" in your mind while you are breathing. Read the following instructions first, then you will be ready to begin.

1. Close your eyes and become aware of your breathing. Become aware of the rate of your inhalation and exhalation. Don't try to regulate it, just breathe naturally.
2. Each time you inhale you are going to say to yourself the word "Hong." Visualize the word entering your face at the point between your eyebrows. If you cannot visualize the word, simply have the feeling of it entering. (See Figure 2).
3. Each time you exhale you are going to say to yourself the word "Saw," and visualize the word exiting at the point between your eyebrows. If you cannot visualize the word, having the feeling of it exiting is fine. (See

figure 3).

4. You'll be inhaling while seeing or feeling "Hong" enter, and exhaling while seeing or feeling "Saw" exit. Remember, just follow whatever your natural breath rate is. If your breath becomes shallow or deep that's fine. If your breath feels like it stopped, don't worry, it will begin again when it needs to. Don't change your breathing deliberately, just continue to do "Hong Saw" for 20 minutes.

5. Take the additional two minutes before opening your eyes.

6. Congratulations, you are now a meditator.

The Key

The key to achieving all the benefits of meditation discussed previously is to do it twice a day. If you're saying to yourself, "I'm too busy, how can I find the time," let me share with you my own experience. I have been meditating for 14 years. For the past 12 of those 14 years, I have not missed a meditation; however, I have done it at some pretty unusual times and in some pretty unusual places. That's because I made a decision and commitment to do it regularly no matter what!

The morning meditation is the easiest to do since it means you just need to get up 20 minutes earlier in the morning. The late afternoon or early evening meditation can be squeezed in as your time permits. For example, if you have a late afternoon business meeting, you may want to meditate at three in the afternoon. If you have meetings all afternoon and early evening, you might meditate at 7:00 or 8:00 p.m. The key is a willingness to be flexible yet committed.

At this point, I am not asking for your commitment to meditate regularly for the next 14 years. All I'm asking you to do is commit yourself to meditate regularly for the next 2 to 3 weeks. This time period will allow you to begin to experience the real benefits for yourself, and once that happens, you'll want to continue.

Conclusion

These Stress Strategy techniques that I have been sharing with you are just two of many that you can use to help you reduce the stresses in your life. Whether your stress comes from the kids mis-behaving, or the pressures of work deadlines, you are the one who will need to take the time to handle your own stress. Stress management is a very personal thing as no one can do it for you!

Oh, by the way, the YPO person I met with briefly in Bogota due to my unscheduled stopover was the Education Chairperson for the Bogota YPO

Chapter. The result of that meeting? A month later, I returned to Bogota and I conducted my seminar for his chapter!

Figure 1

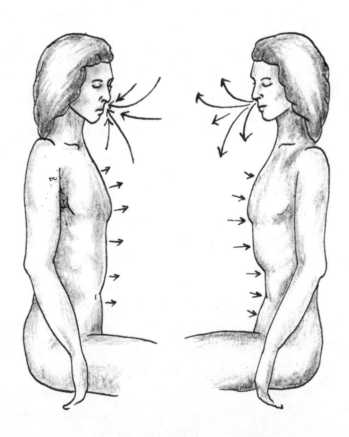

Figure 2

Figure 3

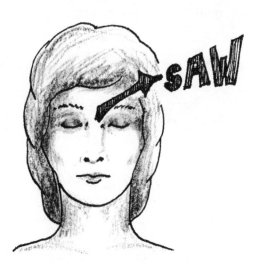

Helen Rose McDowell
305 Corona Drive
P.O. Box 32501
Lafayette, LA 70503
(318) 984-6077

Helen Rose McDowell

Helen Rose McDowell, a health consultant, research writer and speaker for the past twenty-five years, began her career in 1962, testing and developing recipes while completing her degree in Home Economics.

After serving as director for a research foundation in Chicago, she became a faculty member, University of Nevada, Las Vegas. She opened an office as a health consultant during this time, later expanding into Southern California.

Throughout her career she has served as board member and consultant to various health and nutrition-oriented foundations and organizations. During this time, Helen Rose traveled across the United States giving lectures and seminars on health and related subjects. Her media experiences include being a newspaper columnist, a regular on a television talk show, having a daily radio program, publishing a health newsletter and being a writer.

In 1982, she moved to Athens, Greece with her husband. While there she traveled in Africa, the Middle East, Europe, Eastern Bloc countries and the Soviet Union.

Helen Rose now lives in Lafayette, Louisiana where she is a freelance writer. She is continuing her speaking career by presenting seminars on "Stress and Tension Management."

4

The REAL Energy Crisis
by Helen Rose McDowell

*"The fortunate circumstances of our
lives are generally found, at last, to be of
our own producing."*
—Oliver Goldsmith
18th Century English Poet

It was a damp, chilly day in December, 1975, when
I walked down Roxbury Drive in Beverly Hills,
California—looking for the address of one Harold E.
Ravins, D.D.S. As I walked into the building, and
climbed the stairs to 211B, I prayed this would be

the last stop in my long and desperate search for the answer that so far had eluded me.

From the time I could remember, I had suffered regularly with colds and flus—always tiring easily. This was very difficult for me to understand, because also from the time I could remember, good health and eating practices were a part of my life.

By the late 1940's, my parents began making what were considered "drastic" changes in our diet. Out went refined products such as white sugar, white flour, white rice, soft drinks, candy—to name a few. In came whole wheat flour, brown rice, honey, and some brown sugar. There was a lot to learn about proper foods to eat—and in those days, knowledge was scarce. Anyone concerned about diet and eating habits risked being called a "health food fanatic,"or "health food faddist."

Mother read Leland Kordel, Gaylord Hauser and Lee Foundation materials. The local "health food store" was small and carried mainly canned soybean products. So, we were left mostly to our own devices. But that was no real problem since we lived in a small Northeastern Louisiana village and had plenty of room for our own garden and chickens, and there were lots of wild berries to pick. We were almost "self sufficient."

Changing our diet was a start in our health program as my parents began to realize what we ate had a bearing on our health. But this was strange to all the neighbors in our small community. At school, kids laughed at our dark bread sandwiches and cookies; our friends no longer would come and eat at our house—they didn't like our "dirty" food. The brown rice looked strange, and the whole wheat biscuits weren't light and fluffy.

To this day, I am not sure that the people of that small community understand the connection between diet and health.

As I sat in Dr. Ravins' office waiting room, I thought about the nice pretty skin I had enjoyed as a teenager. Now, I was suffering severe skin problems compounded by extreme tiredness, frequent colds and flus. My face was broken out in severe lesions like small boils—tender and painful. Gone were those teenage years. I was now the mother of three young healthy boys. It seemed with each birth, my health had deteriorated.

Why?

Why was I suffering all this? As I went from doctor to doctor, no one had an answer. Dermatologists prescribed tetracycline, but even that would not clear up my skin. I had numerous blood tests and medical examinations. Over the years, each doctor in turn would shake his head and admit he did not know the answer. He could offer no solutions.

Armed with my Home Economics degree, which

included numerous courses in chemistry, biology, anatomy and other related subjects, I set out on my own to find an answer.

I studied extensively and took supplements with numerous combinations of minerals, vitamins, enzymes and herbs along with diets and "detoxifying" programs—you name it, and I tried it in some form. I became an expert in diet, health and health programs—but my own poor health remained unchanged!

As my skin worsened, my energy level dropped. Colds became more frequent. I tried to exercise, but tired too easily and developed severe headaches requiring frequent visits to a doctor for temporary relief, often three to four times a week. By now I was going to chiropractors and osteopaths (the M.D.s were giving no help). They all complained of one thing: "Rose, you are one of the hardest persons to work on that I have ever had!"

Why? No one had the answer.

All this time I continued a rigid natural foods diet—including all the dietary practices recommended for people with serious illnesses and diseases. Yet all the medical tests showed negative—I had no disease. I even went to the extreme nutritional programs that had been helpful to cancer patients, but to no avail!

The Office Opens

In 1975, I opened an office in las Vegas, Nevada, as a Nutrition Consultant. This was at the time when the Laetrile/cancer controversy was a "hot" news item. My intention in opening the office was to work with young people and basic health maintenance. As the only Nutrition Consultant in town, I was soon speaking for clubs and organizations, appearing on radio and television. Cancer was what everyone wanted to hear about—so I talked about cancer.

I was well-versed in nutritional cancer therapy. Several years before this I had begun working with cancer patients and had seen them improve using nutrition. I began to see cancer patients in my office. What I saw was a sad commentary on the medical community. Tragic is a mild word for what I witnessed.

In my zeal to help these unfortunate cancer patients, I searched for everything I could read or hear about. I joined organizations. Soon I was asked to speak at health conventions. I traveled and spoke all over the Western United States.

One day, I read an article about a dentist in Beverly Hills who was helping people's health problems by improving their dental posture— aligning their teeth and jaws properly. This certainly worth a try. I knew I bit the inside of my mouth all too often, chewing was tiresome and one side of my jaw clicked a lot.

It was time for my appointment. I was seated in a dental chair and Dr. Ravins came in. I explained that I was here to see him because I had a skin problem—and understood that he was using an orthopedic treatment that might help me.

He curtly replied, "I am a dentist. If you have skin problems, see a dermatologist. If your teeth need work, I can help you with that. But I do not, as a dentist, treat skin problems."

I matter-of-factly replied, "Fine, you take care of my dental problem, and that will take care of my skin." I knew it just had to!

My Dental History

I proceeded to give him a brief report on my physical and dental history. At thirteen I had a lower right jaw tooth pulled by our elderly family dentist. I remember he seemed so ancient as his strong hands reached in my mouth and in one "heavy" push removed the tooth. There was no mention of replacing the tooth. I never complained about it and soon became accustomed to the empty space it left. Besides, I had the other side for chewing, and one side seemed enough. Of course, the tooth should not have been pulled, but in those days, that was the custom.

Several dentists suggested I get it replaced, but no one had a good reason, except that the hole needed a tooth. There was never so much as a hint that my health was in any way connected to that missing tooth. It seemed to be only a cosmetic consideration, and one missing back tooth was not noticeable.

Later, after the birth of my second son, I had a few small cavities filled. Every time a dentist worked on my mouth, he would grind and file down on my teeth. My mouth was continually uncomfortable, and I tired of the grinding and filing. I wondered if I would have any teeth left after a few years of this.

Then at age 32, I had a tooth crowned (on my "chewing side") that had been filled several times. The crown was never comfortable, feeling like a foreign object in my mouth. But the dentist contended it was fine. I spent the next four years going from dentist to dentist looking for one who would agree that the crown was not right. Peer protection is strong.

Finally, I found one who agreed with me. He removed the original crown and rebuilt it with such artistry that it is a shame it's hidden in my mouth!

The new crown seemed to help in the reduction of headaches, which had become more frequent and severe. This piqued my interest because I knew the answer to my problem was not in nutrition. It was this improvement in headaches associated with the new crown that turned me toward dentistry in my search.

The Work Begins

First, Dr. Ravins did an extensive dental work-up. Then his lab made a "splint" based on my measurements. For almost two days I struggled trying to wear it while he made continual adjustments.

This was not working. As soon as he put the object in my mouth, my heartbeat and breathing increased and I felt pain in my joints—I ached! The afternoon of the second day, I sat waiting to see him for the fifth time that day. He rushed into the room and said, "I know what the problem is. You have an allergy to the plastic."

The next morning, Dr. Ravins' lab had a removable orthodontic appliance ready for me. Made of wires, it was called a "Crozat Appliance." What we could not do with the splint, we would do with these appliances. These I could wear. The following day I was able to return to Las Vegas.

I wore those appliances religiously! Within ten days I noticed my energy level increasing and my skin began gradually clearing. After several months, I noticed I had not had a cold. Friends began to comment on how good I was looking. My eyes were brighter, my face looked more alive. That was good to hear, but I wondered just how badly I had looked before!

It was only after wearing the appliances for some nine months that I began telling anyone what I was doing. I had to be sure. When I did start talking about dental stress and tension and health problems on radio, TV, lectures and private consulting, I was amazed at the number of people who called me to describe health problems, correlating them with their dental history. Many called about their children who were mouth breathers with low energy levels. How good it felt to help them toward finding an answer!

A few years have passed since then. I later worked with Dr. Ravins and his dental research foundation. I saw and talked with numerous patients and heard their stories—and their happy endings.

Why Crozats Worked For Me

I know you're wondering if she's ever going to tell why the Crozat Appliance worked. As usual, the answer to a complicated problem is somewhat simple. Of course, Dr. Ravins would give a more complex response, but this is the brief summary of it all:

1. Because of past dental errors, my teeth were out of alignment. Consequently, the Temporamandibular Joints (TMJ) were excessively tensed, resulting in excessive energy depletion of the body.

2. The Crozat Appliance re-aligned the teeth, releasing excessive tension in the dental area

and subsequently in the whole body. As this took place, my energy level returned to normal.

I solved my energy crisis through persistent determination. I just knew there had to be an answer. What other choice did I have? To learn to live with it was not living—it was existing. And life should be lived to the best of our individual potential.

The real energy crisis is the HUMAN ENERGY CRISIS—not petroleum. Many people are just existing today because of this energy crisis. You, the reader, may be one of those caught up in this crisis. The chances are you are not finding any ready answers, either.

I'd like to share some thoughts with you—some things I have learned that may help. I no longer actively work as a Nutrition Consultant. I closed my office and altered my direction several years ago when my husband's work took him to the Middle East. We moved to Athens, Greece, with our youngest son. My travels extended from the Soviet Union to the Middle East and Africa as well as the Continent. It was an adventure.

My experiences have led me to learn about things I probably would never have known—not to mention the interesting people and pioneers I have met who have inspired and encouraged me.

The Real Energy Crisis

Only recently have we begun to see the impact of the "real" energy crisis—the cost to industry in time lost, productivity loss and related problems that weaken our industrial fiber and competitive edge. This is not to mention the enormous amount of money spent on medical bills—and the personal suffering!

Over fifty years ago, Thomas A. Edison said, "The doctor of the future will give no medicine but will interest his patients in the care of the human frame, in diet and in the cause of disease."

Since then our society has experienced rapid technological progress; the business community has greatly expanded; and our social order and responsibilities have changed. Yet, even today, rare is the physician who conforms to Mr. Edison's hopeful prediction.

Unfortunately, the health and personal energy issue is compounded by our fast-paced, pressured lifestyle. The stress, tension and anxiety that come with it have proven harmful to our mental and physical health and well-being. New problems have been added to the old ones.

"...in accounting for any disease, including heart disease, the modern doctor will no longer focus his attention exclusively on our material make-up, whether derived from heredity, diet or other means, but will consider also how we handle ourselves...proper handling of ourselves is the avoidance of undue tension, provided that we live normally otherwise." (*You Must Relax*, Edmund Jacobson, M.D., copyright 1978, McGraw-Hill, publisher.)

The question is, how are we doing in the areas of lifestyle, diet, the care of our human frame and in understanding the cause of disease? Not too well, I'm afraid.

Our national medical bill for 1984 was $357 billion—11 percent of the gross national product! Drugs to treat anxiety—a tension disorder—represents the biggest chunk of the $1.5 billion psychotherapeutic drug market. And the anxiety-drug market is expected to hold a "window of opportunity" for drug companies. That is, they anticipate a windfall of business. It is estimated that only 23 percent of patients believed to be suffering from anxiety are now receiving drug treatment. This one paramount fact stands out: drug companies and investors are banking on us not being able to cope with our lives.

The Mind and Energy

I hurt when I read such figures. "Anxiety" is a state of the mind. What is the mind? It can be defined as "that energy-expending function of the organism by which it programs its behavior."

Past experiences and information are stored in our brain. But it is our *perception* of events that become our own "reality." This is why two people presented with the same facts can each come to entirely different conclusions. Seeing the same sight, we see different things. How we "perceive" it to be actually determines what we "see" and know.

To come to these conclusions requires a certain amount of energy. It takes energy to think! But what if there is not enough energy available for everything to work properly at the same time? Have you ever said, "I'm so tired, I can't think straight!" That's quite possible, literally. That is, your energy supply is so low, you cannot think clearly.

What is our energy supply? The raw materials come from the food we eat. If our food is poor quality and doesn't contain the necessary ingredients (nutrients) we require, our quality of product (our natural energy level and health) will reflect this.

From the nutrients in food, the body makes its fuel, called "adenosine triphosphate," or "cyclic ATP" for short. Every moment of our effortful life depends on and results from the use of adenosine triphosphate—our energy supply.

Energy Consumption

Following are some examples of how we use energy:
- The body's chemical activity (function, including

energy) performs at an estimated efficiency rate of about 40-70 percent of its potential. This can be improved.

- Of the energy we produce, about 20-25 percent is used for normal brain function. Its needs go up dramatically under stress and pressure. Excessive energy requirements can be controlled.

- In normal, quiet breathing, the energy requirement is 5-10 percent of our total energy output. If the airways become obstructed (as with colds, nasal blockages), the energy requirement rises to 30 percent or more.

- Human muscle efficiency is only 20-30 percent of its potential. Energy needs vary with degree of usage, but with its low efficiency, the muscle requires 2 to 4 times more energy than it produces in the form of work.

- Dental tension disorders such as Temporomandibular Joint problems, mouth breathing or infections in the dental area can require up to 50 percent of the TOTAL ENERGY EXPENDITURE of the entire body.

Does this give you some idea of what happens to our energy when we are not physically functioning well? Moreover, it is important to remember that the body has inherent predetermined priorities on the use of that energy—beyond our control. The brain and breathing are top priorities—

survival. Functions such as digestion are low priorities. These can wait until the crisis is over.

Is it any wonder that back problems and digestive disorders are the second and third most common reasons why people go to hospitals? Pain is the number one reason people go to a doctor or dentist? Too many of us have enough energy to stay alive, but hardly enough extra to cover other needs.

This does not leave us prepared to meet the challenges of life on the outside. With stresses and pressures, tensions and strains bombarding us from every direction, where is the energy to handle it all?

Personal Responsibility

It is the responsibility of us all to learn about the requirements of this complex, sophisticated, wonderful mechanism of the human body. We need to understand that disease and suffering is not a punishment from God. It is the consequence of broken natural laws. With sickness and disease, you are suffering an energy crisis!

Today, my skin is completely clear and my chronic headaches are gone. I still adhere to the natural foods diet and practice the principles of nutrition I studied so long and hard. My parents, who started this years ago, are still alive and very healthy at 74 and 79—a good genetic omen for me!

I was fortunate to find the answer to my energy

crisis—by diligent searching and learning from others. For those of you suffering the same crisis, I hope my experiences can help you find an answer, too.

Receiving thankfully all that Physiology or Chemistry or any other Science can give us, let us still hold that that alone is true which is proven clinically, and that which is clinically proved needs no other evidence.

—Sir James Padget

We must not say, "Let us begin by inventing principles whereby we must be able to explain everything;" rather we must say, "Let us make an exact analysis of the matter, and then we shall try to see, with much diffidence, if it fits with any principle."

—Voltaire

MARIETA P. PICKETT
Concepts Unlimited
R.R. #2, Box 139
Atlanta, IN 46031
Bus. (317) 773-0061 • Res (317) 984-5547

Marieta Pickett

Marieta Pickett is a consultant, speaker, seminar leader for business and industry specializing in Human Relations and Customer Relations Programs. She has taught hundreds of people how to manage stress by taking back control of their life and health. Raise your awareness of how to be happier, healthier, and more productive by attending one of Marieta's lectures or workshops.

Her extensive teaching experience at Anderson College and Ball State University has given her much expertise in using the subject matter as the catalyst to develop the person's self image. With a positive self image and high self esteem, a person can do anything they want in life with a lot less stress and have a much better chance of becoming a highly successful and happy person.

While working on a doctorate at Arizona State University, she became intensely interested in the Holistic Health Care Movement. She is a founding charter member of the American Holistic Medical Foundation and has accumulated many hours of CME credits. She is currently program chairman for the Health and Wellness Special Interest Group of the National Speakers Association Convention.

Marieta, a highly successful businesswoman, currently owns and manages New Age Technics, a business distributing products to enhance our lives and health.

Her extraordinarily effective speaking ability has made her a nationally known lecturer and speaker for workshops, seminars, specially tailored programs, and spouse programs. Current Programs are: TEAM BUILDING FOR BUSINESS, CHOOSING THE RIGHT PEOPLE, USING STRESS CREATIVELY, WEEK-END WELLNESS PROGRAMS, CUSTOMER RELATIONS PROGRAMS, CONTROL YOUR ATTITUDE—CHANGE YOUR LIFE AND YOUR HEALTH, YOU DON'T HAVE A PROBLEM—YOU HAVE A DECISION TO MAKE, RELATIONSHIPS, STRESSORS—WHAT PRICE TO PAY, WORD DIETS.

5

Using Stress Creatively
Increase Your Energy—Decrease Fatigue
by Marieta Pickett

"When there is a problem, there is not something to do, there is something to know."
—Dr. Raymond Charles Barker

Many of us are not aware of the things that are stressors to our body, deplete our energy and cause us to feel fatigued.

In the next few pages, try to recognize:

1. the stressors you have in your life—and the

price you are paying for them,
2. the two major categories of stress,
3. the importance of the mind,
4. and most importantly—that you have the power to control and create your life and your health.

If we start out with a certain amount of energy and then deplete some of it because of poor foods choices, use another portion working under lighting conditions that are not beneficial to our health, and then have toxic elements in our water and air—when we have an emotional drain because of a parent or child being very ill or a spouse announcing that they're leaving—suddenly there is not enough energy left to do all the things we want to do and still maintain good health. That is when we have illness.

If you are doing some things that deplete your energy and are not important to you, with new information you may choose to change those habits and save your energy for an activity you really enjoy.

Two Main Types of Stress

Beneficial Stress

Hans Selye, M.D., the father of Stress Medicine, called the "good" kind of stress, EUSTRESS. This is the kind that helps us be productive and meet our goals. It is the deadline that helps us get a Business Report or Presentation completed, the incentive to meet a quota to win a company trip or the impetus to finish a term paper. It can also be the stress of being Chairman of a Fund Raising Campaign or giving a speech—or just planning a party.

All these things are stressors, but they have a conclusion. We usually feel good for having completed the task. We have that "natural high" that comes from a job well done.

Destructive Stress

The second kind of stress is what most people think of when we discuss stress. To some it may mean smoking, consuming caffeine, eating candy and fried foods. It occurs over a long period of time with no measurable beneficial results. It's like having a rock in your shoe—forever. Many things are not recognized as being stressors—like being in an unhappy relationship or working in the wrong job.

It is not surprising that many of us are not aware of the things that affect our body, for to this date, there has not been a single report of a human body being delivered with an Owner's Manual!

Cars, stereos, appliances, etc. all come with instructions. Do not immerse in water. Keep away from extreme heat, etc. We promote "high level wellness" for our autos and appliances, but what about our personal bodies?

Understanding the events that are destructive is not always easy. Sometimes the use of inexpensive biofeedback equipment is one of the easiest ways to understand what is really "bugging" us.

When asked to relax, it is not unusual for people to say to me, "I am relaxed," and yet they may be *very* tense and tight. Biofeedback equipment does not do anything for us or to us, but lets us know what we're doing. With the use of biofeedback, people understand and say, "Oh, I can do more of that. I just didn't know that's what you wanted me to do."

Can you imagine what it would be like if you were attempting to learn to shoot a basketball through the hoop and you never got to see whether it went in or out—to the right or left of the goal? Without feedback we have no way of improving our productivity or accuracy. In our jobs, we need to know how well we are doing. Failure to have a manager or supervisor tell us about our job productivity produces anxiety.

Managers—the only way a person will improve their performance is to have positive feedback.

While at the University, teaching people how to teach, I often said to my students, "Find something that a person does well, compliment them on that, and they will strive even harder to please you to get another "Warm Fuzzy." (All of us need positive strokes to feel well and survive.)

The feeling of accomplishment that comes from doing a good job reduces tension tremendously.

Non-productive Long Term Stress

Many times we spend our lives in jobs that are not satisfying or in jobs where it is not easy to be effective and productive. Another tool that is very beneficial is a personality evaluation that will help us understand our strengths and weaknesses. Knowing ourselves helps us recognize the different behavioral styles of others in our relationships at home and on the job.

Managers may get the results they want and cause less stress to their employees and themselves if they have learned from an evaluating instrument such as a personal profile the best way to give instructions. One behavioral style may respond best to written instructions, another may learn quickest and easiest from verbal instructions, and still another really wants to be shown how to do something.

If you were a salesperson, can you imagine how much less stressful a sales presentation could be if you knew whether or not the person wanted only the bottom line or if you needed to give them every last detail?

Using tools such as biofeedback and personal profiles enables us to attain self discovery and mastery and helps us to accomplish our goals with much less effort and stress.

Lighting is another kind of stress that Dr. John Ott documents in his book, *Light, Radiation and You.* He reports a variety of startling improvements that occur when full spectrum fluorescent lights are introduced into a work environment. In schools, children who have been hyperactive become calm and co-operative.

Since human energy is depleted under ordinary fluorescent lighting, and since Dr. Ott recommends we all need one to one-and-a-half hours of sunshine each day to have optimal health, he developed full spectrum fluorescent lighting that does not deplete our energy or cause us stress. Eight hours under this type of lighting also benefits us like being in the sun for an hour.

Offices that have purchased this full spectrum lighting from us continually comment on the reduction of stress to the eyes and body and the increase in productivity.

Changing the lighting in offices, schools, and factories may be one of the simplest, easiest, and most effective things you can do to decrease stress.

Sounds also influence our body and energy. Steve Halpern, in his book *Sound Health,* reports that Dr. John Diamond, a behavioral kinesiologist, tested hundreds of persons. He found 90 percent registered an almost instantaneous loss of two-thirds of their muscle strength when they heard the "short-short-long-pause" beat pattern that is standard in much of rock and roll music. The body soon adapts to the stimulus by what has been called "the general adaptation syndrome." Just because the body adapts does not mean it is good nourishment and that no harmful effects may come from it.

Just as people who continue to eat junk food soon become conditioned and even addicted to these harmful substances, so people who continue to listen to music that weakens them and confuses their inner natural pulse soon become conditioned and possibly addicted to that music.

Through addiction, those things which are bad for our body become necessary for us to carry on. Sound and rhythm addiction are much like sugar addiction, nicotine addiction, caffeine addiction or any other drug.

Be aware of what your body tells you and realize how powerful the effect of music is on the body—and make informed choices.

Some simple suggestions for foods that enhance our energy and reduce stress might be to use all whole grains and lots of fruits and vegetables. Avoid sugar, preservatives, white flour and chemical additives to reduce stress. Drink water that is free of chemicals—chlorine, fluoride, and any other toxic materials.

We have seen people remove many toxic minerals and metals from their bodies as we helped them with nutritional counseling, vitamin therapy, and water purification.

An example of the importance of removing these unwanted metals is the fact that Alzheimer's Disease victims consistently have a high aluminum content in their bodies when tested by tricho tissue analysis (hair analysis).

There is much research on the benefits of physical exercise and the importance of doing it regularly to improve the cardiovascular system. Suffice it to say here that the lack of physical exercise is stressful to the body.

Your Mind—Friend or Foe?

Your mind can be your friend and help you create your own future by what you think, or it can destroy all your efforts faster than you can work.

Plan of Action

The first step in the process is to lay the groundwork. Decide what it is we really want to have; secondly, understand the process that will take us there; and thirdly, have total faith that we will get where we want to go.

It is more difficult to replace old ideas with new ones than it is to begin with a good idea from the beginning. Many times we attempt to reconstruct and replace an old habit pattern or a thought pattern. Because it has become so natural and so much a part of us, it is much more difficult than it would be for us to start from the beginning and construct a whole new program.

For it is only a matter of time until we come to the realization that it is a difficult problem to rebuild a habit pattern and so it makes much more sense to begin and construct our habits by a meaningful thought process rather than allowing ourselves to fall into the habits we may have accumulated or learned from our family and friends.

Demonstrations of Mental Stress

In many of our seminars, we use Applied Kinesiology (muscle testing) to determine the relative strength of an individual, then ask them to think of something in their life that is not perfect and while concentrating on that, we re-test. They always test weaker. Then we ask them to visualize or fantasize the solution as they would like the imperfect situation to be or conclude. Immediately, they are stronger.

This is quite amazing to most people, but demonstrates very dramatically that what we think is what we get. A positive mental attitude really does make a difference in the polarity of the human energy system, for as we are positive, we attract universal energy to us and when we are negative, we disperse our own energy.

How often have you known someone who was

negative and depressed and seemed to be in a vicious cycle that led to more and more depression? Most everyone interprets this as severe stress. When we are loving and giving we attract energy to us. When we try to hang on to people and things, we send energy from us.

Think about a time when you helped someone who really needed you. Can you remember how good you felt?

Giving generates that "natural high" that energizes us with abundant life force—and we feel at peace—not stressed.

You and a friend can test this for yourself. Extend the arm straight out from the shoulder and rotate the arm forward until the thumb turns down. (This isolates the muscle used to test.) Have your friend push down at the wrist for two seconds.

Now think of something you don't like to do—somewhere you don't like to be—or someone whose company you don't enjoy. Re-test. Were you weaker? Next, think of something you like to do—somewhere you like to be or someone you like to be with. Re-test.

Are you surprised how much stronger you are? Can you imagine how much happier you could be, how much more energy you could have, and how much less stress you would feel if you could concentrate your mind on what you want instead of what you don't want!!!

Indecision: Another Major Stressor

Think of an example where you haven't yet made a decision. Are you having trouble deciding whether to buy a home or rent an apartment—continue in your current job or take the new job offer in another city—stay in this relationship or start a new one?

Use the "T" Bar and list on the left side all the benefits of staying where you are and on the right side the benefits of making a change. Which list is more important to you?

Whether you stay in the relationship or current job or whether you go on to the new experience is not as important as your attitude about it.

S   Stay
O   get Out
S   Suffer

If we choose to Stay, that's OK. If we choose to get Out, that's OK. But the thing that is most detrimental to our health is the long term stress that comes from saying: "I'll Suffer. I'll stay for the sake of the kids. Our business would fail if I left. It would break Mom's heart if I moved," and then resent staying and make ourselves miserable and ill.

Indecision drains energy and creates stress. Making a decision gives a feeling of power and taking back control of your life. Even if you have to reverse the decision later on—*make a decision.*

Mental Imaging

Now this is not a great revelation, but it is a universal truth that only when we have the mental image of what it is we are trying to create, do we really have a good chance of getting where we want to go.

There is a wonderful saying that the mind can create whatever you wish—for what you think is what you get. Most people are not aware that they are constantly programming negative things by saying, "I always have bad luck, I never win anything, I'm always last in line."

Of course! They *are* always last in line for that is what they expect. If we mentally create that which we want, we are programming for less stress in our lives.

Take Back Responsibility

How did you decide what to have for breakfast today?

A young bridegroom asked his new wife why she always cut off the end of the ham before she baked it. She replied, "I don't know—Mom always did it that way."

The next time the young man saw his mother-in-law, he asked her the same question. "Why do you always cut off the end of the ham before baking it?" She looked rather puzzled and said, "I really don't know—Mom just always did it that way."

Deciding to get to the bottom of the family tradition, the young bridegroom vowed to ask Grandma. And when he did, she said, "Young man, it's *very* simple. The ham is usually about 16 inches long and my roaster is 12 inches long.

How many of you are making decisions based on habit or information that may have been appropriate when you were three or perhaps twelve years old, but may no longer be relevant?

With new information, how will you decide what to have for breakfast tomorrow?

Imagine yourself in line at a smorgasbord of food, and then instead of dishes of food, imagine there are dishes of thoughts. You get to choose any and all thoughts you wish. These thoughts will create your future experiences. Now if you choose thoughts that will create problems and pain, that's rather foolish. It's like choosing food that always makes you ill. We may do this once or twice, but as soon as we learn which foods upset our bodies, we stay away from them; it's the same with thoughts. Choose to stay away from thoughts that create problems and pain.

If we want a joyous life, we must think joyous thoughts. If we want a prosperous life, we must think prosperous thoughts. If we want a loving life we must think loving thoughts. Whatever we send out mentally or verbally will come back to us in like form.

There is no "good" or "bad" weather, there is just weather—and our individual learned reactions to it. Would you like to change your reaction?

"The Point of Power Is Always in the Present Moment."—Louise Hay

The changes take place right here and now in our own minds! It doesn't matter how long we've had a negative pattern or an illness or a poor relationship or lack of finances or self-hatred. We can begin to change today!

Remember: You are the only person who thinks in your mind! You are the power and authority in your world. Your thoughts and beliefs of the past have created this moment and all the moments up to this moment. What you are now choosing to believe and think and say will create the next moment—and the next day and the next month and the next year. YOU are the power in your world! You get to have whatever you choose to think!

Stop for a moment and be aware of your thoughts. What are you thinking right now? If it is true that your thoughts shape your life, would you want what you were thinking just now to become true for you?

Louise Hay says in her book, *You Can Heal Your*

Life, "I believe we create every so called 'illness' in our body. The body, like everything else in life, is a mirror of our inner thoughts and beliefs. The body is always talking to us, if we will only take the time to listen. Every cell within your body responds to every single thought you think and every word you speak."

Many people say they cannot enjoy today because of something that happened in the past. We are only hurting ourselves by refusing to live in this moment to the fullest.

Your mind is a tool you can choose to use any way you wish. The thoughts you choose to think create the experiences you have. If you believe that "It is hard or difficult to change a habit or a thought," then your choice of this thought will make it true for you. If you would choose to think, "it is becoming easier for me to make changes," then your choice of this thought will make that true for you.

The only thing you ever have any control of is your current thought. See if you can say, "I now realize that I have created this condition and I am now willing to release the pattern in my consciousness that is responsible for this condition." Let's stop wasting time and energy putting ourselves down for something we can't help doing if we have certain inner beliefs. Change the beliefs!

Trying to eliminate the symptom without working on dissolving the cause is useless. The moment we release our will power or discipline, the symptom returns again.

Although we are never in control of anyone else, as we learn our lessons, we are now able to take the hand of someone else and help to lead them. Of course, it is not our responsibility to learn their lesson, but we can be of help in guiding and directing—never taking away the opportunity for them to learn what they have chosen to learn.

As we progress, we will have the full realization that we can increase our energy and decrease fatigue. We will understand that we can control the stressors in our lives and decide how many and what price we are willing to pay for those we choose to keep. For only when we are looking at it from above—from having completed the task—do we have a true perspective and knowledge of the whole picture.

It is never enough to watch from afar, for we must be involved. We must be part of the picture in order to learn the lesson. We do learn by experience.

If you think of the hardest thing for you to do and how much you resist it, then you're looking at your greatest lesson at the moment and your greatest current stressor. Surrendering—giving up the resistance and allowing yourself to learn what you need to learn—will make the next step easier and reduce the pain and stress. We all have lessons to learn. The things that are so difficult for us are only the lessons we have chosen for ourselves. If things are easy for us, then they are not lessons but things we already know.

Summary

There are three principles involved in reducing stress in our lives.

The first is becoming aware of the lessons we are attempting to learn and therefore the reasons for creating the stress. For it is only when we understand that there is a purpose for this stress, that we can benefit from it and go on to have real peace. For as we become aware of the lessons we are attempting to learn, then we can eliminate the stress and have peace.

The second step is acknowledging that we are responsible for creating this mess that we are in for no one ever does anything to us. We have created all of this for ourselves to learn what we need to learn. That may seem difficult to understand, but when we realize that as soon as we learn the lesson, the stress is eliminated and we are at peace.

The third step is acknowledging that we have the power and ability to take back the responsibility for our life and our health.

For a self-scoring Stress Assessment Questionaire, send a SASE to:
COUNCEPTS UNLIMITED
R.R. #2 Box 139, Atlanta, IN 46031

Anybody can become angry—THAT IS EASY: BUT TO BE ANGRY WITH THE RIGHT PERSON, AND TO THE RIGHT DEGREE, AND AT THE RIGHT TIME, AND FOR THE RIGHT PURPOSE, AND IN THE RIGHT WAY—that is not within everybody's power and is not easy.

—***Aristotle,*** Nicomachean Ethics

DR. STAN FRAGER
Counselor to Champions
3906 Dupont Square, South
Louisville, KY 40207
(502) 893-6654

Dr. Stan Frager

"Everyone can be an achiever—but first you've got to get out of the locker room."

—**Dr. Stan Frager**

Nationally known as "Counselor to Champions," Dr. Frager's work with professional, Olympic, and amateur athletes has won recognition from Sports Illustrated, Basketball Today, *and others. But his insights extend far beyond athletics. Convinced stress management is one of the keys to self-actualization, he has drawn on his years as a licensed psychologist, marriage/family therapist, probation officer, and award-winning filmmaker to develop entertaining, educational workshops for everyone, from executives to students, who want to reach his or her personal and professional best. Frager Associates, his human resource development consulting firm, enjoys a wide-ranging institutional and industrial client base.*

In addition to his active practice as therapist and speaker, Dr. Frager is a university professor and consultant in sports counseling to several outstanding university teams. He has also fought and won a personal battle with cancer and is a respected contributor to the literature on the special problems of those facing catastrophic illness.

Dr. Frager holds a Ph.D. from UCLA and received a Winston Churchill Fellowship. He has judged the Dale Carnegie International Speech Competition and is listed in Who's Who in the South and Southwest.

6

Turn Your Stress Into Strength
by Dr. Stan Frager

*"I wish to preach, not the doctrine of
ignoble ease, but the doctrine of the
strenuous life."*
—Theodore Roosevelt

Imagine this: You find your lane, bend down,
wiggle your right foot into the starting block. At this
angle the hurdles ahead crowd the horizon. The dirt
under your fingers is as dry as the inside of your
mouth. The runner in the next lane has closed his
eyes. His lips move, but you can't hear him. "Ready!"

Your heart jumps. There's a knot in your stomach. "Set!" Hunch down a little more, your shoulders tense for that final signal...

Or this: After months of patient work, you finally have an appointment with the right person. You're ready as you'll ever be. You walk in with your presentation materials; however, she's not alone. "Thought it would be good for all the department heads to hear your proposal," she says, gesturing toward the six others. "No problem," you reply. You turn to set up the easel. Your palms have begun to sweat ...

Even if you've never been in either of these situations, you know one thing they have in common: the individuals are under "stress." That's bad, right?

It could be—but look again: The runner's a coiled spring waiting for the starting gun: "psyched up." Athletes are trained to use tension to improve performance. The businessperson? This case isn't so clear. They fall apart, go blank, stammer, knock over the easel. Or—turn to that roomful of people more alert, aware, thinking more quickly than ever before.

Toward an Understanding of Stress and Stressors

What is "stress"? We understand it best if we make this distinction: "stress" and "stressor" are not the same.

The boss who humiliates you in public is only a stimulus—a stressor. Your *response* to criticism determines your level of stress. The stress itself is something different.

Look again at the reactions in the runner and businessperson. They're *physical.* Stress is a physiological response to a demand for adaptation to some environmental change.

The three phases of response: In 1936, stress-research pioneer Dr. Hans Selye defined ("A syndrome produced by diverse nocuous agents," Nature), a biological response, the "General Adaptation Syndrome" (G.A.S.). "All organisms depend upon maintaining a sort of internal balance," he said. "When they're exposed to demand for change—whether from the environment directly (an earthquake) or from their perceptions of the environment (is the boss frowning?)—internal balance is upset. The organism's first need is to *reestablish balance*—to "adapt" to the demand." Selye saw adaptation as having three phases, (Figure A.)

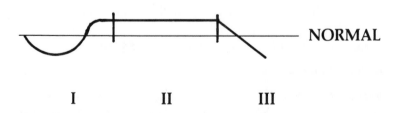

NORMAL

I   II   III

The first, the phase of alarm is the "fight or flight," mobilization response. The second, Selye called the phase of resistance. The organism's energy expenditures remain high as it attempts to keep up the balancing act, by opposing the demand ("catatoxic" response, from the Greek prefix "cata-" or "against") or learning to live with it ("syntoxic" response, from the Greek prefix "syn-" or "with"). Even syntoxic adaptation uses up energy. No matter which response, if the demand lasts too long or is too intense, the organism reaches the third phase: exhaustion, or death.

In human beings stress response produces very predictable physical changes. Figure B gives the physiological nuts and bolts. Think of how you've felt in various situations. You'll recall that not even very pleasureable experiences can be sustained for long. Excitement creates as intense a demand for adaptive energy as running five miles: after a while, you've just got to stop and rest.

Another essential element in our developing understanding of the nature of the stress response is it's *nonspecific*. Whether we face a pleasureable situation or an unpleasant one, *physiological* responses are the same.

"Spending" adaptive energy—the Schedule of Recent Events: How much adaptive energy do we have? There's no scientific way to measure it. It seems likely that each of us has a limited amount. It would be useful to know how much adaptive energy is used up in various activities. Then we could "budget" our expenditures.

In their Schedule of Recent Events, Holmes and Rahe offer a useful starting point for estimating relative stress effects of various life events ("The social readjustment rating scale," J. Psychosom. Res., 1967). Having compiled a list of common life events (everything from taking a vacation to the death of one's spouse), they asked a sample group of raters to use "marriage" as the comparison midpoint (50) and assign a score from 1 to 100 to each event, according to how much more adaptation that event demanded. The consensus on relative individual scores was considerable—sometimes surprising to those of us first looking at the chart. "Being fired" ranked just below "marriage." "Christmas season," "vacation," and "minor traffic violations" were points apart on the low-demand end. *Changes* in status require the same amount of adaptation, if the changes were "positive" or "negative" changes in number of marital arguments, family gatherings, or work responsibilities. The investigators asked a sample group to check on the events that had occurred in their lives over the previous twelve months. When these SRE ratings were added, there seemed to be a correlation between individual scores over a certain number, and those individuals becoming physically ill. The Schedule of Recent Events roughly predicts

SYMPTOMS OF STRESS
Stanley R. Frager, Ph.D.

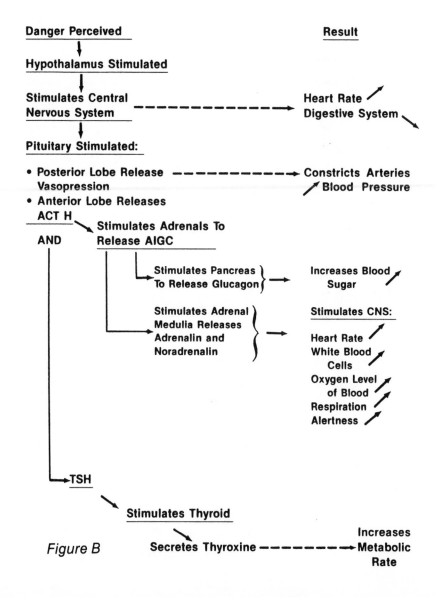

Figure B

Selye's phase of exhaustion—that point when so much of our adaptive energy has been used up we don't have enough to fight off disease.

"Individual" Factor

We all know individuals who seem to be able to withstand anything and keep going. We know people who fall apart at the least stress. Why is individual response to stressors so variable?

Think back to our original distinction between stress and stressor. Rahe and Holmes only identified *stressors,* not stress levels. Stress response is an *individual* matter—affected first by how we perceive the stressor. The ordinary airline passenger and the experienced skydiver (wearing a parachute) see different things in the open airplane door flying at 30,000 feet.

Individual characteristics affect how we respond to stressors. If the amount of adaptive energy available to us is a finite pool of investment capital, the more places we dedicate funds (by choice or necessity) the thinner we spread ourselves. If we fight off acute or chronic physical illness, we have less energy available to deal with a difficult, demanding job. Age and hereditary disorders, particularly those that affect our ability to perceive, also play a part. Personality types and their associated attitudes are important. It's a matter of speculation whether specific traits "lead to" specific diseases. The reason for the seeming correlations is still a mystery. Certain *combinations* of traits do seem to be associated with particular disorders. The best example is the Type A personality—the "one man band" who cannot delegate, suffering from "hurry sickness"— they are considered prime heart attack candidates.

There are other, purely "coincidental" elements in the equation. Is the stressor, regardless of intensity, familiar, like the reporter's daily deadline? Is the individual surprised by the demand? Had some warning? Preparation, however short, reduces stress response. The amount of time available for responding can affect how much adaptive energy is used.

Disposing of Misconceptions: We can bring these into focus by considering what stress is *not.*

A. Nervousness or Anxiety. Feelings are symptoms of stress, beyond the individual's capacity for adaptation—*distress,* not stress. The stress response is nonspecific—a physiological response called up whether the demand is winning a lottery or being arrested for speeding.

B. Avoidable. Since stress response is our means of adapting to an ever-changing environment, we can't avoid it. Even in sleep or deep relaxation, we expend energy to keep our hearts beating, our lungs gilling and emptying regularly. If we *could* fully suppress our stress response, we'd die.

C. Harmful or the result of damage? The demand to adapt varies in intensity. When it is greater than we can deal with, or the stressor outlasts our reserves, we feel the unpleasant, even damaging effects of maintaining resistance.

Stress and Disease: Rahe and Holmes never claimed that scores on the Schedule of Recent Events predicted particular diseases, or illness. A stay-at-home group like Kansas wheat farmers have a statistically low risk of dying in plane crashes. Coincidental "correlation" aside, no thinking person could imagine wheat farming in Kansas would make him immune to death in a plane crash, especially should he fly to visit his mother in Toronto every weekend.

SRE clearly suggests the criteria for predicting "exhaustion" of adaptive energy lies in accumulation of stressor exposures over a short time. We've all heard more than we can digest about the relationship between stress and physical and emotional diseases.

The long list is depressing. On the physical side are heart attack, cancer, ulcers, asthma and other allergy-related problems, susceptibility to infectious disease, hyperthyroidism, rheumatoid arthritis, colitis, premenstrual syndrome—right down to warts. On the emotional side, are addictions (alcohol, caffeine, nicotine, drugs), obesity, divorce, accidents, and the extreme, suicide. More subtle, but no less tragic, is the undeniable effect of stress on aging, the "art of dying young."

Eustress—the Balance Point

Courage is resistance to fear, mastery of fear—not absence of fear.

—Mark Twain

Stress is unavoidable, nor should we attempt to avoid it totally. Even if it were possible, withdrawal from all exposure to demands for change would mean a life so bland as to be virtually worthless.

"Burnout"—the phenomenon we've heard so much about should now have new meaning for you. The other end of the spectrum—"rustout"—presents a problem in professions where responsibility for others combined with an ever-increasing sense of helplessness produces emotional and professional withdrawal, absenteeism, illness, and flight into other fields.

We know that *meaningful* activity like work is necessary to the human animal. Lack of stress is itself a sort of stress. Deprivation withers us on the vine as quickly as spectacular disaster.

It is to our advantage to operate at peak performance for as much of our lives as possible. Alertness mobilization is a pleasurable feeling. The sensation is being in balance—not having to give more than one can give, is called eustress (from the Greek prefix "eu-", meaning healthy. (Figure C).

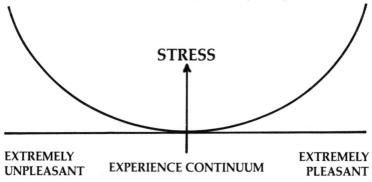

STRESS

EXTREMELY
UNPLEASANT   EXPERIENCE CONTINUUM   EXTREMELY
PLEASANT

In minimizing wear and tear on body and psyche, eustress is what we must seek. It would be wrong to conclude that we should attempt to achieve eustress by eliminating unpleasant or pleasant stressors from our lives, or to think of that point of equilibrium as static—predetermined. Remember: physical and psychological conditioning play an important response in stress reaction, as do familiarity and preparation. We *can* change our response to specific stressors—improving our general response, thus turning our stress into strength.

Promoting Eustress—Workable Strategies

Fortunately, psycho analysis is not the only way to resolve inner conflicts. Life itself still remains a very effective therapist.

—Karen Horney

Our helping profession is *not* helpless when it comes to providing effective, workable tools to those who need management of stress response. Sometimes problems are best dealt with by avoidance. Not dealing with them, is not really evasion of the stressor but substituting a lesser evil, (deciding that working overtime does more damage than would a reduction in pay). Evasion is a possibility, such as abstaining on a controversial vote. However, it's almost impossible to avoid difficult decisions forever, even postponement can create stress.

The most effective techniques I offer my clients and patients involve promoting eustress by improving stress tolerance. These techniques fall into two categories: those we use for ourselves, and those we use as supervisors. We help others manage job-related stress, and avoid the possibility they will become sources of stress for us.

Personal Tactics

Relaxation techniques/meditation/self-hypnosis: Deep relaxation, meditation techniques, and hypnotherapy are far more than moments set aside for passivity, dependent upon "supernatural" power. Remember the businessperson about to give a presentation. Anxiety manifests in muscular tension that plays havoc with functional abilities. The voice suddenly breaks two octaves higher than usual.

Preoccupation with physical discomfort prevents the most competent from thinking clearly—or at all.

I see this kind of reaction frequently among my many athlete clients. One football player said, "Winning in sports is 90% mental." The basketball player who misses the free shot he made a hundred times out of a hundred in practice, the gymnast who misses on the balance beam may be suffering more from concentration problems than lack of athletic ability. I've had gratifying success teaching talented people simple methods of deep relaxation and visualization that constitute powerful mental imagery tools.

The key is to learn how to induce a state of deep relaxation, followed by carefully structured imagining of situations in which you have a pattern of error. Change the situation: Picture yourself performing perfectly. No technique can make you capable of jumping four feet unless you have the physique and conditioning to do so, but if you can jump four feet in one situation and only three in another, deep relaxation and autohypnosis can help.

Diet! Your Mom was right—you are what you eat. The more balanced, nutritious, and sensible your diet the better chance you have for improving response to stress, physical or emotional. Carrying extra weight is a load neither body nor self-esteem can afford. Keep alcohol to a minimum (alcohol represents one of our most potent sources of empty calories). Quit smoking; a stressor in itself.

Exercise: A stressor that is beneficial. The physiological "fight or flight" originally ended in actual physical activity: combat or retreat. Look at the physical manifestations of mobilization in Figure B. Remember, the body will produce them indiscriminately, no matter whether an appropriate response to the stressor uses them up. If they aren't used up, they're potent sources of erosion on other body systems. Exercise as a key to managing stress, provides the body with regular means of using up excess physiological stress-response byproducts—as soon as possible.

Exercise, used as therapy for specific stress-response situations, should be performed as soon as you've been stressed—not a very practical option. The best alternative is regular, planned, vigorous exercise. At least three hours a week. What's best? *Anything vigorous and sustained done consistently.* A game of handball may work to spot-treat times when anxiety overwhelms you, but it's not worth much as part of a systematic attack on stress levels.

Irregular, unsustained exercise won't help get the weight-reduction and general physical conditioning benefits you're entitled to; it may end in just making you hungry. *Regular,* moderate exercise works to suppress hunger. It makes the difference between the stress of having to turn aside tempting food and being able to eat what you want.

Developing Personal Coping Skills

Better time management helps smooth out rough places. Be ruthless with time, be kind to yourself. Whose life is it, anyway? Take a few minutes at the end of every day to plan reasonable goals for the next. Write them down. Review them next morning. See whether they still look achievable. Change what doesn't look within reach, then start checking them off.

Learn to say no. Postpone until you really knov what you want. Don't be rushed into decisions before you have all the facts. It you feel over-whelmed by information, and your thoughts are hopelessly snarled in all the possibilities, buy your-self some time. Just shout "Stop!" (even if it's heard only in your head). Break the cycle of anxiety and increased tension.

No one loves you like you can. If you don't care about yourself, others aren't motivated to care about you either. Commit yourself to getting enough rest—seven to eight hours a night. Take breaks from long-term, sustained activity. Master one of the many relaxation techniques available. Reserve time, even in the middle of the day, for a short quiet time.

Developing a Personal Support System

One of the chief causes of burnout is a pervasive sense of helplessness in the face of responsibility—a terrible double bind. There are situations in which we find ourselves operating at a handicap. Even our best efforts are frustrated.

The perception that you're alone in the struggle is an unnecessary stressor. Draw on your pool of friends to create a personal support system.

That's a tall order for many of us. Pride can make us unwilling to admit that independence can be a burden. Support is best when it's reciprocal and involves mutual feedback. Isolation affects everyone. Concentrate on learning to approach others with a neutral attitude, neither aggressive nor defensive. We're social animals. We are relieved to be able to fit into support systems with a feeling of equity among the members. Respond when you're asked to give support. You'll find it's there for you when you need it. Systems like these get stronger with use.

Get help: Strategy for managing personal stress assumes we are free to make choices. We're not locked into behavior. Sometimes, we're not able to change a destructive pattern. If you bang your head against the same wall, sit down and consider if it is time to consult a professional. There are no rules for deciding when it's time to stop trying to go it alone. If you've developed an effective support system, you'll at least have feedback available from people you trust to be more objective. If you decide you need help, follow through. Life is finite; don't waste time on strategies that aren't getting the results you want.

Institutional/Supervisory Strategies

Helping your people help themselves: Those of us with responsibility for others know how frustrating it can be to watch the decline of an eager, intelligent subordinate succumbing to what the manager suspects may be stress-related problems. Make efforts to salvage such people. Give thought to how to improve communications becoming part of their support systems. You're likely to find you're developing one for yourself at the same time.

"Black Holes:" Managers face another kind of stress-management problem that needs a different approach. Every manager has deduced from the rapid succession of people through a position that there's a "black hole" on the organizational chart. A spot that swallows up one talented person after another. Stressors, built into the organization, play a part in creating "black holes." Fortunately, they're not immune to remedy.

Analyze the position carefully. Are responsibilities clearly defined? Do they overlap or conflict? Both are sources of stress, as is responsibility for people. Territoriality too plays a part. Unfortunately, for administrators, it's often impossible to avoid crossing organizational boundaries. These are all areas in which the organization can take steps to reduce built-in strain that leads to burnout, rustout, and loss of productivity.

Developing an Integrated System for Personal Actualization

> *The management of a balance of power is a permanent undertaking, not an exertion that has a foreseeable end.*

> **—Henry Kissinger**

The good news: Stress can be managed to your benefit. The bad news: In the end, only you can do it for yourself.

I can teach you effective methods of relaxation and coping, but if you leave them in my office, we're not much further along than we were when you walked in. Stress response is physiological; learning where and how strong your personal stressors are means learning to monitor your own internal state. Biofeedback—whether with sophisticated machinery or temperature-sensitive "biodots"—only helps you along the route. Learn to listen to yourself—to care about and for yourself.

The secret will be experimenting with strategies, tinkering with combinations. Come up with the ones that work best for you. Do you have a trick knee? Avoid jogging. Perhaps you'd like to swim, or to walk. Do you smoke? Drink more than you'd like? Carry a "spare tire"? We'd all love to be able to shrug off in a moment the effects of a lifetime of self-abuse. Deep-down, change takes time; stick to your goals, but don't be too hard on yourself. You're less likely to choke to death on your goals if you cut them up into bite-sized pieces. Self-confidence comes with repetitive success, even if the objectives at first look insignificant. Build the habit of doing what you promise yourself.

Finally, define what lifestyle changes you must make to manage your personal stress more effectively. Make a commitment to those changes. It's the stuff of your own life you've got in your hands. You only get one go-'round . . . if you do it right, it's all you'll need! Don't be content with Band-Aid solutions when it's possible to turn your *stress into strength.*

QUO VADIS?

Every man, woman and child is born of Almighty God for a purpose. If you're not fulfilling your purpose, you will never be happy. Find out what that purpose is no matter what your age may be. If you are well along in years, the mere fact that you are still here means that the Lord has a long lingering hope that at least you will do what he had you born to do! Get with it, and happiness will surge through your soul.

—Dr. Norman Vincent Peale

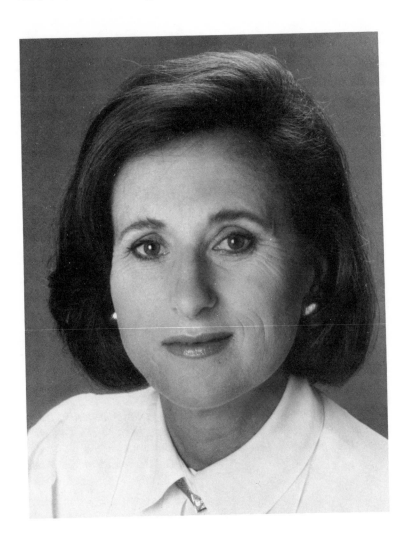

SUSANNE KIRCHER, R.N.
Sans Souci Health Resort
3745 Route 725
Bellbrook, OH 45305
(513) 848-4851 • (513) 435-9778

Susanne Kircher, R.N.

Susanne Kircher, "health trainer" of the Midwest, is owner and director of Sans Souci Health Resort in Bellbrook, Ohio.

The focus of her internationally known spa is improving health by means of stress reduction, fitness, and weight control.

Susanne, a registered nurse with a B.S., is a professional speaker with a vital message for the most valuable possession—good health.

She draws upon 15 years of work experience as a consultant on nutrition and fitness to the Olympic sport teams in her native Rumania. Susanne was the only woman member of the National Ski Patrol in the Carpathian mountains for 14 years.

She emigrated to the United States from behind the Iron Curtain in 1977. Susanne made the most of our free world by building two successful businesses in record time.

She is featured in major national newspapers and magazines and has appeared numerous times on TV.

The two people who have the largest impact in her personal and professional achievements are the ones she loves and respects the most, her husband, Konrad Kircher, and her brother, Otto Schmidts.

Currently Susanne lives with her husband and their children in Dayton, Ohio.

7

Kick the Stress Mess
by Susanne Kircher

"You are born with the potential to achieve greatness. Start by caring for your health."
—Susanne Kircher

High on the snowy mountain top of Davos, Switzerland my life changed. It brought all the happiness I dreamed and hoped for, together with extreme stress.

As a new immigrant from Communist Rumania

to West Germany I worked long hours as a head nurse in a cancer hospital in Bad Wiessee. When my brother, Otto, who is very close to me, called me one day to invite me to a ski vacation I was ready for a break. He asked me to accompany him to a medical meeting in Davos, a prominent ski resort in the Swiss Alps.

On the last day of our ski vacation, I met the man who would change my life completely. Konrad Kircher, born in Germany, now a practicing radiologist in Dayton, Ohio, impressed me as a special person. It clicked! For a full year we enjoyed a transatlantic courtship. Then I moved to the United States and we exchanged marriage vows. I was as happy as a new bride can be.

You might ask, where is the stress? Well, I just added the points from a stress evaluation sheet and came up with the dangerous number of 553. Getting married, becoming an instant mother of three teenage stepsons, moving to a different culture where I didn't speak the language, taking exams and state boards are just some of the stress situations. Stress is energy, which can either produce high blood pressure, ulcers, tense muscles, or it can be directed in a positive way helping us to achieve unusual accomplishments. We grow and change more in times of stress.

I channeled all my energy to build a happy marriage and a successful business, coming out stronger and more able to handle stress. To varying degrees stress is always part of life. It's everywhere. I say, thank God for stress. It can help us grow, adapt and survive.

It is *distress* which causes ill effects on our health. Distress is defined as stress, too much and too often, real or imagined.

Stress Defined

For a better understanding of this chapter, I propose this definition of stress: "Stress is an internal condition of mental and physical strain and tension caused by *our reaction* to external or internal stimuli."

A stressor is the multitude of daily happenings like a new job, getting married, moving, loss of a loved one.

Stress is *our* response to these situations.

Stress is a fact of life! But, what is stressful for one person might be a welcome challenge for another. For example, public speaking is defined as one of the most anxiety-producing stress factors. Many people will develop a dry mouth, perspire, get a knot in the stomach, and find it difficult to concentrate. For me, it was once a disaster to speak even in a small circle of friends. I felt all of the above and then some. Consequently I avoided public speaking. However, for almost 40 years, I lived in Rumania, a Communist country where the English language and the places where it was spoken seemed so wonderful and desirable.

Eight years ago, when I emigrated to the United States, I wanted very much to learn this language that sounded so wonderful. My enthusiasm grew to the point that each time I spoke English, it made me happy. After I opened Sans Souci health resort in Dayton, Ohio, I had the opportunity to give mini-seminars to guests who came to my spa. When I finally joined the Ohio Speakers Forum and National Speakers Association to share my message for health, weight control, and stress reduction with a broader audience, I was ready and happy to speak. Now each time I speak, I experience an elation similar to the "joggers' high."

The intensity of our reaction to stress is determined by our perception of the stimuli and by our beliefs.

II. Causes of Stress

A. **Internal causes,** like thirst, can help us survive and can be life saving. Other internal causes of stress, however, can be self-destructive, such as worry, fear, and anger. Worry can become a bad habit and cause action paralysis. Worrying doesn't solve anything. Creative action does! Fear is a powerful emotion. Fear of failing prevents many from giving their dreams and aspirations a chance. Anger, hatred, envy, jealousy, anxiety, perfectionism, and rigidity drain emotional and physical strength. There isn't anything we couldn't do better without these feelings. Keep in mind that all these negative emotions drain energy, and energy is what keeps us alive.

B. **External causes** of stress, such as a loss or a threat will be filtered through our minds and beliefs and our reactions will differ from person to person. External factors become stressful when we make them so. The same situation can be pleasurable, challenging, or distressful for three different people, depending on their beliefs. Since we are complex beings, stressful conditions will almost always be complex, having physical, mental, and emotional overtones.

III. Solutions

What can we do about stress? We have two options to reduce the ill effects of stress in our lives.

A. **OPTION NUMBER ONE** is to shut off the valves which allow stress to enter our lives, bodies, and minds.

   a. Change our thinking—thoughts create feelings, and feelings lead to behavior, good or bad.

   b. Lower our expectations—unfulfilled expectations will produce stress. By reducing the gap between what we have (reality) and what we want (wish), we can reduce stress. This doesn't mean that we have to lower our standards.

c. Ask the question, is this my problem? If no, let go! How important is it? Will it matter to me a year from now?

d. If you are a "Type A," change to become more like a "Type B."

B.   **OPTION NUMBER TWO.** The stress input valve cannot be shut off all of the time. There are events which will produce stress as an automatic response, no matter what we think or expect, no matter what our personality type or our self-esteem might be. In those situations, we have a second option: to be equipped to handle stress so that it does not result in damaging effects to our body. One key ingredient for this is *good health.* Health is determined, besides the genetic makeup, by three components: mind, body, and spirit.

What is health? Good health is more than being free of "dis-ease." It is a feeling of vibrant energy and being happy to be alive. We accomplish this by making knowledgeable choices about the food we eat, the exercise we do, and the thoughts we harbor. The first step toward good health is to assume responsibility for what or where we are. Proper food and exercise for the body, positive thoughts for the mind, and love for our spirit are key ingredients to keep us well.

The Mind Is Powerful

It directs our lives. If you need any enforcement as to what your mind can do, try this: tell a friend to raise her arm at shoulder level and to make a strong fist. Now suggest to her that she think about something positive, happy. Let her know that you will try to push her arm down and that she should resist you. While you attempt to push her arm down, repeat the word "energy." See how strong she is! Now, tell her to think of something negative, ask her to picture the word weakness and then push her arm down. There will be very little resistance. The difference will astonish both of you. I do this sometimes at Sans Souci with my guests. It is a convincing and amusing experiment.

Our minds can make or break our health. Positive thoughts and positive words create a positive energy field around us. We have the free will to choose, for example: yes-no, can-can't, hope-fear, rich-poor, I will-I won't, belief-doubt, eager-anxious, challenge-problem, the best-the worst, love-hate, health-disease.

Develop a positive attitude. Know that being healthy, happy, and successful is your birthright and it is achievable. Define your goals; most of us have a yearning for fulfillment. To leave a mark upon this world is a powerful yearning. We all have the potential to grow and to leave this world a better place.

The Magic Is You

The past can be limiting. Close the door to it. I worked for eighteen years in Rumania as a medical practitioner caring for injured and sick patients. At that time I liked my work. Then I emigrated to the United States where my profession didn't exist. This produced anxiety and stress in me. I asked myself what did I really want to do at this point of my life. I had changed in the meantime and began focusing my energy on health rather than disease. I decided to open a health resort where people could come to exercise, let go of extra weight and old habits, and improve their health. After being in business for seven years, Debbie Goebble, a guest and friend, put it this way: "Susie, Sans Souci has a great program and a charming setting, but the magic is YOU. When you are not there, there is something essential missing." Everyone has a magic, unique part to fill in life's puzzle. The magic is YOU! I love what I am doing now. It gave my life a whole new dimension and purpose.

Determine what you really want to achieve.

Write it down. Be specific, revise your goals from time to time, and adjust them to the changes in your life. Keep in mind that you have the free will to choose your goals. Most of us don't realize how much we could accomplish if we would move out of our own way. Success is just an attitude away. If you have a problem, state it only *once*. Never repeat it again! Direct your energy in a positive way and find a creative solution to it. Transform your problem into a challenge. Repeat to yourself over and over again, "I have the tools to handle this challenge."

Food, the Stuff Our Body Is Made Of

I grew up eating meat and desserts. My father was a veterinarian and brought home the best cuts of meat from the meat bank. Our family was overweight and "healthy" looking, at least from the point of view of our anxious mother whose anxiety got relief with every pound we gained. I grew up being overweight and sickly, and was in and out of hospitals. At the age of seventeen, I developed a chronic kidney disease which, I was told by my doctor, would lead in a few years to kidney failure.

I made it through college and as fate would have it, I was selected by a health department official to work in an international sports resort in Poiana Brosov, Rumania, as a medical practitioner. Here I worked with national and Olympic sport teams to assure first aid and counsel nutrition to people who were in top shape. I graduated at the top of my class but my health and physical condition were deplorable. For the first time in my life it dawned on me that I had input into the way I looked and felt. At that time I was fifty pounds overweight, couldn't touch my toes, and huffed and puffed going up stairs. I don't want to say it was easy, but I made the transition from what I have just described, to a level of health and fitness which is beyond my wildest dreams. I feel, at the age of 49, I am at my personal best.

Yoga postures like the head stand, the shoulder stand, and the plow position, years ago were for a lucky few, but not for me. Today I am in awe and wonder each time I perform them. Such is the recuperative power of our bodies!

Raw Material

Of all the external factors, food has the biggest impact on our health and on the way we cope with stress. Every minute millions of cells in our body die and are rebuilt with the food we eat. Our body uses food as raw material to build new cells, but it needs good raw material, meaning good food, to build healthy cells. These cells form organs which have to perform a function. If the quality of the cells is not good, the function of our organs and body will suffer.

Following this line of thinking, it becomes evident that indeed we are what we eat. This makes it easier to choose an apple over apple pie. My nutritional philosophy is to eat food as close to its natural state as possible. The more we cook, bake, process, and can our food, the more we lose nutritional value. By eating a variety of whole grains, legumes, fresh vegetables and fresh fruits, we assure that our body gets all the necessary aminoacids, vitamins, minerals, fiber, and energy it needs.

Eliminate or reduce the intake of red meat, sugar, white flour, fats, caffein, alcohol, salt, artificial sweetener, and drugs. Drink six to eight glasses of water every day. Last but not least, listen to your body. Some people are allergic to the healthiest food. Your body will tell you, with specific symptoms, if that's the case.

When planning and preparing the meals at Sans Souci, I choose for the first half of the meal a raw salad. This aids digestion, brings vitamins, minerals, fiber to the body, and it has few calories. The second half balances the salad by adding protein and complex carbohydrates in the form of legumes, whole grains, vegetables, some seeds, and nuts. All of the fat we need is already in this type of food so I don't add any oil or butter.

At Sans Souci Health Resort we usually start the day with a glass of lemon water. This aids elimination of metabolic waste products. After a 20-

minute stretching-breathing and wake-up exercise, we have a balanced breakfast of fresh fruits followed by a whole grain cereal like sprouted wheat berries or rolled oat porridge with skim milk. For variety we have egg white omelets with bran muffins or whole wheat crepes filled with lowfat cottage cheese.

After walking on the Parcourse we have a snack consisting of a fruit drink made from fresh fruit, water, ice cubes, and almonds blended in the blender. It's refreshing, tastes good, and gives us the necessary energy for the next exercise class.

Lunch usually consists of an assorted fruit plate with cottage cheese, musli, or a vegetable based dish. After pool class, we have at 4 p.m. a snack consisting of fresh vegetables with a low calorie dip or broiled mushrooms. For dinner a raw salad followed by a legume—vegetable dish.

As you can see, the pattern is not to mix fruits and vegetables at the same meal. The first half of the day has fruits which are easily digested and provide energy for the day's activities. Most fruits have a slight acid pH. In the afternoon we switch to vegetables which have an alkaline pH and aid the body in neutralizing metabolic waste products.

Evenings we relate to each other by having group discussions or some fun activities.

At the end of the week guests feel and look so much better that this experience is exhilarating and self motivating.

Emotional Eating

Most of our eating beyond physiological hunger is emotional eating. Let's go back to the time when we were a baby. Each time we felt discomfort and cried, we were fed. At the same time we were also cuddled and felt the closeness, warmth and love given together with food. As we grew older high calorie food was often given to us as a reward for an expression of love. Each time the family gathered for a holiday and celebration in a loving, safe atmosphere, high calorie food greeted us. As we grew up, we learned to associate food with love. Now as a result, whenever we feel the need for comfort and love, we might crave food.

We all need a certain number of positive strokes a day to stay emotionally balanced. For example, we know that a baby does not develop well if not physically touched and cuddled. As adults, we still need touching and love just as much. If we don't get it, one way to feel loved might be food. It is always available, and most importantly, it never rejects us. Fear of rejection prevents many of us from taking the risk to reach out to others and then we seek comfort from food, an immediate, no risk gratification.

Love keeps us emotionally balanced. If we want love in our lives, we have to give love. Create and collect "gold stars" that life has to offer by cultivating friendships, doing something creative, admiring a flower, listening to your favorite music, giving yourself the gift of a healthy vacation, exercising, having a massage and yes, enjoying food. Make food ONE of your pleasures, not THE pleasure in life.

Letting Go of Extra Weight

Weight control is the most critical long-term stress factor in America. In spite of better knowledge of nutrition than ever before, we eat too much, too often selecting the wrong type of food. Overeating creates a new stress factor—overweight. Then the vicious circle closes; overweight as a stress factor leads to more eating.

Proposed solutions to overweight seem simple, but developing self-discipline and the insight necessary to break old habits are not.

Overeating can be a habit. It is easy to start a habit, positive or negative. It starts like a thin thread which becomes thicker and thicker by repetition. In time it becomes thick like a rope, strong like a cable, and difficult to break. Other reasons for overeating could be: anxiety, boredom or denial. While we eat we don't have to cope with whatever is unpleasant or stressful.

Hiding behind fat can be one of the reasons for overeating. It might be safer for some of us not even to enter the contest of life. Obesity then becomes an excuse to put off realizing our dreams. For example, "I will do that when I lose thirty pounds."

Losing weight is a national obsession. Wherever I go, I hear people talking about losing weight. Let's stop and think about this. Have you ever lost a ring or a pin? What would be the first thing you would do if you lost anything? ... probably you would look and try to find it! We are culturally conditioned to find what we lose. If you lose weight, sooner or later you will find it right back in the same places! Instead of thinking and saying, "I am losing weight," say to yourself, "I am letting go of extra weight." This means that you let go of something you no longer want or need at this point in your life.

Diets Don't Work

Dieting is another negative term. DIETS don't work! The first things that come to my mind when I hear the word diet are: deprivation, limitation, short term. It sounds terrible because of these negative connotations, and therefore assures failure. Most importantly, dieting is an external cue. Overweight people eat according to external cues like the sight, smell, or thought of food, a schedule, the clock, company, and parties with emphasis on food. When dieting, somebody is there to tell us what we can or cannot have on the diet.

Instead of going on a new diet, resolve to make it a lifelong commitment to good health. Establish a new relationship with food, *a positive one.* I thoroughly enjoy biting into a ripe apple. It's juicy, sweet, and feels wonderful in my mouth as I eat it, and on my hips when I look at them.

We become overweight from the apple pie, not from the apple; from the potato chips, not from the potato; from the peach cobbler, not from the peaches. The apple, potato, or peach are "healthy choices" which also keep us thin. Thin people eat according to the internal cue which is hunger. Newborn babies eat to this internal cue. They will eat only when hungry. Eating to external cues is a learned behavior and can be *unlearned.*

Reinforce Good Behavior

Charlie, my Collie dog, has taught me quite a few lessons. He was well house-trained; for emergencies, he had a corner in the basement laid out with newspapers where he could relieve himself when I couldn't be home on time to take him out for a walk. He is a smart aleck and found out soon that he could use that corner to show me his discontentment whenever I didn't give him enough attention. I would scold him, drag him to that corner, and tell him what a bad boy he was. This approach didn't bring any results whatsoever. One day I read about using positive reinforcement in changing behavior. I changed my approach with Charlie. I would check the corner at random and whenever I found it clean, I called Charlie in a happy voice, praising him while pointing to the clean corner. Lo and behold, after a few times it worked like magic. Our basement corner has been clean ever since. I repeat this "happy corner" routine from time to time just to reinforce his wonderful behavior.

Rewards are essential for any kind of progress. Each time we reward ourselves, a pleasure-producing chemical is released into the blood stream which makes us feel good. Therefore, we seek to repeat experiences associated with these good feelings.

Practice and positive reinforcement of the new behavior are the key ingredients for changing behavior. Practice makes permanent!

Exercise, Health, and Stress

We live at a time when we can go to the moon, have computer and complicated technology at our fingertips, but still we live in a body which has the same biochemical response as that of our caveman ancestors. It prepares us for fight or flight as if our very lives were at stake, each time we encounter stress. This powerful automatic response speeds up our heart and respiratory rate. Cholesterol, fat, and sugar in the blood stream increase. The immune system and digestion slow down. This can make us more vulnerable to heart disease, cancer, ulcers, or depression.

The fight or flight response helped our cave ancestors to fight *physically* or run for life. In our culture it is no longer appropriate to fight or run away each time we feel threatened. Instead, we are taught to "control ourselves." Tension and adrenaline can no longer be released in the way they were intended and so build up and cause damage. To prevent this, aerobic exercise like jogging or walking are excellent. These exercises stimulate the brain to release a chemical called endorphine. This chemical produces a feeling of well being and is responsible for the "joggers' high," and can become the base of a "positive addiction." A fit body is well equipped to handle stress. It's like having a bank account of energy. Choosing an exercise which is pleasureable makes it play, not work. Life is movement and the more active we are, the more we are alive.

I exercise six days a week. During the winter when Sans Souci is closed and I don't teach exercise classes, I keep my body fit by doing stretching exercises and race walking. In addition, I practice Hatha Yoga. I find Yoga one of the best ways to stay flexible. Only the soft can be strong, like a branch on a tree. If the branch is hard and rigid, it breaks. If it is soft and pliable it can resist the storms. In addition, Yoga taught me to breathe properly, to relax, and to keep in touch with my body.

In most religious philosophies our body is the temple in which we live. To keep this temple healthy and flexible is our first responsibility towards life.

Meditation

Guests at Sans Souci often ask me: Susie, what is meditation? It is a state where we transcend physical boundaries of time and space. It is achieved by sitting in a comfortable position in a quiet place, relaxing the body and focusing the mind. Deep rythmical breathing centers the energy.

Meditation is a natural state like sleeping or walking.

At Sans Souci we have a special place for meditation in a pine forest. Attending there is the highlight of our day. It is like a quiet retreat. We are surrounded by the song of the birds and by the mellow scent of pines. The sound of the wind in the trees relaxes body and mind. As the mind quiets, we tune to the inner wisdom where we find peace and happiness.

Meditation can be helpful in coping with stress and in achieving and maintaining good physical, mental and spiritual health.

The Gift of Life

I close every one of my meditation sessions with a

short prayer, which translated from my mother langauge goes like this: "God, I know that I am born to be healthy, happy, and successful. I know you gave me the potential to achieve greatness. Please show me the way and give me the physical and emotional strength to walk it so I can realize my full potential. Thank you for a loving relationship with my husband and our children. Thank you God for the wondrous gift of life and for the changes and challenges which come with it."

DR. MELVIN J. LeBARON
Behavioral Fitness Institute
P.O. Box 9361
Brea, CA 92622
(714) 990-1637

Dr. Melvin J. Le Baron

Dr. Melvin J. LeBaron is President of Humanistic Consulting, Inc., a management consulting organization specializing in team development. For nearly two decades he was a faculty member and administrator at the University of Southern California, School of Public Administration. He has been a consultant to state mental hospitals, correctional organizations, police departments, voluntary organizations and to city and county governments throughout the United States.

Dr. LeBaron pioneered, and conducted numerous management and team development programs. He has a national and international reputation in the field of executive development and manager training and is author of several publications. He has held more than a dozen part-time faculty positions at various colleges and universities.

In addition to training of local officials, he has had hands-on experience as a member of the city council and mayor of his home city of Brea, California. He has also served as chairman of the Brea Human Development Commission. He has served on several state and national committees and task forces that developed plans and materials for training of public officials.

During recent years, Dr. LeBaron has concentrated his consulting activities on business and industry while he developed the new concept for personal and managerial coaching he calls "Behavioral Fitness."

8

Behavioral Fitness: The Stress Remover
by Dr. Mel LeBaron

"Man has come to control all other forms of life because he has taken more time in which to grow up; when he takes more time, and spends this time more wisely, he may learn to control and remake himself."
   —**Will Durant, The Story of Philosophy**

E ver been flying high one minute—soaring to the crest of accomplishment, basking in self-worth—and then suddenly found yourself crawling through the sucking mire of embarrassment or depression?

Then you know what it's like to plummet from arrogance to humility.

You know it isn't easy. You know, in fact, that it's painful...and stressful.

In today's fast-paced world, it is difficult to develop and maintain balanced behavior that will fit the constantly changing social and work situations. With the speed of travel, communications, and creativity, the world is growing smaller. Just as new technology has replaced old, we need new patterns of behavior to replace the old. We have undergone tremendous value and cultural shifts to become a society of individualism, self-expression, and freedom; our behavior must reflect those changes and must enable us to keep pace.

Unless you've been living in a cave during the last decade, you've witnessed an astounding switch in emphasis toward physical fitness. Joggers don athletic shoes and terrycloth sweatbands and clog the edges of streets and highways across the nation. Corporations have cleared out the vending machines and filled employee break rooms with exercise equipment instead. Stately gentlemen with Bostonian accents glare at us from our television screens and admonish us about polyunsaturated fats. Cancer researchers plead with us to munch on broccoli and cauliflower.

The result of all this physical frenzy? Longer, healthier lives, we are told.

So much for physical fitness.

What about behavioral fitness? It, too, is a key to a longer, stress-free and healthier life.

Is it important? Absolutely! Has it been neglected? Probably. In an age when fitness is emphasized, it is essential to include behavioral fitness—the values and attitudes you promote and defend, the social responsibility you accept. It's critical that you strike a balance, that you become behaviorally fit.

Behaviors In The Workplace

Of all the places you exhibit stress behavior, perhaps the most difficult is in the workplace. Why? You are torn between the invitation to assert yourself over others and the necessity to maintain restraint and humility. On the one hand, arrogance beckons; on the other, humility threatens. Balance—the delicate middle ground between the two—constantly evades.

The workplace provides you with work, and work provides you with identity. Consider the impact work has on your life; your workplace, more than any other factor in your life, determines your time schedule, lifestyle, anticipations, fulfillments, successes, and failures. No institution so organizes, structures, and perpetuates your growth and development like the workplace does. And in no situation is your behavioral fitness so challenged as in the workplace. Why? The workplace is where your success and growth as a human being is put on the line.

It sounds pretty simple; figure out where you want to be, decide how you're going to get there, and behave accordingly.

Ah, it sounds simple, but it's not. Why? Because nothing is what is seems—the workplace, more than any other situation, is a stressful paradox. We are top in efficiency, but elaborately shoddy. We have the greatest number of regulations, and the greatest number of violations. We have accumulated the greatest variety of material goods, but are profoundly uncertain about our needs. Our technology is a fantasy, and our unsafeness is unparalleled. We are leaders in growth, but we are leaders in uncontrollability. We boast the fastest speed, but experience the greatest fatalities.

We enjoy enormous power, but increasing alienation. We are soothed with the greatest abundance of assurances, but we suffer the fastest rate of inadequacy. Our most obvious wealth can be found within blocks of our most devastating poverty. Our advanced communications broadcast our high volume of distrust.

In the middle of all the inconsistency and paradox is a painfully personal one: our emotional fire extinguishers are surrounded by unbreakable glass! We seek in the workplace a refuge from the frustrations of life, but we find there the greatest frustrations of all.

Polarized Behavior

Nowhere in life is stress so evident as in the workplace. On the one end is excessive arrogance—behavior that inhibits otherwise free and open people, that restricts acceptance of ideas, that rejects the perceptions of others, that discounts others' values and discards those values without emotion. At the other end of the spectrum is extreme humility—a condition of vulnerability and servitude, a posture of giving in or giving up.

You'll find both arrogance and humility in your organization—and chances are, you won't have to look far. The arrogant ones are those who are climbing to the top—and who are using others in the organization as the rungs on the ladder. Ask these climbers what they think of humility, and they'll spare no emotion: they will tell you that humility is weak and spineless. Want the other side of the story? Look for those in your organization who are crippled by humility, those who falter at the bottom in self-doubt, refusing to get involved in the organization. Ask them what they think of arrogance, and they'll mumble that it is unbecoming and untrustworthy.

Now look at the way the organization functions.

Most of it is likely polarized around those who think they are more important than they really are (the arrogant ones) and those who don't think they are as important as they really are (the humble ones). Complicating the whole picture is a simple fact of human nature; those at each end resent those at the opposite extreme.

People are rushing toward the two extremes. Why? They are fleeing from displacement and uncertainty. The fast pace of living and the rapid changes we encounter have plunged us into unfamiliar transitions. Too many situations are either too complicated to handle or too far out of control to rely on. To survive, we do whatever we can to avoid being ambiguous or uncertain: we head for the extremes of arrogance and humility, trampling any bystanders in the stampede!

The result? *Stress!*

It's a scary situation. We yearn for person-to-person contact in the workplace, but the organization wants more advanced technology. We are robbed of human experiences in order to produce goods and services that no one may want. We are faced with the blunt realization that any company capable of giving us everything we want is also capable of taking everything we have.

Many workers are trying to free themselves from conditions they don't like—but, at the same time, they are becoming enslaved by situations they do like. Some started out working with the notion that the world owed them a living; they now blame the world for their failures. Valuable workers have moved from wondering if there is a promotion in their future to suspecting that there is no future in their promotion. By the time a worker achieves success, he also earns a nervous breakdown or a heart attack. They are bound by the "golden handcuffs"—lured into a position of servitude by the benefits of the job.

And here's the greatest paradox of all; at a time when we most need behavioral fitness, we are the most behaviorally out of shape. At a time when we have the greatest need for behavioral strength, we are plagued by behavioral weakness. Our unfit condition has become epidemic.

It doesn't have to be that way. Each of us—one at a time—can fight back. Each of us can become behaviorally fit, and we can reverse the trend.

It all starts with an understanding of the two extremes: arrogance and humility.

A Mound Of Arrogance

Arrogance isn't new. It's been around since the beginning of time—but our rapidly changing times have finally forced us to come to grips with it.

What is arrogance?

Arrogance is most common among those who have climbed the ranks rapidly. It starts out as a kernel of thought—and, like a cancer, it spreads insidiously to consume the entire person. Want to see arrogance on center stage? Watch how an arrogant person interacts with others. The arrogant one is totally self-centered and self-concerned, consumed by the trapping of his own glory; it is as though the other person exists only as a minor irritation, a fly on the wall. He is of little consequence, and may as well be flicked away or smashed underfoot.

But wait a minute—don't get confused. A moderate amount of arrogance can result in *confidence,* an obviously desirable quality. Confidence allows you to take prudent risks. As those prudent risks gradually pay off, you develop enhanced self-confidence. You get into trouble only when your self-confidence soars beyond control, when you lose a sense of respect for your fellow human beings.

A Dip Into Humility

At the other end of the spectrum is humility. If arrogance can be compared to sitting smugly atop the highest mountain peak, extreme humility can be compared to wallowing in the deepest mire.

Humility is an extremely positive quality. It keeps us ever mindful—*respectful*—of the world around us, and it reminds us that we are only a part of the world. It helps us recognize and appreciate others. It provides a moderation to self-esteem at a time when ego is invited to go on a rampage. But, at it's worst, extreme humility debilitates. A person crippled by extreme humility becomes convinced that he is worthless. He has played the humility role to such an extent that he has talked himself out of self-value. He believes that he is less than acceptable as a human being. Obscure. Nothing. Look around for the people who are devastated by humility: they are the ones that are submissive, passive, withered, and withdrawn. Unfortunately, they are often victims of the arrogant—they have been robbed of their vitality, sapped of their strength and identity.

But remember—a moderate amount of humility is a positive quality. Humility is based on respect for others; properly used, it carries great power. It can enhance awareness, increase sensitivity, and promote understanding of self.

The answer?

It lies in *balance*. You need enough arrogance to have confidence in yourself, but not enough to become crushing and hurtful to others. You need enough humility to maintain respect for others, but not so much that you lose respect for yourself. That balance—that careful combination of courage, conviction, strength, tenderness, and concern—is what behavioral fitness is all about.

Stress Removal Behavior

The basic task of behavioral fitness is to get rid of the stumbling blocks—the stumbling blocks that cause you to not appreciate your full value or that cause you to pay a greater price than necessary just to survive. It helps you get over the tendency to size everyone else up while ignoring your own out-of-shape behavior. It helps you stop blaming others for your problems—and it helps you stop discounting or inflating your abilities.

To find out where you stand, ask yourself six quick questions. But just because they are quick, don't assume that they're easy! They are, in fact, loaded. They are designed to force you to privately examine your own behavioral image. So don't scrimp. Don't cover up. It's just you...and you need to know the honest answers. It's also just a start...

1. Do you think that looking for sympathy qualifies as looking for help?
2. Does subjecting yourself to another person feel like a violation of your rights?
3. Do you feel that your problems are so unique that no other person could ever understand them?
4. Do you debate issues because your desire to be right is greater than your desire to solve a problem?
5. Do you ever get in over your head and

remain unwilling to acquire the necessary skills and behaviors?

6. Do you test, grade, and compare yourself to others?

Philosophically, stress removal behavioral fitness was captured perfectly by Erich Fromm in *The Art of Loving* when he said, "The idea expressed in the Biblical 'love thy neighbor as thyself' implies that respect for one's own integrity and uniqueness, love for and understanding of one's own self, cannot be separated from respect and love and understanding for another individual. The love for my own self is inseparably connected with love for any other being."

Go back to the quiz you just took. Think about your responses carefully. The simplest form of stress removal—behavioral fitness—is to ask yourself following *every* encounter or *every* activity: Did I show a proper amount of confidence and respect for myself? Did I show a proper amount of confidence and respect for the other person?

Those two simple variables can be used to measure *every* situation. Those same two variables can also be used to *change* every situation. How? You can show more self-confidence or demonstrate more respect in the other person, depending on which direction you've slid in. Remember these two variables—they are your basics.

Okay. Time to start.

Identify one behavior—a way you respond, a way you react—that is keeping you from accomplishing some goal. It should be a behavior that you want to change because it is causing problems for you and for those around you.

Now write it down. Underline it. Look at it. And do the following exercise:

1. List all the prices you pay for your out-of-shape behavior—things that result from your behavior until the price is too high. (When the price gets too high, obviously, you discontinue the behavior.) Now second-guess yourself: list the ways that you can—or do—minimize the prices so that you are free to continue your out-of-shape behavior.

2. List the techniques you use to activate your out-of-shape behavior. It might be discouragement. Comparing yourself with others. Impatience. Stress.

3. List the fears you may have when you think about eliminating your out-of-shape behavior. Sound ridiculous? It's not! Fear is incredibly powerful. And, whether you realize it or not, fear may be making you cling to that out-of-shape behavior.

   What kind of fear?

   Let's look at some examples. If you get rid

of your out-of-shape behavior, you might be afraid of finding out that you are a person you truly don't like. That you are dumb and incompetent after all. That you are weak and vulnerable. That you are unable to handle responsibility. That you are inadequate. That you are cold and unfeeling.

This is a tough one. Up until now, it's been easy to ignore it, avoid it, hope it will go away, redirect it to others—by making them look bad through casting blame, intimidating, or being the victim and yielding. We all have lots of practice hiding who we are. We are masters at it! One of the most difficult things you can be asked to do is to face up to your fears. But, while difficult, it is supremely important for a behavioral change.

4. Now face your fears by testing them against reality. How? Let go of the out-of-shape behavior, and see what happens.

The first few times will be scary. You might even be a little shaky. But take the plunge! Keep at it, no matter how different or difficult it is. It will probably take half a dozen tries before you start feeling a renewed confidence in reshaping your behavior. Step by step, you'll find that you can overcome your out-of-shape behavior. You'll find that you're becoming more comfortable without it than you were with it. You'll find yourself contributing to the workplace in new and satisfactory ways.

Remember, behavioral fitness stresses confidence in self, balanced with respect for others. It sees both conceit and meekness as dangerous positions. It predicts tragedy for those crushed by excessive arrogance and extreme humility.

Remember, too, that you are what you are—plus what you hope to be, plus what others force you to be, *minus* what you are not able to be. You can be behaviorally fit—keep reading and find your next step!

Clearing the Deck

You just finished an exercise that involved one out-of-shape behavior. It's an exercise that can apply to every out-of-shape behavior you identify in yourself. But, before you go on too far, you need to clear the deck of your old problem behaviors and make way for your new, stronger, more positive behaviors. it's up to you to identify the criteria you will require of your new behaviors. Remember that you have to keep practicing your new, in-shape behaviors until they become firmly entrenched—habit is difficult to break, and difficult to reestablish. Remember—give yourself half a dozen tries!

As you get ready to clear the deck, you need to

remember an important point: self-examination is the starting place for creating new behaviors. It's not a new message—Christ told us, "Know the truth, and the truth will make you free." Shakespeare wrote, "To thine own self be true." Several thousand years ago, Socrates penned, "The unexamined life isn't worth living."

What does that tell you about the need to search yourself? The need for penetrating self-examination?

You're the only one who can do it, because anything else is second-hand experience, second-hand knowledge. If you go on second-hand experience—without truly knowing yourself—you are at risk of extreme arrogance or excessive humility. You are at risk of becoming so big on yourself that you believe you never make a mistake—or so down on yourself that you are always correcting your "mistakes."

One company president commented that some of his best people were like "a horse that had never been ridden hard." What did he mean? His people took responsibility for work, but not for themselves. Another corporate executive lamented, "we need to reexamine the motivation menu we feed to our people. A person is worth more to this company when he finds himself and stops giving the impression that he is more or less than he is." Still another manager maintained, "Our people need to find themselves and recognize what they stand for."

It's a universal cry: we all need to overcome the obstacles we find in ourselves so we can find a more comfortable—and contributory—way to perform our work.

If you haven't done it yet, take some time for that crucial self-examination before you try to clear the deck.

Follow these suggestions, step by step, to clear your deck:

1. Write down up to six recent critical incidents that are troubling you; now list some significant involvements that were part of these incidents. (You'll want to use a separate sheet of paper for each incident so that you have room enough to complete all nine steps.)

2. For each incident, determine the kinds of arrogance-humility behaviors displayed by you and the other people involved. (Write them down.)

3. Take a long, hard look at the behaviors you listed for yourself. Are you proud? Were they positive behaviors? Did you slip into the trap of conceit, arrogance, meekness, or withering self-doubt? (Take a few minutes to think about it. Take a few more minutes to recognize your need to change.)

4. Here's a tough one: own up to your out-of-shape behaviors. Take responsibility for them.

Refuse to avoid them, blame others for them, or attack yourself or someone else as a result of them. Simply take ownership.

5. Look at your list of out-of-shape behaviors associated with each incident. Circle the ones that are—or could be—destructive to you or someone else.

6. Take the steps to strengthen yourself by sizing yourself up. Are you leaning on someone else as a "model" of fit behavior? Assert your independence! Use what you have observed to list some fit behaviors you could have substituted in each of the incidents you described.

7. Go a little easy on yourself. No one is perfect—and no one expects you to be perfect, either! Be willing to accept the fact that you have some out-of-shape behaviors. Your objective is moving toward becoming *better* rather than becoming *perfect*.

8. Now look at the incidents you described. They are likely to be the general kinds of incidents that are repeated countless times in the workplace. Your task? Look for commonalities. What's the cue that initiates the behavior? Is it the person? Situation? Time? What specific act, set of words, place, condition, or time sets it off? Once you figure that out, you're closer to being able to

do something about it. Figure out, in writing, a systematic and workable method for dealing with the situation in a positive way, using fit behaviors. Be specific—write down your solutions!

9. Put aside your "incident" papers. Develop, in writing, a plan and program for continued behavioral workouts. You can use some of the suggestions you came up with as you tried to solve the incidents. Be creative, and let your mind run free!

Greg, a project manager, who was disturbed by the company's tendency to stray from the basic goals of the project at hand, complained that managers and employees were always torn between company growth and production. Disorder was the typical condition, particularly in staff meetings.

Greg was shown the nine-point method and was challenged to record in writing the behaviors that were surrounding the critical incidents at work. As part of his resolve, Greg decided to keep a journal of what happened at staff meetings over a three-week period.

Three weeks later, Greg's journal reflected a variety of revealing incidents. In particular, his journal provided a pretty clear idea of what behaviors were contributing to the problem. He shared the following excerpts:

- We all have varying attitudes toward how to manage and supervise. We argue over our approaches, and our way becomes a part of our personal ego. We fail to discuss concepts, big-picture issues, and a perspective of where we are going. *(I need to do more to respect the contributions of others at the same time that I have confidence in myself to create a common vision of where we are going.)*

- Hidden agendas and uncertain messages tend to grow into debates and philosophical discussions about people. We don't deal with frustrations, anger, negative behaviors, and so on. We claim we can't do the job because of the system, the president, and others. *(I need to take the philosophical position that our strengths are given us to respect and serve, not to fight with.)*

- We each have our own patented methods for doing things, and most of our conversation goes to convincing others and ourselves that we are okay in what we are doing. Responses and giving others feedback tends to bring on defensiveness and justification. *(I need to listen better so I can determine the difference between arguing over who is right and pursuing what is right.)*

- We use abstract statements about issues and how we handle our world. We don't accept feelings. We talk about the company historically, but no one owns the problems of today. *(I need to require those who work for me to prove themselves worthy before I allow them to take on bigger jobs.)*

- We tend to get frustrated and burn up energy over all that's wrong. Little energy goes toward learning and listening to what we need to do to change the situation. *(I need to see myself more as a servant to my people and less as a master over them.)*

Greg had successfully identified and verified some out-of-shape behaviors.

Greg had started to clear the deck for behavioral fitness!

Revitalizing Behaviors

If you rub your hands on a rough surface for awhile, one of two things happens: you either get callouses or blisters. A callous is the constructive result of stress; a blister indicates that the stress was destructive.

It's the same way with behavioral fitness! The stress you impose on yourself must be great enough to cause new, constructive behaviors to occur, but not so great that it destroys your "good self." To gauge how much stress you can tolerate, you need to consider three variables: *intensity* (how much behavioral fitness is enough?), *frequency* (how often should you work out?), and *duration* (how long should each workout last?). And, just as in exercise, you need to start out with a warmup—a period of loosening up that allows you to recognize your behavioral condition and where you want to change.

Let's look at the way these three variables work in real-life situations. The intensity is the degree to which your self-belief has been inflated or deflated. The duration is the length of time you have been exposed to the arrogance—humility polarization. The frequency is the number of times you have been affected by imbalanced situations.

Your ability to maintain a balance depends on these three variables. The longer the duration of humility, for example, the more severe will be your inflicting self-doubt. The more sustained and intimate the experience, the more difficulty you will have in gaining a balance.

Behavior: It's Your Choice

If behavioral fitness is going to work for you, you have to incorporate four factors:

Awareness: Obviously, you must be aware of the need to change.

Acceptance: You must create a climate in which it is okay to change.

Ease: If you want your behavioral change to be successful and permanent, you should remember an important fact: Do what you can to make the change easy.

Knowledge: You'd never forge into the wilds of the Canadian Rockies unless you had some basic knowledge about survival skills—how to build a fire, how to cook over an open flame, how to protect yourself from the elements.

It's the same way here. Don't try forging into a new behavior until you get some knowledge about it! You can utilize talent, but you also need to employ skill—and skill comes from taking the time to learn and practice the facts. You may recognize a need for change, but you may flounder helplessly, not knowing *how* to make the change.

There are some basics you should find out:

- What do you do to people?
- What are the consequences of your interactions with others?
- What are others saying about your behavior?
- How much support do you have from your peers?
- What is going on around you?
- What are your ego blockages?
- Do you tend to partially listen to others, and then tend to react based on that partial information?
- Do you come across like you know more than everyone else?
- How much of your success has been achieved as a "Lone Ranger"?
- Do you have fixed ideas that you stubbornly

cling to, failing to be flexible or to see the bigger picture?

• Have you gathered everything around you—and do you refuse to let loose?

• Do you attack people instead of problems?

Use these questions as a basic checklist. When you've finished answering every question, honestly and completely, you will go into your behavioral change armed with the basic facts!

Do It!

Regardless of which approach you decide to use, make a commitment: Commit that you will DO IT. If you do, you will find meaning in your life. You will stop going faster, working harder, spending more money, and dying more quickly. If you have the spark of genius but can't work the ignition, behavioral fitness can start your engine roaring.

Regardless of which approach you take toward looking at your own behavioral condition and the need for behavioral fitness, you need to remember one thing: there is no school for living, and there are few teachers of life. We each have to make our own way. As John Gardner told us, "Man is a stubborn sucker for meaning." Each of us has the same challenge: to find meaning out of our pursuit. Behavioral fitness is a response to the lament of poet Wordsworth when he penned, "The world is too much with us; late and soon, getting and spending, we lay waste our powers."

Ready for some behavioral fitness workouts?

TRESSA CHAMBERS-MEYERS
Thought Motivation Institute
2966 Diamond Street, Suite 151
San Francisco, CA 94131
(415) 821-6334

Tressa Chambers-Meyers

Tressa Chambers-Meyers, president and founder of THOUGHT MOTIVATION INSTITUTE is a highly successful Education/Communication Consultant and a leader in the Knowledge/Education/Communication industry. The Institute specializes in developing Motivational, Educational and Persuasion Training Seminars.

Tressa Chambers-Meyers attended Fisk University in Nashville, Tennessee and graduated from Eastern Washington University in Cheney, Washington, with degrees in Language Arts and Social Studies.

Professional experience includes teaching public school in San Francisco, working in direct sales, a cosmetic consultant and a successful San Francisco fashion and photography modeling career (modeling for Brooks Camera, Photography Unlimited and Damon of North Beach). In addition to the above, Tressa Chambers-Meyers taped a state-wide TV commercial for California Superintendent of Public Instruction, The Honorable William (Bill) Honig's successful bid for office which focused on "Returning Public Classroom Teaching Back to Basics."

She has devoted her life to helping others and volunteering her services where needed. She is divorced and the mother of two children: a daughter, Monica Denise Meyers, who received a B.A. degree in International Affairs from Spelman College in Atlanta, Georgia, presently employed at the World Affairs Council of Northern California in San Francisco; and a son (J.R.) Jon Raymond Meyers, a senior in pre-med at Morehouse College, also located in Atlanta, Georgia.

9

Stress Survival Techniques
by Tressa Chambers-Meyers

*"We shall steer safely through every
storm, so long as our heart is right, our
intention fervent, our courage steadfast,
and our trust fixed on God."*
—St Francis De Sales

S tress is unavoidable in all our lives. When we are
under stress, our blood pressure increases, our blood
vessels constrict and our heart pounds. Learning
how to cope with stress is an important part of
keeping healthy. But, first we must determine

exactly what stress is. Stress can be defined not just in terms of excessive demands. It can arise when people do things they are not equipped for. Stress is, therefore, too much of the wrong sort of pressure. It can be thought of as a reaction to change of any kind. I am not just referring to large scale upheavals, such as death or divorce. Even some pleasant events, such as moving to a better house, may have subtly adverse effects on both mental and physical health. Now that you know what stress is, and how your body reacts to it, you'll be ready to fight it when it strikes. Here are some general STRESS SURVIVAL TECHNIQUES everyone can follow.

When I was an active young wife and mother, age 29, I walked into my physician's office for my yearly "routine" checkup. After examining my blood pressure, he looked at me and said, "Your pressure is up." Then he proceeded to send me home with no instructions or medication. Well, I began to read about Biofeedback and Meditation exercises that had been used successfully in hospitals and clinics to reduce high blood pressure. Being the daughter and granddaughter of high blood pressure sufferers, in addition to being Black (High Blood Pressure is one of the leading killers of Blacks according to *Ebony* and *Essence* magazines). I seriously set out to find ways that did not involve daily medication to keep my blood pressure "normal." I began Transcendental Meditation. When I returned to my physician a year later for my "routine" checkup, he stated my pressure was normal. From that visit until today, the prognosis for my blood pressure is still "normal."

After that experience, you can understand why I was very concerned whether my body would withstand a situation as stressful as a divorce after 22 years of marriage, with two college-aged children depending on me for financial and emotional support.

Always I have been an avid reader. On more than one occasion, I had read that next to losing a spouse, divorce is the most stressful experience a person can have. It is also an experience that gets very little, if any, community support, as still today, divorced women are not held in high esteem in a community. Many times the attitude appears to be "I will pretend you don't exist, and please, bring as little attention to yourself as possible." As tragic as the situation is for a widow, the feeling is that it is not her (the widow's) fault that she is left without a husband (an act of God), and for a "brief" period she has some understanding. For divorced women, it is another story. The statistics for severe illness, and mental and physical problems (most believed to be stress related) for women after divorce and widowhood are astounding. I looked at the picture. It did not look pretty. One friend said to me, "Tressa, you have two choices. You can go up or down." Since down was never an option for me, I decided to go up.

The following are some STRESS SURVIVAL TECHNIQUES that have worked for me:

Goals, Exercise and Diet, and Relaxation

GOALS: I sat in a quiet place in my house and wrote a list of goals, Then I read the list and rewrote my goals in the order of priority. At the top of my goal list, I wrote where I wanted my final destination to be. On my list I had things such as keep my children in college, become financially independent, be happy, find peace in my life and so on. **THE IMPORTANT THING IS TO WRITE IT DOWN. GET IT ON PAPER.**

It is important to set aside time to organize your day. Make sure you're not interrupted when you are drawing up your schedule. Make a list of all of your tasks. Put them in order of priority. Set realistic deadlines. Concentrate on one task at a time and consider each problem in depth. Eat lunch away from the office if you work outside the home. Expect the best from people and give them the benefit of doubt. Improve your communication skills with your superiors and your subordinates. Listen without interrupting. Learn from your mistakes. Always keep your sense of humor. Spend time with your family. Get involved in a hobby that demands your total concentration.

I learned to patiently bear what I could not change in this manner, without fear or restraint. Protecting our children from temptation or harm is not to be confused with living their lives for them, which is a great harm. I had to learn that with love, we shield our children from subtle involvements with others until they come to see their way clearly and are strong enough to follow it in spite of temptation. Overconcern conveys to a child (regardless of age) that he/she is an asset of positive or negative value to you. One kind of concern, criticism, offends their vanity and makes them resentful. Excessive praise, on the other hand, finds them with false self-esteem. Resentful, or intoxicated with pride, they cannot discern clearly to deal with life. And so we produce the problem we fear or secretly conspire to bring about. The resentful, pressured, over-protected child will often seek trouble in which to grow. The child is drawn to the very trouble imagined by the parent, in the name of love.

The Shield of Love

Now I had the opportunity to test that theory. Many friends suggested I withdraw my children from out of state private colleges, ask them to come home, live with me and get jobs to help with financial support. Instead, when my children came home for summer vacation, we had many conversations. The major issue to decide was what to do about their education, in the event there was a financial shortage. My daughter, Monica, wanted to stay home with me. She did not want me to be alone. My "friends" again strongly suggested I take my children ("young adults") out of private colleges in the south, bring them home and put them to work to help out financially.

I said an emphatic NO!!! I sat down each "young adult" and asked them if they would be willing to join the Armed Forces and take advantage of the educational program to finance their education. Each "young adult" said, "Yes" without hesitation. It was unthinkable to me to even consider taking them out of school. In addition, I suggested they not worry about me. I said, "Remember, I am a credentialed California School Teacher. If there are no teaching jobs, I am going to go to an agency and apply for the job of a 'Nanny.'" I had read that the new "Yuppie/Buppie" parents were interested in having someone to care for their children who could also read to them and teach them skills, in addition to guiding them in certain creative/growth exercises, games, etc. Also, the job provided "room and board." I did not want to become weak and return to a situation I had found unbearable because I needed a roof over my head.

I told my "Young Adults" that Plan A was for

them to remain in private college with their father paying tuition, and for me to live in the family home, with their father paying my expenses. Plan B was for my "Young Adults" to join a branch of the military, letting the government educate them in exchange for military duty. I would take a job as a Nanny with room and board included in the package.

In September my children ("Young Adults") returned to private college. I remained in the family home. Plan A was in action. My "Young Adults" and I had no further discussion on the subject.

EXERCISE AND DIET: Millions of words have been written on the subject of diet and diet-related stress. These attempts to understand how our diet may or may not cause heart disease, high blood pressure or high cholesterol levels have resulted in a confusing list of do's and don'ts.

There is no absolutely right diet for everyone. But in times of stress it is important to good health to eat a balanced diet of healthy food. So what I want to do here is offer some basic principles which you can use to tailor your own personal eating plan. Aim for a balanced diet. Eat a mixture of foods, and control your intake. Cut down on fattening items that the body can easily do without, such as sugar and sugary foods, alcohol, fatty foods (especially animal and dairy products) and processed carbohydrates.

Reduce your intake of fats. Cut down on fried

foods. Avoid butter, margarine, cooking fats and oils, cheese, cream, fatty meat, pastry, cake, potato chips, nuts, rich sauces or soups, salad dressing and mayonnaise. Eat less salt. Salt can aggravate high blood pressure. Salt is found in many foods, especially processed packages. A single hamburger, for example, probably contains as much or more salt than the body needs for its daily intake. Forget the idea of dieting. If you eat along the lines I am suggesting, then you will eat both sensibly and adequately, with great enjoyment. To maintain a healthy body, you do not have to subject yourself to some rigid diet.

The way in which you prepare and serve food is very important. People tend to automatically serve food dipped in butter or dressing, thus adding more fats and calories to the meal. With a little more thought and experimentation, for instance, using herbs and spices in cooking, the flavor of food may be enhanced without extra fat. As a general rule, grill instead of fry. Fry only with vegetable oils like sunflower or olive oil; never use lard. Try to cut down on roasting meats. Broil, stew or grill meat rather than roast it in its own fat. Make gravy from the drippings left after the fat has drained off. But, cut down on meat-based gravies in general.

Make sure cooking oil is hot enough before adding food, otherwise excessive fat will be absorbed. Stir-fry Chinese-style. This is a much healthier and tastier way to eat fried foods. Nonstick pans are preferable because they need little or no oil. Use paper towels to absorb surface fats on all foods before they are eaten. I cannot emphasize the importance of eating properly when faced with a stressful situation such as divorce. This is a time our bodies need proper nourishment, and is usually the last thing thought of. Especially if you live alone, as I did.

My Hobby

So, to motivate myself to cook and eat properly, I decided to make cooking a hobby, and each day, I would "test" dishes around mealtime that I planned to serve at "dinner parties at a later date." And it worked. I did extensive library research on nutrition in addition to extensive research in my volumes of personal cookbooks, and had a wonderful time. I had something to do each day that needed to be done, giving my life structure, and I ate regularly.

Thus, eating meals "alone" each day became a "big event." I was so busy shopping, researching and "testing" my recipes, I had little time to feel sorry for myself. I shopped every day for that day's meals (as Europeans do), therefore I was forced to get out of bed, dress and go outside my house.

The Importance of Exercise

There is now evidence showing that some of the

established risk factors in coronary heart disease including elevated cholesterol levels and high blood pressure, are all actually decreased by exercise routines. This means that exercise can have dramatic effects in improving your health. In fact, a modest but regular amount of exercise, say, a few miles walking, swimming or maybe running four days a week is all that is required to stay in good physical health. Swimming in particular is an excellent form of safe exercise for the body.

Each morning I would exercise with the SHAKLEE SLIM PLAN CASSETTE, because, in addition to being excellent exercises, it also suggests "cool down" time to check your pulse and see if you are working too much. I liked this program especially since I lived alone. Because the question always comes up, how much exercise is enough?, it is good sense to exercise on a regular basis. The most dangerous thing you can do (and the danger increases in direct proportion to your age), is to rouse yourself from a state of total inactivity, such as a week at the office, to a sudden hour or two of violent activity.

Try to get 20-30 minutes of continuous exercise a day, or at least every other day. Supplement exercise with everyday substitutes such as walking up flights of stairs rather than using an elevator. You do not need much exercise at all to meet the requirements of a health promoting exercise and diet. Don't let your whole life be dominated by an obsessive urge to sweat and strain. Be sure to check with a doctor before you begin any exercise program.

RELAXATION: I approach this section on relaxation with gentle care, because it is so important, yet so personal. With the subconscious mind, you see things more clearly, and one of the things you see is that you have to LOVE to SURVIVE. You can't love anyone else unless you love yourself. The world is in such a mess now because so many people hate themselves and take it out on others.

According to Dick and Trenna Stuphen, "Fear is the one problem that exists between human beings. Fear is responsible for all disturbance, large and small, international and interpersonal. Hatred, anger, possessiveness, greed, inhibition, stress, frustration, hangups, phobias, insecurities, are all fear-based emotions. Fear paralyzes us and keeps us from acting when we need to act. It can stop us from making a growth choice when it would be in our best interest. In accepting the fear and living with it, you are imprisoned within it."

Lately, medical journals, TV programs and newspapers are saying "stress overload" may be hazardous to your health. It is believed by some authorities that 80-90 percent of all illnesses are "stress" related. One thing that causes stress is change. Our society is changing rapidly, family structures are shifting, there are changes in women's and men's roles, threat of nuclear war, etc. Many people suffer stress because they are unable to adapt. Thus physical disease such as high blood pressure, peptic ulcers, headaches and anxiety occur. Or you can simply be depressed, frustrated, restless, more tired, have problems sleeping or a problem with fluctuating weight. These are all outer responses to inner stress.

The antidote to "stress" is to learn to relax, to become calm. When you are calm you can see things clearly. Problems become solvable and not over-whelming. There is much evidence that biofeedback, Transcendental Meditation, hypnosis, yoga and many other relaxation diciplines on the market will help.

Everytime we allow ourselves to resist emotion-ally to pressure it takes a little less pressure to cause us to respond with more violence or more unbear-able repression, until small irritations can make us explode or makes us withdraw until we become insensitive to feeling. Progressively we lose our grip over our mind and body, becoming conditioned and molded by outer demands. Our only alternatives are to become upset and hurt others or to become upset and repress that emotion to the detriment of your own health and well being.

That is essentially what happened to me when I filed for divorce. I was unable to communicate my feelings about our relationship to my husband. Thus I was influenced by fear of the unknown to envision every possible unwanted thing happening to me and my children. As a result the only thing awful was my fear. Few if any of the awful things I envisioned happening as a result of divorce happened. However, instead of listening to my own inner voice, I listened to every horror story I heard or read about the harshness of divorce. What rid me of the fear was writing down my goals. The first goal I wrote was that I wanted to meditate twice a day for 20 minutes each. You see, today I am convinced that if I hadn't written "meditation daily" as a goal it would not have happened.

Relaxation Techniques

However, I did meditate and do relaxation exercises twice daily, and the stress and tension began to leave. Thus I was able to make plans for myself and my children based on clearly defining the problems, solving them and moving on with my life. I am attracted to relaxation exercises because there are dozens of techniques to choose from. Here are some simple methods you can try:

Select a comfortable sitting or reclining position. Close your eyes and think about a place where you have been before that represents your ideal spot for physical and mental relaxation. It should be a quiet place, like the sea shore, the mountains or even your own back garden. If you can't think of an ideal relaxation place then create one in your mind.

Now picture yourself in your ideal relaxation place. Imagine that you are seeing all the colors, hearing the sounds, smelling the aromas. Just lie back and enjoy your soothing environment. Feel the peacefulness and calmness. Imagine your whole body and mind being renewed and refreshed. After 5 to 10 minutes, slowly open your eyes and stretch. Remember, you may instantly return to your relaxation place whenever you desire and experience a peacefulness and calmness in body and mind.

Sit quietly in a comfortable position. Close your eyes. Beginning at your feet and progressing up to your face, relax your muscles. Keep them relaxed.

Breathe through your nose. Become aware of your breathing. As you breath out, say the word "love" silently to yourself. Continue the pattern; breathe in...out "love;" in...out, "love"; and so on. Breathe easily and naturally.

Continue for 10 to 20 minutes. You may open your eyes to check the time, but do not use an alarm. When you finish, sit quietly for several minutes first with your eyes closed and later with your eyes opened. When some distracting thoughts occur, try to ignore them and return to repeating "love." Practice the techniques once or twice daily but not within two hours of any meal, since the digestive process seem to interfere with relaxation response.

Sometimes things really get to you and you need to back off in a hurry before you blow an emotional or physical gasket. Here is one method for giving yourself that initial breathing space: When you are getting all worked up, say stop to yourself. Breathe in deeply and breathe out slowly. As you do so, drop your shoulders and relax your hands. Breathe in deeply again and, as you breath out, make sure your teeth aren't tightly gritted together. Take two small breaths.

SUMMARY: I do hope the STRESS SURVIVAL TECHNIQUES suggested in this chapter will be of use to you. I know they work, because they worked for me, and are the foundation of my "Highly Successful Balanced Living Seminars and Workshops."

The STRESS SURVIVAL TECHNIQUES I listed above played a primary role in emerging successfully from a marriage of 22 years duration dissolved by divorce, and left with two college age children and no visible means of support. I called on all of my resources, support of friends, family etc. But the most important key was I sat down, decided my priorities, and proceeded to WRITE MY GOALS. I can not say it strongly enough. The one most important thing I did was WRITE MY GOALS.

By writing down my goals on paper, I was able

to establish a sense of direction. "I knew where I was going." Perhaps I hadn't figured out the rough details of how I was going there. BUT, I DID KNOW WHERE I WAS GOING.

The importance of writing GOALS ON PAPER is from that moment on you innately have a sense of direction. The process makes you innately see things more clearly. The process innately guides you to make the right choices along the way to your destination as clearly stated in your goals.

My guides at this time were *The Power of Positive Thinking* by Dr. Norman Vincent Peale and *Think and Grow Rich* by Napoleon Hill, books I had been reading for several years but had NEVER REALLY PUT THE THEORIES INTO PRACTICE until I was forced to do so by life changes I found overwhelming. I had tried everything else over the years to "cope" with life changes. I said, "What do I have to lose by trying the principles revealed in the *Power of Positive Thinking* and *Think and Grow Rich?*"

As a result, I began to really believe I could make it. I began to really believe I could keep my children in private colleges to complete their education. I began to really believe I could become financially independent. I began to really believe that the most exciting, rewarding years in my life were in the present and in the future. Then I put those "thoughts into action" because I had a "burning desire to succeed." And I did succeed.

Because of those experiences, I strongly suggest *The Power of Positive Thinking* by Dr. Norman Vincent Peale and *Think and Grow Rich* by Napoleon Hill as supplemental reading to everyone who takes my BALANCED LIVING WORKSHOPS AND SEMINARS. Because of my personal experience, I know the principles set down in those books are sound. BUT YOU MUST USE THEM.

Conclusion

I am concluding this chapter with a process that combines physical exercise, relaxation exercises and a way to set goals that is simple but sure to reduce stress. I recommend that you record it on a cassette. Make a duplicate you can put in your briefcase and/or purse, and one to leave at home next to your bed or in your special quiet place. These are physical and relaxation exercises recommended by Dr. Charles Faulkner that have helped me: You can use them to change your response to stressful situations:

Physical Exercise: Walk: take casual walks daily. Start off by walking around the block. Increase the speed and distance each week until you are walking at least one mile each day, EVERY DAY.

Breathing and Relaxation Exercise: Breathe in slowly and deeply. Hold your breath for five seconds. Exhale slowly. Tighten your legs for three seconds then relax them very quickly. Next tighten your stomach and cheek muscles for three seconds, then relax them very quickly. Then do the same thing with your arms, shoulders, neck muscles, face muscles and scalp. Repeat this procedure five consecutive times. Carry out the entire procedure as often as you wish, preferably every half hour whenever a difficult situation arises. Your body will eventually become relaxed for hours even when you do not do the exercises. Initially you must do the exercise often.

Goal: Make a cassette recording in a quiet room. Record all the wonderful things you want to accomplish, your hopes and dreams. Tell exactly how they will be accomplished, why you know you can and will do it. Describe how wonderful it feels reaching your goals and being the person you want to be. Listen to this tape daily with your eyes closed, while you sit or lie down in a quiet comfortable place. Dream about your happiness, day dream about your strengths and abilities. Write letters to support yourself. Put happy signs and pictures on all of your walls. These procedures will gradually eliminate and control your stress. The symptoms and stress indicators will slowly disappear. You will gain control of your life. You may not be able to make all your problems vanish, but you can improve your mental and physical health as well as change your negative responses to tough situations. But it will only happen if you begin by doing the above exercises each day for thirty days. Then and only then will you begin to develop the discipline to relax each day and begin to see results. It worked for me. It can work for you. Give it a chance.

Hellen Keller said, "Security is mostly a superstition. It does not exist in nature, nor do the children of men as a whole experience it. Avoiding danger is no safer in the long run than outright exposure. Life is either a daring adventure or nothing."

I knew I would succeed. My attitude became one of success. An "I CAN WIN ATTITUDE." To initiate this change in attitude, I went inward for personal strength instead of looking for help from others. I didn't expect someone else to "fix" things for me. I looked for solutions on my own with GOD's GUIDANCE. I discovered SURVIVAL is not a miracle, but the ability to use adversity to discover unexpected abilities and new strength within. I began to see change more as a CHALLENGE than a threat.

My cooking daily meals was important to my success. I believe psychologists have a name for it. It is called "compensatory self-improvement." That is when a person has suffered a severe stress that they can't do anything about. It is important to give their life structure as a way of regaining a sense of effectiveness and control. I don't know if there is such a thing as a "Survivor Personality." However I became less concerned about security and more focused on now...on my children...and the world. In essence, as Shakespeare said,"To be or not to be, that is the question." I decided to BE.

And, I had to SURVIVE. You see, I intended to SURVIVE, and not only SURVIVE, but be more in every way than anything I had experienced. And, finally, it is the INTENTION TO SURVIVE and do so in better shape, that brings it all together.

Many, many stress-free successes.

IRA KLITZNER
Financial Consultant
1248 23rd Street #3
Santa Monica, CA 90404
Bus. (213) 858-4040 • Res. (213) 829-5077

Ira Klitzner

*Ira Klitzner has spoken all over the world including the high
seas. He is popular with audiences as diverse as corporate
executives, retirees, doctors and C.P.A.'s; as well as almost
anyone with a thirst for knowledge in the fields of Financial
Planning, Investments and many other related topics.*

*He lectures aboard the Princess Cruise ships, teaches
business and finance courses in colleges and graduate
schools, and can be seen regularly on television.*

*Ira began his professional career as an accountant with
two National Certified Public Accounting firms. He is a
Financial Consultant/Stock Broker, beginning his investment
experience in the stock market at the ripe old age of thirteen.*

*His uncle called him a 37 year old midget at 8 years old,
his jokes are worse than a bear market, and he is a David
Brenner, Barry Manilow look alike. Ira was born in Brooklyn,
New York, schooled in California and works for a major
international stock brokerage firm in Beverly Hills, California.*

*He is the kind of man you want to advise you on handling
your money. Ira is a silver tongued investment wizard, with a
heart of gold.*

10

Conquering Financial Stress
by Ira Klitzner

"This is the best country in the world but you can't live in it for nothing."
—Will Rogers

If the most stressful moment in your life was when you looked desperately upon a stack of unpaid bills, then you understand the need for a successful personal and business investment strategy.

Money is pleasurable to most people. It can also be one of the most uncomfortable stress producing factors of our lives. Many psychologists tell you money is the number one cause of stress in Americans today.

First Hand Stress

I was a seasoned front lines veteran of the stock brokerage business, overextended and living on 110% of my income (the American Dilemma). The stock market was reaching new all-time highs. My income looked a sure bet to reach six figures for the first time in my life. I had a wonderful relationship with my girlfriend. I was scuba diving, skiing, eating at the "in" restaurants, traveling at my whim, patronizing the best discoteques, taking flying lessons, and obviously (at least to me) having a heck of a good time.

Boy, Was I On A Roll!

So I decided to "take the plunge" and make a major financial commitment. I purchased a beautiful tri-level condominium in a prime location and paid a handsome price. I was very happy since I could finally afford to buy a place to live that would be in keeping with the image that I had grandiosly perceived I was not only entitled to, but deserved. The tremendous tax advantages associated with home ownership were also enticing.

Escrow was closed. I was to move in, in 48

hours. It was then that I received a telephone call at 2:00 a.m. while fast asleep. Larry, my best friend, was calling me from Italy to announce that he was getting married in Rome in 48 hours. My response was as expected. Even though I was moving into my home at wedding bells time, I would of course be there for this happiest of occasions. The next night at 2:30 a.m. Larry called again; this time to tell me to bring a lot of money, for he had found a great leather clothing store, and to also see if it was possible to take his fiance's best friend along to be the maid of honor.

Four thousand dollars worth of airplane tickets and twenty-four hours later, the maid of honor and I were in Rome. My girlfriend, along with a moving company, moved me into my condo. My friends got married. We drove to Cannes, France. I had a marvelous time on my American Express Gold Card, and flew back to Los Angeles on "cloud nine."

That's When It Happened: "STRESS!"

I had borrowed the 20% down payment for the condominium, received a bill for $7,000 from American Express, and paid $2,000 for fixing-up and moving-in expenses. Then the stock market stopped going up. It started "Heading South," unfortunately not just for the winter. Gone was the six figure-plus income expected that year, as well as the next.

How do you repay all of the loans, mortgage payments, credit cards and lines of credit? How do you pay for skiing, flying, scuba diving and all the other wonderful "fast lane" extras that had become necessities? Not only was my income becoming extinct, but my stock market investments put out a shingle, "gone fishing!"

I didn't need a psychologist to tell me that the breaking-out on my face, the nervous habits that were forming, the lack of ability to concentrate, and the break-up with my girlfriend were all because I was "stressed out."

Since personal bankruptcy was out of the question, charity and I do not mix, and borrowing was like asking for blood, I decided it was time to change my life. From that day forward it was time to get serious, more serious than I thought I would ever have to be.

After spending a great deal of time thinking, planning, and juggling different ideas and concepts, I came up with a "plan of action" that has worked so well for me and my clients, that I want to share it with you. If you care enough about your financial future to spend the time to read this chapter, you will find the answers here. I know they will do for you as much as they have done for me.

It Works !

I prepaid the condominium's first mortgage holder

upon the simultaneous acceptance by them of a $12,500 principle reduction, and obtaining a new loan from a new mortgage lender for 115% of the old mortgage. In other words, I took $25,000 out of the property, and only increased my payments a small amount. (You would be amazed at the flexibility real estate appraisers have).

I then increased the limits on my lines of credit, renegotiated my notes (to lower the principle payments), increased my credit card limits, and started my new investment program.

Strategy

Next on the agenda was to work on keeping up my lifestyle, yet lowering the cost. I began by giving finance lectures aboard the Princess Cruise ships. I was traveling in style, eating gourmet meals, mingling with the world's wealthy and attaining mini-stardom through these lectures. What a great way to see the world, build a clientele, meet wonderful people, enjoy myself tremendously and have the price tag fall from heaven.

Life's Tough

I also began teaching undergraduate and graduate university courses in business and finance again. This afforded me the opportunity to meet very interesting, successful, wealthy people, while increasing my knowledge, since I was studying in order to teach my class and also for my primary business. Most importantly, the school paid me to teach, and I found I had no time to waste any money since I was always so busy.

Financial Victory

I bounced back quickly, and had not altered my lifestyle. My strategy had increased my liquidity, my income, my knowledge, my exposure and put my financial house in order. I was now in a perfect position to succeed in the barbarous world of personal investments. I had also unconsciously put myself on an unwritten, yet very important, budget. *Financial Victory* was just around the corner.

Over the next several years I did well in investments. I am very pleased to report that the game plan I am about to share with you worked. My income is increasing, my investments are growing, my bankers love me, and my net worth has increased substantially.

Most importantly, I am now free from my financial problems. The stormy stress situation has turned into a sea of calm wonderful waves.

For those of you who realize that you often learn more from failure than you do from success, I have written my *Eight Point Strategy To Financial Success.* It worked for me, and it will work for you.

If You Plan, You Win!

Eight Point Strategy To Financial Success

1. Prepare Financial Statements

The best way to conquer Financial Stress is to begin by preparing personal financial statements. They do not have to be fancy, just complete and accurate. A balance sheet shows where you are financially, today. An income statement states how much you expect to have available next year to invest, barring any major unforeseen event. It is most important to write all your figures down, rather than keeping it in your head. It is easier to remember things when they are in front of your eyes. Lastly, be honest with your entries, as they are for your benefit, and completely confidential.

BALANCE SHEET

Assets (own)	Liabilities (owe)
Cash	Credit Cards
•	•
•	•
•	•
Real Estate	Mortgages
TOTAL ASSETS	**TOTAL LIABILITIES**

Total assets minus total liabilities equals your net worth.

List your assets, most liquid (how easily they can be turned into cash) first. A money market fund is almost as liquid as cash, yet much more liquid than real estate.

List your liabilities, longest maturities last. A one year bank loan is due prior to most real estate mortgages.

INCOME STATEMENT

Income	Expenses
Salary	Interest
•	•
•	•
•	•
Dividends	Mortgages Payments
TOTAL INCOME	**TOTAL EXPENSES**

Total Income minus total expenses equals additional capital available for investment.

I recommend that you update your financial statements no less than once each year.

2. Set Realistic Goals and Expectations

Crystalize in writing exactly what your financial goals and expectations are. Be realistic. Fantasy may lead to financial disaster and a great deal of unnecessary stress. If you have a spouse, I recommend this be a joint effort. Your spouse's goals and expectations may differ from yours.

If You Want To:

A. Be wealthy? How wealthy? How do you expect to achieve wealth? Do you know the odds of winning the grand prize in the lottery? Are you prepared to work that hard?

B. Start a business in the near future? Are you aware of the cost of starting the average new business? Do you know the mortality tables in regard to new businesses?

C. Quit working in 5 years, and travel around the world with your family? How long do you plan to travel? What will you do when you return? Have you figured out the realistic cost of this trip? What if your children hate traveling?

D. Earn 25% per year on your money? Are you aware of the risks associated with investments that potentially can return 25% per year? Are you aware that over the last 50 years, stocks, bonds and real estate have appreciated, on average, less than 15% per year?

E. Retire at age 65 on $50,000 (present value) tax free income per year? How do you expect to achieve this? If you are 50 years old today, earn $70,000 a year (before living expenses), you have a net worth of $200,000 (most of which is in your home) and you are a risk-averter, are you being realistic?

F. Live modestly? Take no risks by leaving your money in guaranteed certificated of deposits? Are these C.D.'s protected from inflation? What if you got sick, and your insurance only covered a portion of this major expense? What if you got divorced?

I recommend that you periodically review your goals and expectations. They may change.

3. Diversify

John Templeton said, "The only people who should not diversify are those who are right 100% of the time!"

Diversification refers to investing your capital in several different opportunities. This is very important, because you never know when things will not turn out as you planned. Murphy's law states, "What can go wrong, will go wrong!" If you have only one investment and it fails, you will lose a large percentage, if not all, of your money.

Lets assume you invest $100.00 in each of four

opportunities. One becomes worthless, one remains at $100.00, one doubles, and one triples in four years. You now have $600.00 and a 50% profit. This represents a very respectable 12½% average return per year. There are also tax advantages, such as depreciation in real estate, that might make the return look even better.

100	100	100	100	=	400
0	100	200	300	=	600

How To "Get Lucky"

Luck is often a very important factor when it comes to investments. By diversifying, you put yourself in a much better position to be lucky. If you owned a quality piece of real estate in the late 1970's in the United States, you got lucky. You did not have to be a real estate genius to participate. If you were fortunate enough to have owned stock in one of the companies that was a target of a takeover specialist in the 1980's, you got lucky. If you owned silver coins when the Hunt brothers ran up the price of silver, you got lucky.

You can't win the lottery,
if you don't buy a ticket!

Purchasing investments that are *uncorrelated* is

also a very important diversification strategy. Uncorrelated refers to investments that react differently in the same financial climate. Real estate tends to fare well in periods of high inflation. Stocks fare better in periods of low inflation. In recessions "retail liquidators" (companies that run "going out of business" sales) do very well, yet retail stores fare better in good economic climates.

It is also wise to diversify by making investments of different types within each investment category. Purchasing two properties, one in a downtown area and one at the beach, is very prudent; a recession might have a greater affect on the downtown property while a tidal wave might only affect the beach property.

4. Invest Proportionately Less in Speculative Investments

Your investment portfolio should consist of a combination of speculative, growth and conservative opportunities.

Speculative investments have high risk and high reward potential. They include aggressive stocks and mutual funds, and low quality (junk) bonds, among others.

Conservative investments have lower risk and lower reward potential. They include certificates of deposits, government securities, and high quality bonds, among others.

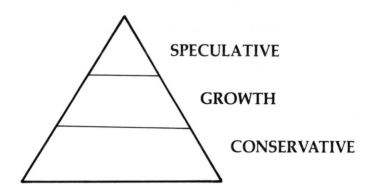

SPECULATIVE

GROWTH

CONSERVATIVE

Depending on where you are in life, what your financial statements show and what your goals and expectations are helps determine what portion of your assets should be allocated to each investment category.

Examples: If you are a 45 year old upwardly mobile corporate executive earning $100,000 a year, with a family and a country club lifestyle to support, you might consider a more aggressive investment posture. Perhaps:

> 30% speculative
> 40% growth
> 30% conservative

If you are 60 years old and looking forward to the luxury life of retirement, you might consider a more conservative investment posture. Perhaps:

> 10% speculative
> 30% growth
> 60% conservative

These are arbitrary percentages. If you are a risk taker you might be more aggressive, and vice-versa.

The rationale behind this orderly concept is to balance your portfolio in order to take into consideration your own personal situation, to protect a comfortable percentage of your wealth, and to always allow you the opportunity to be lucky.

5. Be A Contrarian

"The non-conformist businessman who follows his own counsel, ignoring the cries of the pack, often reap fantastic rewards!"
—J. Paul Getty

If everyone is buying, consider selling. If everyone is selling, consider buying.

Skis go on sale in the summer, umbrellas are cheapest when the sun is shining. Stocks sell at their lowest when "everyone" has sold. They sell at their highest when "everyone" is fully invested.

The stock market was at its lowest point in 1932, the depths of the depression. It subsequently went up for 6 years.

In 1974 real estate prices were plummeting, "For Sale" signs were everywhere. Homes were selling at "fire sale" prices. That was the time to buy real estate. The next five years proved to be one of the greatest times in modern history to be an owner of property. Fortunes were made between 1975 and 1979.

In 1980 real estate was perceived to be the greatest investment on earth. your barber was an expert in buying apartments. Real estate was the number one topic at every cocktail party. *That was the time to get out of most real estate.* It has been a tough market ever since.

In 1931, John D. Rockefeller began building Rockefeller Center in New York. People thought he was crazy. It became one of the most successful and prestigious properties in America, proving he was right, and the majority was dead wrong!

During the depression, the stock market crashed, but J. Paul Getty became a large oil stock buyer. Over the next several years, he made a killing!

In 1980 Chrysler was almost bankrupt. The stock sold as low as $3.00 per share in 1981. In 1985, it sold for over $40.00 a share.

During 1981 Pan American Airlines barely escaped bankruptcy after purchasing National Airlines. C. Edward Acker was brought in, the stock went down as low as 2⅝ and rebounded to $9.00 in 1985.

Post Disaster Investing

Buying stocks after a corporate disaster takes place

and panic selling of the stock sets in, is another type of contrary investing.

In 1980, a major fire in their Las Vegas hotel sent MGM Grand Hotel Corporations stock plummeting. Many people died. Lawsuits were filed. The stock dropped to $7.00 a share. When the reality was revealed that MGM's insurance (they were able to add additional retroactive insurance) was enough to cover the problem, the stock went up to as high as $14.00 in just two years.

An American Airlines jet crashed at Chicago's O'Hare Airport in 1980. Over 100 people died. Their stock fell to $7.00 a share. It was $20.00 just two years later. It hit $40.00 in 1985.

When a leak at General Public Utilities Three Mile Island Nuclear Power Plant was discovered, G.P.U's stock collapsed to $3.00 per share. The stock hit $13.00 within just a few years.

In 1984, a gas leak at Union Carbide's Bhopal, India, plant killed over 1,000 people. The stock sank to $33.00 in the same year, and rose to past $70.00 in the next.

When panic or excitement sets in, opportunities arise!

6. Bet on People

People make ideas happen. You may have a great idea, but if you don't have the right person to see the idea through, there is a much greater chance of failure.

Peter Ueberroth made millions building "Mister Foster," a travel agency. He then turned the 1984 Olympic Games, notoriously a financial nightmare, into a major money making venture (a first!). Herbert Hoover got us into the depression. It took F.D.R. to get us out. Steven Wozniak and Steven Jobs turned the idea of building a home computer for the masses (starting in their garage) into a Fortune 500 company in just five years (Apple Computer Corp.) It was Lee Iaccoca that took Chrysler Corp from the brink of destruction and made it into a very succesful automotive company. It is your surgeon who you bet your life on!

Why do you think the president has a "cabinet," corporations have boards of directors and municipalities have elections?

7. Do Your Homework

Before making any investment, do your homework. Do as much background research as necessary to be comfortably assured that your decision is a correct one.

In choosing a surgeon, would you pick up the phone book and choose the doctor whose name appears first? Of course not! You might ask a few friends for their recommendations, or ask your personal physician for his. You might check with your local Board of Medical Quality Assurance. Then you could meet each prospective candidate before making a final decision on who will "use the knife," assuming at least one of the surgeons met your criteria.

Before I purchased my condominium, I looked at every single family home for sale in the area I wanted to live in that had a sales price within $100,000 of my price range. I then decided to purchase a condominium, which started a new research process not dissimilar from the first. Real estate values have not done well in this area, yet my condo has increased in value.

An investment decision to buy 1,000 shares of common stock requires almost as much research as if you wanted to buy the entire corporation, if you are to be successful. You should speak to the heads of the company. Read their annual report, 10K, 10Q's, proxy statement and any other information available. You should personally visit the company's facilities. Talk to some employees. Speak with friends and trusted business contacts about what you have learned. Find out their thoughts on this company, as well as the entire industry it is in. You should also prepare your own economic forecast and see how this company/industry would fare under your expected scenario. Now you have a fighting chance to be successful.

Investing is not a game, it is a serious, strategic business.

Do you think General Electric Co. would pay over 6 billion dollars to buy CBS before they did their homework?

If you haven't the time to do the homework yourself, hire a qualified person to do it for you.

Before you bought your last automobile, did you look at many other cars? Did you drive a number of makes and models? Did you ask several car owners how they liked their car? Did you read consumer reports? Did you visit two or three dealers to negotiate a better price? If you did, *you did your homework.*

You are competing against thousands if not millions of other investors. The more homework you do, the better chance you have of being successful at "financial combat!"

8. Be Patient

Invest by the seat of your pants, not the balls of your feet! Be patient!

John D. Rockefeller and his family owned Rockefeller Center for over 50 years before selling a large part of it.

Mr. Irvine bought the "Irvine Ranch" in Southern California in the late 1800s for approximately $100,000. His family sold it for over $100 million dollars about 100 years later.

How long has it taken for most of the business people you know, including yourself, to become successful? Many people say 5, 10 or even 20 years. Why should you expect a substantial investment profit to materialize in just 6 months?

Albert Einstein once remarked, "The greatest invention of mankind is compounding!" He was emphasizing the need for time to pass for great things to happen. An example of compounding is; if you invested $100,000 at a compound annual rate of 20%, in just 40 years you would have *150 million dollars.*

If you had been fortunate enough to have bought stock in several of the growing corporations of Japan after that country's World War II devastation, you would have been privy to one of the greatest turnarounds in modern history. If you had been PATIENT, you might have made a great fortune.

Conclusion

If a successful investment strategy would lower your level of stress, then follow my guidelines. I certainly can't give you all the answers, yet I feel very strongly that what I have shared with you works. I know first hand!

I wish all of you happiness in your life, and success in your investments, I hope I have helped in alleviating some of your financial stress.

I would like to leave you with a thought by John D. Rockefeller, *"If you want to become really wealthy, you must have your money work for you. The amount you get paid for your personal effort is relatively small compared with the amount you can earn by having your money make money."*

Harness Stress

Nothing left loose ever does anything creative.
No horse gets anywhere until he is harnessed.
No steam or gas ever drives anything until it is contained.
No Niagara is ever turned into light and power until
*   it is funneled.*
No life is ever grown until it is focused, dedicated,
*   disciplined.*

—Harry Emerson Fosdick

KATHERINE E. BURY

TALMAR ENTERPRISES

16720 W. 63rd Place

Golden, CO 80403

Kathy Bury

Stimulated by the fact that an arsonist's flame destroyed her home and all she had, Kathy Bury turned to Numerology and positive thinking to gain insight into her victimization and come to grips with her seeming defeat. Ignoring the fears of friends and relatives, she determined to start over on the same ground, but with new energy and inspiration. Three years later her Phoenix was up; Kathy was back in TALMAR, the name given to her Arabian horse estate and enterprises.

At this writing, Kathy has devoted more than ten years coupling the ancient philosophy of Numerology with the powers of positive thinking to bring new meaning and new direction to her life. Encouraged by personal correspondence with the reputed Numerologist, Dr. Juno Jordan, Kathy spent time on comparative analyses of astrology, Tarot, Chinese philosophy, motivational studies and parapsychology. Today her clientele include the rich and famous, the not-so-rich and not-so-famous, small businesses and large corporations.

Born in Minnesota, Kathy attended Palomar College in California and the University of Colorado. She polished her theatrical skills at the Arvada Center for Arts and Humanities in Colorado. Kathy currently lectures nationwide using Numerology as a tool to inspire and educate. SO YOU WANT TO BE COUNTED! An Every Person's Guide To Numerical Sanity *is her current book in progress with co-author Susan Von Till.*

11

Numerology Unlocks Stress
by Kathy Bury

"Forewarned is Forearmed."
—Unknown

It was two fifteen a.m. Flames whipped around the house. People were screaming. The outside water hoses lay rigid in ice. House guests tore open the door to my bedroom where I lay sleeping. They yelled, "Get out!" I remember tearing off the cover. Dazed, I ran out of the room, my lungs choking from the hot smoke. Pictures of my loved ones were burning on the piano near the living room window. The front porch was ablaze. My stomach tightened, perspiration ran cold, my throat parched. I couldn't think.

I recall turning, running, back into the bedroom, dialing the phone and crying to my best friends, "Fire! Fire! Call the Fire Department! This is Kathy!" I dropped the receiver. I could hear the rumble of footsteps in the upstairs hall as guests grabbed personal belongings and rushed to get out. There was no time. I yanked clothing out of my closet, put a different boot on each foot, hurried out the door with what I could carry and threw it into the snow.

Ten degrees! Bitter cold! Empty darkness! Darkness now suddenly raped by raging fire. The house was old, a piece of kindling sparking one room after another. A structure so old that as the walls peeled down, aged newspapers curled like snakes from insulated panels. A structure so old that rooms I never saw before appeared out of the flames. Rooms hidden behind years of make-over and reconstruction. What secrets they must have held!

I shivered in the cold, staring in amazement at what was happening—my life crumbling, burning, being washed by fire hoses. I felt drained, like in a nightmare with no resolve. Then, something strange happened to me. As I stood watching my hopes for the future go up in flames something took hold of me and I said out loud, "I WILL come back!" I made a decision right there and then to overcome. I did not say, "I will TRY to come back," I said, "I WILL come back!"

Numerology—A Discovery!

I had never studied or learned much about positive thinking, but my words resounded in my ears and became my cornerstone for the challenges of the months to come. I had heard of stress, but until then, I had never really experienced the fullness of it. I had felt stress over new jobs, new relationships, competition at horse shows, expectations of my mother and the death of my father. But FIRE? It changed everything! It left no finger-prints, left no memories. It erased every clue to my existence. They said it was arson! Was my life in danger? Who would do this? Why me? My life became riddled with questions. All questions with no answers.

I was filled with stress. I couldn't sleep and, when I did, nightmarish flames burned my phyche. I would talk too fast at times; I would jump at the slightest sound behind me. I cried all the time. I began to know fear. What to do next? Where to begin? How to pay for a lawyer? Where would I live? How could I ever work at my job under these conditions?

All I knew for sure was I had made a commitment to myself to "come back." That gave me a goal, a place to start. In my search for answers I found I read everything I could get my hands on from Astrology to Tarot to psychology to parapsychology to philosophy. Numerology made sense! It was mathematical, I could relate to it. I couldn't put it down. For me, it answered questions about myself that I needed to understand. Later I would make it my life work but now it helped me plan my stress strategy. I had made up my mind, I was going to control this stressful situation, this disruptive influence, I was not going to let it control me.

Endings Are Often Beginnings In Disguise

I would soon learn that apparent endings are often new beginnings in disguise. A whole new life was about to begin for me. I didn't know it then, but through the study of Numerology I would soon understand the timings for these changes and see the direction I would soon take from dental assistant to designer to contractor to theater to author to speaker. Had that fire not happened I would never have dreamed of designing my own home or even having the capabilities to do so. The pressure of the stress of that situation brought hidden inner abilities to the surface, abilities that would form a ladder stepping in new directions. I was obviously not meant to be a dental assistant all my life, yet before that happened I would have sat contented, never pushing myself or believing myself to be more.

In the months that followed I searched by travel, researched by books, delved into the mysterious, meditated until I passed out, and began to get my sense of humor back. I layed out my Numerology Chart and began to see myself as a whole and complete person having a real and systematic plan for my existence. There were actually years planned for more stress than others. The two years around my fire were very stressful. That was exactly how long it took to get the insurance settlement, design the house and contract to have it finished. Strange! Could there actually be something to this thing called Numerology? Does it actually have the key to the identity of me? Could Numerology possibly unlock stress? Can it open the door to emotional balance and activate the best in me?

What Is Numerology?

I had to take a deeper look at Numerology. First of all, what is it? Studies show modern Numerology dates back to the time of Pythagoras in the year 590 B.C., yet it is as new as the moment you place your pencil to paper and add up your own name! Pythagoras was that mathematical wizard who put together a blend of philosophy and arithmetic to create the study of numbers. It is a philosophy of life designed to open the mind, expand opinions, broaden expectations, and reach for full personal potential.

If it's been around so long why haven't more people used it? Actually, they do, or did. After Pythagoras developed it Julius Caesar planned his campaign to overtake the world with it. Then during the Dark Ages it was abandoned, and later it was labeled mysterious and hidden in metaphysical studies. Today it is understood to be a mathematical process used to find the Personality, Heart's Desire and Destiny in the Name at birth by adding up the numerical values attached to the letters in the Name. Motivating influences can also be seen in what is termed the Birth Force, the addition of the month, day and year of birth.

Perhaps it was the fire that triggered it, but ten years later I have been motivated, educated, rewarded, raised and expanded by Numerology. Do I still look for answers? Of course! Always! No matter how much I learned or experienced, it was no longer enough to just understand myself. I wanted to formulate a long range plan for others to be able to use it also. Numerology is not for the moment, it is for always. It is a way of seeing yourself on paper, in black and white, for the first time. I wanted to show others its value.

Why Numerology?

I often have business men ask me how to make their

businesses run more smoothly. Numerology will never tell you exactly what to do, it will tell you the timings of when to do, when to strike, when to wait, when to plan, when to market, when to buy, when to sell. TIMING IS EVERYTHING!

Knowing that timing can relieve stress or activate it, knowing that I am in control of how I handle the stress that life or other people throw my way creates a happier me. Knowing that I can create stress myself and that I can do it when it is advantageous to me also creates a happier me.

Stress is part of life, part of the living experience. The dictionary says it puts the subject under pressure or strain, it disrupts, it shakes things up. Think about it! If there were no stress, life would have no challenge, no incentive, no reward. Stress triggers choice! It never leaves things status quo. The result is change. The change is either positive or negative, active or passive. The choice is always individual. Stress asks you to risk something. It challenges you to go beyond your limitations, to rise above what is normal, to push you just a little farther.

Numerology can help. It opens a way for you to get to know yourself. By adding up the numbers behind each letter in your name and learning the meanings of those numbers, your name takes on a new meaning. You become special, individualized, unique. You can understand for the first time why personal actions, reactions and interactions all have individual meaning within the structure of your full name at birth. To know and understand yourself is a major break-through to self-esteem, self-confidence and accomplishment.

When you can see through a simple mathematical lay-out a pattern for your life, it takes on new meaning. You now have a reason for your existence. No longer is your course uncharted. You now have a map, a plan, something to hold on to, something to sustain. You can reach for the stars, take a chance, plan for tomorrow. The answer is and always has been in your name. Knowing that alone is a stress-saver.

Know Thyself—Numerology Reassures

Your name is so close to you. It is with you all the time. It never abandons you, it is never jealous, never envious, never fearful, never guilty. It is always there for you, always supportive, always a quick supply of energy JUST FOR YOU! ALWAYS FOR YOU! Even when you seem to give up on yourself it still remains ever pushing from behind the scenes, ever moving you in the right direction.

Let's take a closer look. Several indications in the chart of a name show innate qualities. Your First Name can be used immediately upon birth, causing its vibrations to influence and motivate at an early age. A vibration is just another word for movement, qualifying the energy behind the numbers in your name. How you use or do not use this energy is up to you. Free-will, as always, is the mentor. If used to its optimum you may hear mom or dad saying, "Look, she's so independent!" or, "Look, dear, how he loves to share his toys!" These qualities will vary upon the number vibrations that are indicated in your name, but strong responses can be seen even at any early age as to whether you are acting positively or negatively.

Your Middle Name is a passive parachute to lift you and inspire you like a Guardian Angel in times of need. It is always there for your use. Your Last Name, no matter how many times you have tried to bury it, marry it or scratch it off your birth certificate, is with you to stay. It is the heritage you were born with and with it comes the courage to grow past it if not up to your liking. It gives you the satisfaction of learning from its standards or the challenge to show others you could and will do better.

Another innate number in the chart is taken from the date of birth. The total of the day, month and year is your Birth Force Number and is what motivates you to get out of the womb and out into the world. The direction of your early years will be influenced by this number. These innate Numbers should be used positively to lead you towards your

Heart's Desire and your Destiny and to aid in the development of your Personality.

Pythagoras used a very simple arithmetic process to find the different major parts of the name. Your Heart is the vulnerable side of you, therefore he used the soft sounds in the alphabet in deciphering it. Your Heart's Desire is what you really want out of life. You must risk to get it. It is found by adding together all the vowels in your name at birth. Keep in mind, you must use First, Middle and Last Names. On the other hand, your Personality could either be soft or crusty, but it is the way that you present yourself to the world, so it is usually tougher. Therefore, Pythagoras decided to use the consonants to find it. Add all the consonants together in your First, Middle and Last Names for this Number.

Another vibration that includes risk is the destiny, that which you MUST DO in this life. It is not innate and must be nurtured, polished and accomplished. It is life's biggest challenge and contains much inner stress until it is attained. I hear people ask me all the time, "If only I knew what direction to take next. I feel like I should change, but what can I do?" When you can look at your name and see in a mathematical way indications for change, needs for risk, values within the name that stabilize and qualities that energize and motivate, you not only are reassured that the timing is right for change, but that you have within you all the ingredients necessary for executing that change. What does Numerology give you? Confidence! Absolutely! And confidence relieves stress!

You must remember that you never have to develop, nurture or risk for anything in your life. Too often I see people just grabbing the bus of life and going along for the ride. They feel that nothing they do makes any difference, so why make waves? Life is going to take them where it will and nothing they do is going to make any difference. How sad, yet how true! With that attitude that is exactly what will happen to their life. Others will influence all their decisions, probably even make most of them. Others may even isolate themselves and remain unapproachable, never allowing the world to see or benefit from the really beautiful qualities they hold within.

Numerology shows you are responsible for your own life. It not only demonstrates what you have to work with, but just as importantly, explains the timings in your life. By bringing your attention to specific numbers for each year it stirs and excites you to see what you can really be or do with your life. Depression lifts, stress relaxes, challenges excite, planning ahead creates goals, timing sets deadlines, accomplishment is victory.

Timing Puts Stress in Perspective!

Timing puts stress in perspective in two ways. First, the study of numbers shows four major timing changes in the life, each asking for you to work under a different number and going from nine years to up to thirty or more years to accomplish. Each person works at a different pace and is always given the energy and time needed to finish what was to be accomplished in that cycle. These are called Pinnacles and relate important changes in the individual. Some will have more emphasis on marriage, work, travel, buying and selling, the arts, etc. The indications will be strong; each individual will be influenced by the innate qualities in their chart, their style and talents.

As your Pinnacles unfold the need to be more than what you started out to be will be increasingly stronger. Housewives go back to school, men have mid-life crises, people reach and stretch and realize the need to grow beyond where they are. Actually, you are realizing that you cannot keep taking from the world, from mom and dad, your first teachers, your first jobs, you must give something back. Now you are reaching, risking for your Heart's Desire and your Destiny.

Secondly, each person works constantly in Personal Years. This is an ever-changing barometer of how the weather is in your life. Cloudy or sunny is up to you. Again, attitude has everything to do

234 / The Stress Strategists

with your year and each year has specific stress indicators, so learning about each one gives you the edge. Personal Years are found by adding together the month and day of your birth plus the current year that you are living in right now. Double digits are always added together one more time to eventually get only one digit (1986 = 1+9+8+6 = 24 = 2+4 = 6).

Personal Years create quick stress. The pressure is really on. There are only 365 days to accomplish, not years and years. As each New Year proceeds ahead to the next number so does your Personal Year. Eventually you journey through all the numbers, one through nine, in a normal lifetime. This gives you the chance to experience each number's influence even if you didn't find it anywhere else in your name.

Stress—The Challenge

Numerology teaches stretching. It comes to terms with who you are, what you want, what pleases you, and gives you the confidence to risk to get it. When you risk you create stress. Not only have you created a challenge, but you have decided to meet the challenge and reach for the victory. This is positive stress. Scary? Yes, but more than scary, it stimulates a certain excitement that outweighs the fear. This is being in charge of your stress. This is being in charge of your life.

Every time you make a change you put yourself on the line. Keep in mind, change is what makes you grow. Welcome it! Delight that you have given yourself a chance to broaden. Your growth and development is the only real handle you have on life. You can stimulate, educate, love, administer to others, but often it is only temporary, transitory. Others move in and out of your life. You are really the only one you can count on to stay with you. I am not saying people, places or possessions are not worth the effort, but if you are not developing yourself as well it is devastating when they leave your presence. You are worth developing, nurturing, loving.

Stress—The Victory

Numerology wants you to create your stress, to want to learn more, to want to do more, to grow beyond taking, to keep working to improve those wonderful qualities in your name. Why? Only when you are working at your optimal can you ever really relax, can you say "Yes" or "No" with real conviction and clear commitment. Stress is never easy, but you can be the champion. I did finish my home, I quit my job as a dental assistant, I did take up a new career. You can do it too! Numerology will help you know yourself. It is not the size of the victory that creates self-esteem, it is the victory itself.

So whether the tycoon building an empire or the clown spreading smiles from ear to ear, the wealth of you is all you have to take on. Make stress work for you, use it for your benefit. To do this, first you must know yourself and what better way than with the study of Numerology? Count yourself lucky. Count yourself to a better way of life.

SIMPLE NUMEROLOGY CHART
Use Name At Birth—As Is On Birth Certificate
Use Month, Day And Year Of Birth

ALPHABET
VALUE KEY

A-J-S	= 1
B-K-T	= 2
C-L-U	= 3
D-M-V	= 4
E-N-W	= 5
F-O-X	= 6
G-P-Y	= 7
H-Q-Z	= 8
I-R	= 9

DATE AND TIMING KEY

JANUARY	= 1	JULY	= 7
FEBRUARY	= 2	AUGUST	= 8
MARCH	= 3	SEPTEMBER	= 9
APRIL	= 4	OCTOBER	= 10/1
MAY	= 5	NOVEMBER	= 11/2
JUNE	= 6	DECEMBER	= 12/3

SIMPLE KEY

	YOU	ADD
HEART'S DESIRE	WANT	VOWELS
DESTINY	MUST	NAME
PERSONALITY	APPEAR	CONSONANTS
BIRTH FORCE	ARE	DATE

PERSONAL YEAR	TIMING	MONTH + DAY OF BIRTH + CURRENT YEAR

SIMPLE VALUES

1 = LEADER

2 = PEACE-MAKER

3 = JOY-GIVER

4 = DEPENDABLE WORKER

5 = FREE-SPIRIT

6 = HUMANITARIAN

7 = SERIOUS THINKER

8 = ORGANIZER

9 = IDEALIST

SIMPLE TIMINGS

1 = START!

2 = AGREE!

3 = PLAY!

4 = WORK!

5 = BREAK AWAY!

6 = CARE!

7 = PREPARE!

8 = DO IT!

9 = FINISH!

REMEMBER:
ALL DOUBLE DIGIT ANSWERS ARE TO BE ADDED TOGETHER FOR A SINGLE DIGIT TOTAL
(12 = 1 + 2 = 3)

THE FACTS

1. You're the one with the bright idea! You've got the will and determination to stand on your own. You're a starter, not a finisher. Try not to be overbearing or cynical, others have opinions too. At your best, others will admire your strength and your ideas can spur the world to better things.

2. You're true cooperation! You love to share, are a good friend and companion. You don't appear to be the leader, but are the power behind the throne. Partnerships give you stability. At your best, others will admire your diplomacy and look to you as the peacemaker.

3. You're the joy of the world! Words are your power and your delight. You are creative and magnetic, the eternal optimist. You're the life of the party, yet sometimes too easily imposed upon. At your best, you attract the help you need.

4. You're the one we can count on, you're dependable! You're wholesome, love nature, cautious, hard working, judicial, and industrious. You manage, apply and construct. Change can be difficult. At your best, others will bestow pride and honor for a job well done.

5. You love freedom! You're restless and need progress and growth for survival. You're active, witty and curious. You love travel, people, law,

sales, and government. The unexpected seeks you out. At your best, you are truly vivacious.

6. You're the symbol of truth and justice! You are the humanitarian who gladly takes the responsibility of home and family. You have strong principles and are a loving teacher. At your best, you are the family, the backbone of society.

7. You're the analyzer! You observe and think. For you, knowledge is power. You are the reserved loner, but your inner magnetism attracts what you want. Success comes to you. You are selective. People feel important in your presence. At your best, you are one of the worthies.

8. You are the executive! Your knowledge and power are well earned. No one hands you anything. Your inner need to govern and direct overrides disappointments. You are the mental worker. At your best, you are the spine of the economy.

9. You are the idealist! No one understands empathy, tolerance or compassion quite like you. You are the sign of forgiveness. You love art and theater. You have the ability to really contribute to the world, service and generosity are your paths. At your best, you add more light to the universe.

AL J. LANE
Counseling and Learning Centers
3575 Cahuenga Bl. West, #213
Los Angeles, CA 90068
(213) 850-1160 ● (818) 242-5111

Al J. Lane

A native Californian, Al Lane was born and grew up in the San Jose area, graduating from the University of California, Berkeley.

Somehow he always knew he would become a teacher but did not realize this career would not begin until his 60s. A great deal of preparation intervened as Al moved through various vocational experiences, including being a food chemist, Naval officer, food plant manager, plant engineer, bank officer, salesman, store manager and restaurant owner. During this time he also experienced a family with 5 children, and gradually his habit of continual study and searching led him into metaphysical fields, with particular interest in the thing we call Mind.

After reviewing and studying many New Age modalities, Al decided that some form of Hypnotherapy would teach him the most. He was right and soon discovered that Mind, Body and Spirit are so closely related they must be considered simultaneously if he was to unravel some of the Mind's mysteries. Al never realized how fascinating the quest would become, especially in the realm of the Spirit. Fortunately for Al's clients, answers come readily and rapidly when they are ready for them. Hopefully, there will be some answers arising from this writing.

12

Stress Is Such A Bother— Or Is It?
by Al J. Lane, B.S., C.H.

"When an evil spirit pursues you, your legs cannot carry you fast enough to escape—but if you turn around and face it, it will disappear."
—An old American Indian saying

I once heard a man say, "Thank God for a little stress in my life." Obviously he realized that stress could be beneficial for him in some ways. On the other hand, most people seem to go along with

Webster's definitions that characterize it as a weight or burden. Thus, it follows that stress is to any one person what he perceives it to be, or how he reacts to it. Most often, discomforting reactions occur without much knowledge of the source within us.

Stress—What Is It To You?

We may find our job or our relationship stressful and wonder why other people under similar circumstances don't have the same feelings of anxiety we do. Some people seem to dip into their anxiety bucket wherever they go, while others don't appear to even have a bucket. This is particularly true of young children, and you may agree that your life wasn't so much of a burden for you either when you were very young. So, what has changed? Your answer may well be that you have more responsibility now. Yet we know that many leaders thrive on superhuman loads of responsibility. Then what is it that permits some people to handle well or even enjoy stressful conditions? Hopefully, you will have some of the answers by the time you finish this chapter. And, by applying a few of the ideas you will read, you will then find your life becoming more enjoyable.

Stress—What Is It To Me, Now!

Many years ago when I had a large family, lots of

bills to pay, and I would find myself out of work with little savings, anxiety would sleep with me many a night. Now, the family is grown and gone. Things have changed, but life still presents me with burdens. The difference is that I don't even allow anxiety into my house. Having become a hypno-therapist, I've had the opportunity to observe anxiety in many forms in my clients. What I have seen and learned now helps me to avoid the disturbed feelings that used to result from the stressful conditions around me.

I've learned, for example, it doesn't help much to blame people or conditions for my poor feelings. Life will go on bringing me people and conditions that I'm not very fond of. Instead, I've assumed respon-sibility for my feelings, and I came to know there was some cause within me for them. Eventually, I rooted out of my subconscious mind a lot of these fear, anger and guilt causes, and found I no longer reacted to stress in the old way. Life for me has become much more enjoyable, and I feel better when life is throwing challenges at me. Therein is a change in attitude—what used to be problems are now challenges.

Negative Emotional Reactors

Understanding reaction to stress has been enhanced by work with agoraphobic (anxiety complex) clients.

This kind of person has a whole complex of phobias or fears in the subconscious. A situation perfectly normal to most of us, such as shopping in a supermarket, could bring on an anxiety attack producing a host of physical, mental and emotional symptoms that are completely disabling. In therapeutic treatment the agoraphobic person gradually comes to understand the symptoms, to release the fear energies, and then the symptoms become less severe, ultimately disappearing.

Although the stress reactive person may also be triggered by fear in the subconscious, the emotional base is usually broader and more diverse. Emotions like anger, resentment and guilt may be underlying causes. Somebody who chooses to repress or not show anger in a relationship is adding fuel to a fire under his emotional boiler. As time goes on he will feel increasingly stressed, maybe demonstrating the increased tension as an ulcer or ultimately exploding with violence. Resentment of authority figures is often transferred to bosses in a job situation. This kind of person may still be resenting the coerciveness of a parent while he was a child. The pattern in his subconscious tells him to resent anyone who orders him around, no matter how well intentioned. Since he may have to repress his feelings for fear of being fired, the tension inside grows.

Another example is the tension produced by an aged parent using guilt against a middleaged child.

The parent becomes sickly (mostly imaginary) attempting to control the child with a "poor little me" script. The child feels guilty if he doesn't take care of the parent, but in doing so feels stressed because he resents the control.

In each of the aforementioned examples we see one or more negative emotions underlying the stress reaction process. Even when the emotion in the subconscious is partially understood, consciously it may be difficult to cease reacting. This is usually because there are other negative factors hidden in the subconscious, particularly belief systems.

The False Belief Reactor

My work with the subconscious area of the mind has led me to characterize the energies there as patterns or structures in the memory bank. In dealing with energies in the mind, I attempt to identify and trace specific emotion patterns (as I call them) in the memory. I've discovered that the emotional energy is connected to or surrounds a specific belief. If the emotion is negative the thought or belief is both negative and false. A simple example is fear of spiders connected to the idea that all spiders are dangerous. The idea is false because, in fact, very few spiders are dangerous and are rarely lethal.

There are numerous instances of generalized

negative belief systems underneath stress reaction syndromes. We usually label these attitudes or prejudices. A person may have a strong belief that certain kinds of people can't be trusted and may apply it to all those of a particular race or color. In this case there may not be a lot of emotional energy; rather most of the energy is just the deeply ingrained prejudice. Confronting someone of that race or color could produce considerable tension. In a similar way, imagine the stress on a mother when her daughter announces she is going to marry a man who the mother is convinced will be no good for her daughter.

Deactivating the Reactors with Hypnotherapy

The process of removing unwanted belief and emotional energies in the memory is similar to the learning process. A young child learns rapidly, because the memory slate is relatively clean, and the new information does not have to fit into, be matched with, or agree with existing data already in the memory. However, as more data crowds onto the slate the mind begins to run into dissimilar or conflicting ideas. Now the mind has the task of deciding which information is most valid—except that the bio-computer does not reason nor make decisions; it only receives and catalogs data.

When a client finds himself acting in unwanted ways and asks for help, it is the existing and conflicting data that we search for with hypnotherapy. We have discovered that working with this old data in terms of energy (which it really is), if the amount of energy is simple and slight, it is easily overcome and replaced with the new more appropriate and correct idea. On the other hand, when an old idea energy is large, such as a firmly established prejudice, or if it is heavily layered with an emotional charge like fear, then replacement may be more difficult. This is particularly true when other similar energies are overlapping in the mind creating a more complex pattern.

The process in hypnotherapy of effecting the change may vary either with the client or practitioner, but the objective is the same—to remove the offending energy and replace it with a more acceptable, healthy energy (idea, belief, etc.) The advantages of a therapy approach are that it takes less time to make the change and there is a good likelihood of a complete and irreversible change. Time is reduced because in the relaxation process, the conscious mind becomes sharply focussed on the task at hand, while the subconscious becomes more open and receptive to the good change. Further, it is important to remove all of the undesirable energy, especially the original root or first cause. This first cause as well as subsequent experiences often exist in the memory in past lives. Rarely can such energies be reached by conventional means.

In dealing with reaction to stress, the situation causing the stress is usually apparent, but the why of the tension build-up may be well hidden. Survey reveals that relatively few people really love or are totally comfortable with the work they do. Most of us simply put up with the job not realizing that certain changes in our mind could make the work more comfortable. One client discovered the stress factor was working for and with "men." She had a total distrust of all men arising from several traumatic experiences with her father, husband and other men. Another common stress factor in work is resentment of authority—stemming from experience with the first authority, a coercive or disciplinarian type parent. In both of these actual client situations, the root or first cause was a past life experience, indicating the desirability of delving deeper than just for surface reasons.

Do-it-yourself Deactivation

Since we all constantly are re-learning and changing old ideas, we are in the habit of using our own chosen methods—some being quite effective while others may be less so. There are several reasons for the differences in effectiveness. First, we must recognize that each of us is unique, differing in the ways we think and act. One person may learn to meditate readily, while another may never learn how. A positive thinker may welcome change, while a negative thinker can find many excuses for not changing. Second, re-learning techniques vary widely in structure and in the way they are applied.

There are some basic guidelines that can be helpful in learning what may work best for you. Initially you must take responsibility for any stress you feel. It is yours, and no amount of blaming or finger-pointing will change it, except very temporarily. Next, evaluation or analysis of the stress producing situation may provide some clues as to what needs to be changed. Observing a client afraid to drive freeways, I discovered she had little sense of direction and she virtually ignored all freeway signs—things she was able to learn.

A truism is that knowledge and fear cannot be in the same place. I also note in my work that an essential ingredient to change is motivation and the decision to make the changes. Lip service, in terms of an affirmation to think differently will seldom have much effect on a firm, internal desire to think the same. This factor is the reason addictions are so hard to overcome; worry itself is a type of addiction.

Assuming the decision to change has been made, the next step is to find out how to make it. Many techniques or processes are available to the person ready and willing to expend the effort. In general, the degree of success in applying the technique depends on two factors. First, success is roughly proportional to the amount of energy applied. This means much more than just physical energy or effort. It includes all of the sensory energies, e.g. seeing, hearing, smelling, tasting and feeling. Second, technique effectiveness depends on how deep into the mind one can get with the process. Working on the surface with just conscious affirmations is not as effective as adding self-hypnosis or meditation. Of course, repeating the process adds energy too, but here moderation is best. The mind has a tendency to tire if the time span between applications is too short, or it may forget if the span is too long.

Choice of the technique may be guided by what feels best. Fighting a resistance will certainly dilute the energy being applied. Most of us find it easy to read a book, go to a seminar or listen to a lecture or tape, but we note that distractions often interfere. A quiet time each day, devoted to the process, allows more concentrated effort and minimizes distractions.

Visualization is widely used, because the conscious mind can be focussed on a desired result. Starting in a relaxed position with the eyes closed, most of us can form pictures through our imagination. Since almost anything is possible in the imagination, the picture may be created as a superbly happy, exciting, supportive scene—something opposite to what has been causing discomfort. The subconscious mind is not selective; it simply accepts the scene as real and when enough positive (though imagined) input has built up in the memory bank, it can then neutralize or override the negative.

It is good to add energy with the senses. For example, if lack of money has been causing stress, then see yourself with a new pocketbook filled with green currency, smell the leather of the pocketbook, feel and hear the currency crinkle in your hands, smell and taste the luxurious meal you are enjoying in a fancy restaurant, feel generous as you leave a large tip for the waitress. One caution—do not say this is only imagination, for it is real to your subconscious! If you happen to be a person who doesn't visualize easily, you may still hear, feel or sense otherwise.

There are many extensions of the visualization technique. One is termed focussing, where attention is focussed on feelings in the body. Tensions caused by stress always take form in some part of the body, such as the head or stomach. By concentrating on that feeling and following it as it changes or moves, words or pictures will usually pop into the mind— clues of the nature of the problem. Many similar techniques fall under the general heading of self-hypnosis. Most of these involve some form of self-directed, creative visualization along with a relaxed state of mind and body. Under the heading of meditation are many processes that are less active or creative. The purpose of meditation is to quiet the mind, releasing it from the constant flow of thoughts that often bombard an anxious person. By focussing on a specific, simple object or sound, and with lots of practice the mind becomes disciplined to the objective of clearing itself of external sensations and input at the conscious level. This then allows eventually a flow of truth up from the spiritual center of our being. Even if the ultimate purpose is not achieved, at least the mind has the chance to become quiet and rest—much more than when we sleep, and that is therapy in itself!

Attitude Is Everything

The first time I heard that statement proclaiming the importance of attitude, I had just started working for the man who stated it, Jim Rohn. As a speaker, seminar leader and motivator, it was Jim's job to show people how to become happier, more successful and actualized. I can now concur that a positive, healthy attitude is paramount to stress-free living; in fact, with this kind of attitude stressful situations may be welcomed as opportunities to learn more about life and to enjoy it more. This kind of thinking is similar to that of the adventurer who is excited about what he may find over the next hill.

The pessimist may argue, "How can I have a

positive attitude when everything is going wrong around me?" The person suffering from stress, for like reasons, may find it nearly impossible to act happy when he feels tense with every part of his body. Perhaps part of the solution is that most of us do not feel out of sorts every moment of the day. We tend to cycle emotionally, feeling down at one time, but much better at another. If we are not a good enough actor to "act as if," i.e. in the opposite way to that which we feel, we can at least use those moments when we feel good. Then we should deliberately move into high gear, programming this extra positive energy into our subconscious while we have the opportunity.

A program of moving toward a more positive attitude should start shortly before retiring for the night. Read something inspiring, or simply reflect over some of the good things that happened during the day. Do not get drawn into negativity in the TV, such as the late news. Just before going to sleep ask your mind for some pleasant, upbeat dreams. Even if you don't remember dreams well now, your mind can be gradually trained to allow you to recall exciting and instructive scenes when you awaken. When you do first awaken stretch a little to get the blood circulating better before getting out of bed. If it fits, say a short prayer of thankfulness for another day of living—it could have been otherwise! A short session of stretching exercises or calisthenics can be refreshing and stimulating if you are not into jogging. If the weather is good, be grateful; if the weather is not so good, be grateful! As you move out into your busy day greet those you pass with a smile or nod—for all you know they may need it. When someone asks, "How are you?" respond with, "Great" or "Wonderful." Fake it at first, if you have to; it will get easier with practice. Try to ignore bad feelings or small aches or pains; above all, do not talk about them. During the day catch yourself if you begin drifting into any kind of negativity—in thought, speech or emotional reactions. Disciplining your mind may take some effort, but the rewards of a happier, tension-less existence are well worth it.

The Values of Stress

It may be difficult for someone coming home dead-tired, after a stress-laden day on the job, to feel there is any value in stress. However, the first thing one must realize is that it doesn't have to be that way. If others can endure or thrive on stressful situations, why not you? The tension or fatigue is valuable, because it is a message saying something is amiss or out of balance. It is indicating, as we've seen, some false ideas or negative emotional energies in the subconscious mind. The struggle to keep things under control takes energy and produces fatigue. The underlying anxiety produces tension, aches, pains and even illness. When personal responsibility for reaction to stress is accepted, and the decision to do something about it is made, the way is open for change. As change for the better does occur, other values begin to appear. The benefits may be subtle at first, but continuing comparison with the way things used to be will point out the differences. Body tone, feelings and general health will improve. Emotional feelings like anger, fear or depression will gradually subside, giving way to more positive feelings. Attitude in general will improve, and circumstances from day to day will appear brighter. One often begins to lose interest in so-called friends who remain negative in attitude; at the same time new, more positive friends begin to appear. As feelings of well-being grow, so does a zest for living!

Like the fellow at the beginning of this chapter, who found value in stressful situations, you will also accept these challenges more gracefully. Much of mankind's progress has been made by those willing to ask why and then to search for the answer. Such people regard otherwise stressful experiences as opportunities—chances to change and grow. Life itself is much less a noun than a verb of action; living is not meant to be passive but a system of constant movement and growth.

How boring if stress did not exist at all—to spur

us into thinking and action. If stress bothers you, then do something about it!

MALCYE W. JENSEN, Ph.D., R.N.
3800 S. Figueroa Street
Los Angeles, CA 90037
Bus. (213) 746-5751 • Res. (818) 282-5048

Malcye W. Jensen, Ph.D.,R.N.

A graduate of Loma Linda University, she holds a B.S. and M.S. in nursing with a major in Medical Surgical Nursing.

The early part of her nursing career involved working in many large hospitals in acute care, namely the emergency room. While working in this crisis setting, she became increasingly aware of occupational stress inherent in the work place.

A large span of her professional career has involved teaching in nursing programs at community colleges and universities including her alma mater, Loma Linda. Presently, she teaches community nursing at the University of Phoenix in the Registered Nurse B.S. program.

In addition, she is an Occupational Health Consultant for California State Department of Industrial Relations, Division of Occupational Safety and Health, better known as Cal/OSHA. This Department is mandated to enforce rules and regulations that ensure the health and safety of workers.

It was this concern for the worker and interest in employee/employer relationships that motivated her to enter the doctoral program in Psychology at California Graduate Institute in West Los Angeles. After receiving a Ph.D., she focused on stress management, writing articles and conducting workshops. These workshops have been held with State personnel in various positions throughout the state.

In addition she has conducted stress management workshops in the community in connection with her private practice.

13

Work—The Universal Stressor
by Malcye W. Jensen, Ph.D, R.N.

*"Though little, the master word looms
large in meaning. It is the "open sesame"
to every portal, the great equalizer, the
philosophers' stone which transmutes all
base metal of humanity into gold. To
youth, it brings hope, to the middleaged
confidence, to the aged repose. It is the
measure of success in everyday life. The
master word is WORK."*
—William Osler

Work occupies a significant aspect of our lives and can be both exciting and satisfying. In addition to physical and mental activity, work provides income for our survival and comfort. There may be increased self esteem based on feelings of competence and effectiveness, and the need for social contact can be met through our work. Working has been one of the most constructive expressions of living. Today, however, we are beset with the problems of stress.

Occupational stress has always been in the working population. However, due to changes in industry, it has now become a serious problem. Job-related stress contributes to absenteeism, and as a result adversely affects employee's production and mental health. The problems generally arise when work is unsatisfying, frustrating, monotonous and unsuccessful. Singer (1960) comments on accidents, absenteeism and alcoholism as functions of stresses. It is one of the costly by-products of excessively stressful situations in industrial life. For some, these by-products provide the only relief they know for increasing tensions and represents a last defense against complete breakdown.

The following are current statistics by Charlesworth Nathan (1982) that illustrates the seriousness of the stress syndrome.

Disorders

30 million Americans have some form of major heart or blood vessel disease.

1 million Americans have a heart attack every year.

25 million Americans have high blood pressure.
8 million Americans have ulcers.
12 million Americans are alcoholics.

Drugs

5 billion doses of tranquilizers are prescribed each year.
3 billion doses of amphetamines are prescribed each year.
5 billion doses of barbiturates are prescribed each year.

Dollars

$19.4 billion is lost by American industry because of premature employee death.
$15.6 billion is lost by American industry because of alcoholism.
$700 million is spent each year to recruit replacements for executives with heart disease.

Historical Perspective of Stress

Stress is universal since it effects all of us. It is also individual as our response varies.

The concept of stress was first introduced by Hans Selye (1956). Originally, he defined stress as all nonspecifically induced changes in response to stressors.

Selye more precisely defined it as the well-known general adaptation syndrome of alarm reaction, resistance and exhaustion. He was careful to underscore that these were changes in adaptation. He took a physiological approach to stress.

A more recent concern is the issue of psychological job stress and individual well-being. Three separate trends converged to give the concept of stress great vitality, engendering renewed interest in Selye's earlier work on stress and the general adaptation syndrome (Selye, 1956). These are represented by Brenner's analysis, particularly employment rates, as a determinant of changes in rates of mental illness; the development by Holmes and Rahe of a Stressful Life Events Questionnaire; and the appearance of studies indicating the effect of the contribution of stressful life situations to heart disease (Brenner, 1973).

The patterns of stress are often complex and can be exacerbated or diminished by the conditions in which they occur and by intervening psychological events.

French and Caplan (1972) have developed a model for stress research. In their model, occupations or roles are the loci of stress in organizations. Role overload, role conflict, and responsibility for people are examples of job stressors. These stressors lead to psychological and physical strains, such as job tension, low self-esteem, elevated blood pressure and high cholesterol. The amount of strain the individual experiences is mediated by personality.

Personality and Stress

Several studies of specific occupations analyzed the relationship of stress to the physical and emotional well being of its practitioners. A study by Cobb and Rose (1973) provided evidence that the psychological stress experienced by air traffic controllers resulted in elevated risks of hypertension, peptic ulcer, and diabetes. Researchers studying tax accountants found marked increase in cholesterol levels as the April 15th deadline for filing tax returns approached (Friedman, Rosenman, & Caroll, 1957). Similarly, a number of studies have shown that the cholesterol level of medical students is elevated on days preceding examinations (Sales, 1969).

One of the major issues is the effect that the personality of the individual has on the perception and experience of stress.

In one study, introverts reacted more negatively to severe conflict than extroverts; flexible people experienced more conflict than rigid ones. Positions involving creative problem solving in contrast to routine supervision and management positions were also more conflict ridden (Kahn; 1974). Welford concludes that introverts represent greater chronic arousal than do extroverts. Therefore, introverts tend to perform better under monotonous conditions where arousal tends to sag and to be less affected by loss of sleep and by narcotic drugs than extroverts. However, unlike introverts, extroverts tend to seek stimulation in order to sustain arousal and tend to remain stable under pressure and perform well under such conditions (Welford, 1974).

Person-Environment Fit

The interaction between the individual and the environment was defined by Lofquist and Dawes in 1969 as the "Person Environment Fit" (Cooper & Marshall, 1976). Cooper and Marshall stated that outside relationships such as family problems, financial problems, and life crises, may affect the interaction as well.

Some studies have been conducted to determine what personal characteristics are important in the stress response.

Pepitone (1976) emphasized the need to understand the individual's motivations, competitiveness, and persistence as they restate one's performance in the stressful situation. In a study of seven astronauts in the Mercury Space Program it was found that the keys to successful adaptation to stress were past experiences and professional competence (Ruff & Korchin, 1967). In general, health problems have been related to unpleasant work conditions, the need to work fast, the need to use a lot of physical effort, and excessive and inconvenient hours. Physical health problems have been shown to be related to repetitive and dehumanizing work (Cooper & Marshall, 1976; Rogers, 1977).

Gross (1970) stated that specific forms or reactions to stress exist within an organizational environment. This includes the stress of organizational careers, task stress, and structural stress. The stress of an organizational career includes the uncertainties of losing one's job, the future of the organization, and lack of advancement opportunities. Task stress refers to the difficulty of performing tasks delegated by the organization for the achievement of its goals. Structural stress refers to the problems of working with others, accepting orders, and cooperating with colleagues.

These role problems lead to a general state of high tension and low job satisfaction. Role ambiguity also leads to a depressed mood, lowered self-esteem, dissatisfaction with one's life, low motivation to work, and the intention to leave one's job (Cooper & Marshall, 1976).

Working conditions, including workload, pace, and hours, have been shown to significantly affect job-related stress. Following his study of 113 Canadian, male, upper-middle managers, Rogers (1977) concluded that workload is highly correlated with stress. In particular, he identified the following factors as related to stress: too heavy a workload, the conflict between quantity and quality demands, and the workload's interference with family life. Burke (1976) reported similar findings and concluded that too heavy a workload was the third most stressful condition that confronted his sample of engineers and accountants. Cobb (1974) similarly stated that workload was among the key factors in job strain.

Work pace, similar to workload, has been found related to stress in jobs. It is one of the general working conditions that affect mental health and create feelings of loss of control. This leads to low job satisfaction (Cooper & Marshall, 1976; Gross, 1970).

Relationships at work have an important role in the increase or decrease of reactions to stress among workers. Studies by Argyris in 1964 and Cooper in 1973 concluded that good worker relationships have an important impact on employee health (Cooper & Marshall, 1976). The need to work with others, accept orders, and cooperate with fellow workers whom one might dislike provides ample opportunity for the arousal of tension, anxiety, and reactions to stress (Gross, 1970).

Occupational Stressors

In the Work of America report, the authors noted that the area of heart disease (which accounts for about one-half of all deaths in the U.S. annually), such factors as diet, exercise, medical care and genetic inheritance may account for as little as 25 percent of the risk factor. On the other hand, the work role, work conditions, and other social factors were suspected of contributing heavily to the "unexplained" 75 percent. Along this line, Kroes and Margolis, citing work undertaken by the Institute for Social Research, indicates that the following occupational stress conditions are generally correlated with coronary disease:

- **"Role Ambiguity"**—having unclearly defined objectives, being unable to predict what others expect one to do, only vaguely understanding the scope of one's responsibility (Kroes & Hurrell, 1975, p. 118);
- **"Role Conflict"**—being torn by conflicting demands, feeling pressure to get along with people, having differences with one's supervisor (p. 118);
- **"Role Overload"**—having too much or too little to do, or too difficult or too easy a level of work assignment (p. 118);
- **"Responsibility for People"**—feeling responsible for the health and well-being of others, for their work performance, career development, and job security (p. 118);
- **"Poor Relations with Others"**—not getting along with supervisors, peers or subordinates; and

- **"Participation"**—having influence on decision making process in one's organization (p. 118).

Other significant occupational conditions identified as stressful included changing work shifts, unnatural work-rest regimens, frequent geographic moves, and inequities in pay and job status.

Occupations with little opportunity for decision making and autonomy tend to be high stress areas. Executives and high level managers in lower stress jobs should be aware of the workers in high stress jobs. They should be able to intervene and decrease turnover, absenteeism and illness.

Stress Management Techniques

There are no simple or universally effective solutions to the problem of stress management. We are all unique, and what works well for some of us may be totally ineffective for others.

The knowledge about stress is one method of increasing your level of awareness. In recognizing and accepting our vulnerability, we can anticipate stressful periods and plan for them. Your stress level can be reduced by having alternate plans available, increasing your options.

Stress management is a problem-solving process. When faced with a stressful situation you can deal with it in several ways. First, you may be able to avoid the problem by delegating it to someone else.

Another approach is to alter it, that is change the situation by negotiation. Finally, you may have to accept this situation as it is and work within that framework.

Problem solving is an action-oriented approach to stress management. Stress is reduced, eliminated, or minimized by taking action. Looking at a problem alone will do nothing. You must take action, that is, make a decision based on all the information you can garner. Your production at work will certainly increase knowing that you feel both competent and effective to cope with the daily stresses of life.

Many problems encountered in the work place are interpersonal, to put it simply, learning to relate meaningfully with difficult people at difficult times. Being competent is not enough. It is also necessary to be effective, and to be effective is to be able to relate to others effectively.

Other problems may be environmental conditions such as noise.

Noise may be defined as "unwanted sound." The effects of noise on man include the following:

Noise may have phychologic effects. For example, noise can startle, annoy and disrupt concentration.

There may be interference with communication by speech and, as a consequence, interference with job performance. Since noise is a critical problem in industry, effort should be made to establish a hearing conservation program. This intervention will help to reduce stress from noise.

Come to Terms With Your Feelings

Accepting your feelings is an initial step in accepting yourself. Feelings are neither good or bad, they just are. All of us have two basic feelings; feelings of happiness and feelings of sadness. These two feelings embody all the other feelings such as love and anger.

Anger can serve a very useful function. Anger is feeling that results in stress. It can be an alerting sign that you are upset and that effective action is necessary. Knowing that you are able to control your anger, you will become less upset. When angry, some of us become irrational and act impulsively. Acting in this manner gives power away. Managing and/or controlling anger is a necessary aspect of stress management.

The more confident you are in a situation the more likely you are to be flexible and adaptive. To be flexible requires that you are able to view a situation from many aspects. You are able to weigh both the positive and negative aspects of a situation and be able to sometimes give up your position and yield to another.

To be flexible also requires taking risks. Risk taking requires confidence and also the knowledge that you may be responsible for the consequences. Risk taking may also indicate that you may not be right all the time but are willing to try new approaches at work with new employees, alter a budget and be adaptable when necessary.

A Five-Stage Program of Behavior Control

There are five stages in this program to reverse dysfunctional habits of behavior:

1) Observe yourself.

Become aware of the nature of the habit and the context in which it occurs. First you should study the habit carefully, spending a week a month observing yourself to discover exactly when, where, and under which circumstances the habit started. Carry a paper with you and record when certain types of habits and feelings appear. This chart will serve to make you aware of how prevalent pain or stress is in your life.

2) Commit yourself to accomplish a specific goal.

List as many reasons as you can for your undesirable habits. This list should contain all the environmental factors that tempt or persuade you to keep the habit, including people, situations, and feelings and it also should include the benefit obtained from these habits. Next compile another list of reasons to change. Since it is not uncommon to feel a sense of loss when you abandon a habit that might be pleasurable, you may need to make a third list in which you create a new strategy for obtaining each of the benefits you derived from your bad habits.

3) Create a change strategy, and a contract for specific action.

This stage of the program is critical. It involves examining your lists of positive and negative incentives and designing a program for change. To heighten your commitment, the program should be in writing and signed by you and a person who can help in the program.

4) Adopt new and healthier habits.

There is an initial break-in period in which it seems unnatural. During this time, it has to be earnestly practiced and soon it will become automatic. Consider the situations that give you trouble, and work to create now responses.

Health

Health status may be viewed in three ways. Firstly, it can affect the extent to which one is exposed to stressors. Secondly, good health is in itself a significant generalized resistance resource by definition. Thirdly, being healthy can facilitate the acquisition of other general resistance sources.

Seven habits can significantly determine a person's health status and life expectancy. Life expectancy is highly correlated with how many of these habits a person follows. A forty-five-year-old man who practices three or less can expect to live to age sixty-seven, while a man of this same age who follows six or seven should live to seventy-eight. The following habits can add much time and health to lives:

7 Health Habits

1. 3 meals/day at regular times, with no snacks.
2. Daily breakfast.
3. Moderate exercise, 2-3 times weekly.
4. 7-8 hours sleep/night.
5. No smoking.
6. Moderate weight.
7. No alcohol, or only in moderation. (4 oz./day)

5) Make sure you have continual support for the new responses.
Beyond the family, the best way to support new behavior is through a self-help group of men and women with the same problem. Gaining internal control over damaging habits demands hard work to look closely at these patterns, understand their roots, and restructure the environment to create incentives for new behavior.

In the past few years, many support networks have failed. Increasing mobility, both social and geographical, has made it more difficult for people to establish relatively enduring friendships. Many are reluctant to involve themselves deeply in friendships, to avoid the later pain of separation. The extended family unit is less likely to be found living in the same geographical area where family members can turn readily to each other for social and other recreational activities.

Affiliation with an organization in which a person works seems to have become a major device for developing a support system. Many employees identify with organizations whether a company, church, university, or governmental department. Many people move every five years, the work organization can be the trend of continuity and may well become a psychological anchor point and reduce stress.

Support groups are very important in helping people to manage stress. The nuclear family may not be in close contact with the extended family. Therefore, a concerted effort should be made to formulate and maintain other friendships. Friendships are like bank accounts. You need to make a deposit in order to make a withdrawal. Friendships need to be maintained in order to be able to use them in a time of crisis. Maintaining friendships takes both time and energy.

These support groups are vital in reducing stress and maintaining self esteem.

Concentrate on Positive Development

- Adopt the attitude that no problem is too monumental to be solved.
- Establish a sense of purpose and direction.
- Learn to transcend stressful situations.
- Increase your awareness of the interdependences of all things in the universe.

Generally, research indicates that individuals who believe that they can exercise some control over the events that happen to them are more likely to take steps to maintain their health. Coping is taking charge of one's circumstances. These four strategies can help you be in charge: *Psychological* coping includes: counseling, personal growth, and therapy. *Physical* coping includes exercise, weight control and diet. *Social* coping includes enlisting family support, friends, co-workers, and professional organizations. *Relaxation* coping includes vacations, hobbies, and meditation.

Plan and Execute Successful Life-style Changes

- Expect to succeed.
- Approach projects one step at a time.
- Keep change projects small and manageable.
- Practice each change rigorously for 21 days; then decide whether to continue with it.
- Celebrate your success; reward yourself.

Stress touches the life of everyone of us and in many results in complete psychological and physical breakdown. There is a need that we learn to manage stress and feel confident that we can implement strategies necessary to control stressful situations.

REFERENCES

Pepitone, A. Self, Social Environment and Stress. In Appleby, M.H., & Trumbull, R. (Efs.), *Psychological Stress: Issues and Research,* New York: Atherton Press, 1967.

Ruff, G.E. & Korchin, S.J. Adaptive stress behavior. In Appleby, M.H., & Trumbull, R. (Eds.), *Psychological Stress Issues and Research.* New York: Appleton-Century-Crofts, 1967, pp. 299-323.

Rogers, R.E. Components of organizational stress among Canadian Managers. *Journal of Psychology,* 1977, 95, 265-273.

Gross, E. Work, organization and stress. In Levine, S., & Scotch, N.A. (Eds.), *Social Stress.* Chicago: Aldine, 1970

Burke, R.J., & Weir, T. Marital helping relationships: The Moderators between stress and well-being. *Journal of Psychology,* 1977, 95, 121-130.

Friedman, M., Roseman, R.H., & Carroll, V., Changes in the serum cholesterol and bloodclotting time of men subject to cyclical variations of occupational stress. *Circulations*, 1957, 17, 852-861.

Sales, S.M. Organizational roles as a risk factor in coronary heart disease. *Administrative Sciences Quarterly*, 1969, 14, 325-336.

Kahn, R.L. Conflict ambiguity and overload. Three elements in job stress. In *Occupational Stress*. Springfield, Illinois: Charles C. Thomas, 1974.

Welford, A.T. *Man Under Stress*. London: Taylor Francis. Ltd., 1974.

Cooper. C.L., & Marshall, J. Occupational sources of stress: A review of the literature relating to coronary heart disease and mental ill health. *Journal of Occupational Psychology*, 1976, 49, 11-23.

Singer, H.A. *The Management of Stress*. Advanced Management, 1960, 25, 11-13

Charlesworth, E.A., & Nathan, R.G. *Stress Management: A Comprehensive Guide to Wellness*. Houston, Texas: Biobehavorial Publishers and Distributors, Inc., 1982.

Selye, H. *The Stress of Life*. New York: McGraw Hill Book Co. 1956.

Brenner, H. *Mental Illness and the Economy*. Massachusetts: Harvard University Press, 1973

French, J.P., & Caplan, R. D. In A. J. Morrow (Ed.), *The Failure of Success*. New York: Amacon, 1972.

Cobb, S., & Rose, R.M. Hypertension, peptic ulcer, and diabetes in air traffic controllers. *Journal of the American Medical Association*, 1973, 224, 489-492

Cobb, S. Role responsibility: The differentiation of a concept. In *Occupational Stress*. Springfield, Illinois: Charles Thomas, 1974.

Kroes, W. H., & Hurrell, J. Job Stress and the police officer: *Identifying Stress Reduction Techniques*. Paper presented at the meeting of the Symposium of the National Institute of Occupational Safety and Health, Cincinnati, 1975.

The body must be repaired and supported if we would preserve the mind in all its vigor.

—Pliny the Younger

FRANK WM. VARESE, M.D.
24953 Paseo de Valencia, Suite 7C
Laguna Hills, CA 92653
Bus. (714) 837-1510 • Res. (714) 496-7255

Dr. Frank Wm. Varese

Dr. Frank Wm. Varese was born and educated in Europe where he obtained his medical degree from the University of Bologna, the most ancient medical school in the western civilization. He pursued his postmedical training in the U.S., and completed a medical internship, and a residency program in the specialty of internal medicine. He maintains a medical practice in Laguna Hills, California.

Dr. Varese is also a teacher, writer, and public speaker. He has taught nutrition and holistic health for a California college for twelve years. His upcoming book, "Tools of Wellness: How to be Well in a Sick World" awaits publication in the spring of 1986. He lectures and presents workshops on preventive medicine, stress management, and holistic health methods in the U.S. and Europe. He is also known for his knowledge of comparative religions, Eastern philosophies, and the ancient Kabbalah.

Dr. Varese is a cofounder and charter member of the American Holistic Medical Association. His many other associations include the American Medical Association, the California Medical Association, the American Society of Contemporary Medicine, and the Royal Society of Medicine of Great Britain.

14

A Holistic Approach to the Stress of Life
by Frank Wm. Varese, M.D.

"The abolition of disease will depend upon humanity realising the truth of the unalterable laws of our Universe and adapting itself with humility and obedience to those laws, thus bringing peace between its Soul and itself, and gaining the real joy of happiness of life."
—Edward Bach, M.D., 1931

A Simple Biology Lesson

A man, a butterfly, an eagle, and an amoeba have something in common. They are all members of the animal kingdom. These organisms are made up of microscopic structures named *cells*. Cells are composed of a special substance called protoplasm, the living stuff which exhibits the properties and activities of life.

Animals have special characteristics which distinguish them from members of the mineral and vegetable kingdoms. They have the ability to move parts of their bodies and change their position with respect to their surroundings. They also possess the ability to respond to change in their environment. If we place a drop of a dilute acid in the water in which a quiescent amoeba lives—or if we heat that water, we observe an immediate response. The one-celled amoeba starts to move by means of pseudopods, which are protrusions which it forms from its own protoplasm. The characteristic of all protoplasm to respond to a stimulus is known as *excitability.* Organisms are equipped to respond to many stimuli—including heat, cold, light, sound, and chemical stimuli.

The French physiologist Claude Bernard (1813-1878) made the observation that all living organisms, including man, possess the ability to preserve a constancy of their internal milieu—despite changes in their surroundings. For instance, a human being can endure intense heat or cold and still maintain his usual constant body temperature. He can ingest relatively large amounts of acid or alkaline substances and still retain the usual, constant composition of his blood. The great American scientist Walter B. Cannon (1871-1945) called the ability of organisms to preserve constancy "homeostasis," the capacity to remain the same. As long as an organism is able to preserve homeostatic balance, it is able to survive and experience a state of wellness. However, when stimuli are too intense, they cause stress: they overwhelm the organism's ability to cope, therefore destroying its homeostatic equilibrium and creating disease and eventually death.

Stress results from an individual's inability to adapt to an environmental event. It can result from a positive event. For instance, a person who wins a ten million dollar lottery may suddenly die due to the stress of happiness. And it can result from a negative event—such as losing a job, being infected by viruses or bacteria, or experiencing the death of a spouse.

Hans Selye, M.D., a world famous endocrinologist, permeated medical thinking and influenced medical research in every country with his concept of stress as the principal contributor to disease, premature aging, and death. Professor Selye stated, "No one has seen stress, but when the lining of the stomach is raw with ulcers, when the adrenal glands are swollen, and the thymus shrinks, we know we are encountering stress." Selye explained that continual exposure to stressing agents or stressors can make a person look older than his years and accelerate the aging process. Stress diseases include high blood pressure, headaches, cardiovascular disease, gastric ulcers, pains in the neck, aging, and others. Stress consumes the body and destroys it. The thymus gland, an important organ of the immune system, is one of the first targets of stress and atrophies at an early age. Anatomists used to think that it didn't serve any biological role in humans and therefore it naturally shrank. The digestive system responds to stress with ulceration and bleeding. Skin hardens and becomes very thin. Stress affects skin by deterioration and its reduction to a small fraction of its original weight.

"As A Man Thinketh..."

The human body is made up of some one hundred trillion tiny cells which biologically are very similar to the amoeba cell. The amoeba adapts to many stimuli surrounding it and survives. But, when stimuli are too intense, the amoeba succumbs. Biologically, humans are very similar to the amoeba. Man, however, is an extremely complex organism. He has developed an intricate nervous system with a brain structure that has no equal in the animal kingdom. Homo sapiens seems to know no limitations in the exploration of the universe. He has visited every remote corner of the earth and landed on the moon.

He has a mind that can penetrate the most distant star or planet. Clearly, the human mind can think. But thinking creates feelings that often become stressors.

The role of thoughts and emotions in producing illness has been known since the earliest recordings of medical thought. Plato, in one of his *Dialogues*, wrote, "Hippocrates, Asclepiad, says that, 'The nature of the body can only be understood as a whole; for this is the great error of our day in the treatment of the human body, that physicians separate the mind (soul) from the body.'" Galen first called attention to the fact that women who were melancholic, who had too much black bile (Greek, *melas chole*), appeared to be particularly predisposed towards cancer. Many 18th and 19th century English physicians viewed emotional distress as the major cause of malignancy. Relationships between emotional stress and angina and coronary disease were noted by William Harvey, John Hunter, Sir William Osler, Walter Cannon, and many others.

How Do We Cope with Stress?

Hippocrates and other medical thinkers of the past clearly stated that man has physical, mental, and spiritual components. They advanced the concept of holistic medicine that is now revolutionizing medical thinking in many countries. We can control stress only when we comprehend the real nature of man and the many factors that are capable of upsetting his balance or homeostasis. These factors can originate from within or from without. They can be physical, chemical, mental, or spiritual.

How To Cope with Physical Stress?

Physical stressors—such as heat, cold, or the impact of an accident can cause disease. We can avoid or minimize such stressors. Excessive sunlight may become a stressor and cause disease. But we do need light for health. Researchers at the top health research facilities are suggesting that some people experience mental depression due to a light deficiency. Dr. Steven Potkin, who has won national recognition for his work at the National Institute of Mental Health and as the first in the nation to set up collaborative research on major mental illness with China, has begun a series of experiments at UCI Medical Center to determine the effectiveness of treating a type of depression with light. Excessive exercise can exhaust the body and even cause death. But inactivity is also a powerful stressor. If we put a healthy, young athlete to complete rest for one week, we upset his or her body homeostasis and therefore cause "dis-ease."

The adrenal glands and the sympathetic nervous system respond to stress by producing certain hormones that can be measured in the laboratory. For instance, cigarette smoking is a very powerful chemical stressor. We can measure the level of catecholamines in the blood of a subject before smoking. After smoking one cigarette, a twofold or greater increase in the level of catecholamines of the blood will be found. Also coffee, sugar, and many other substances are stressors. They upset body chemistry and alter homeostasis. No matter what the nature of the stress—physical, chemical, or emotional—the body reaction follows a similar pathway, which leads to the fight or flight response. If we smoke a cigarette, eat excessive sugar, or feel anger, fear, or depression, we signal the pituitary gland to produce ACTH (Adrenocorticotrophic Hormone)—which, in turn, stimulates the adrenal glands and the sympathetic nervous system to secrete more adrenaline and noradrenaline, two powerful catecholamines, and produce more cortisone. These chemicals increase blood pressure, pulse, and blood sugar. The pancreas responds to the increase of blood sugar by producing more insulin to metabolize it.

Reduce Stress by Balancing Body Chemistry

In balancing body chemistry, good nutrition is extremely critical. Dr. Roger J. Williams, former director of the Clayton Foundation Biochemical Institute, stated, "The nutritional microenvironment of our body cells is crucially important to our health, and deficiencies in this environment constitute a major cause of disease." When stressed, we need larger amounts of several nutrients which are essential to manufacture the stress cycle chemicals. We have greater need for vitamin C and magnesium. We need more of all the vitamins of the B complex family, especially vitamin B_6 and pantothenic acid. If we do not have adequate zinc, we are not able to make enough ACTH. We need the frequently lacking essential amino acid tryptophan in order to produce adequate serotonine. We must have enough of the trace mineral lithium which is frequently deficient in the diet of many individuals.

In the words of Roger Williams, "...the most basic weapons in the fight against disease are those most ignored by modern medicine; the numerous nutrients that the cells of our body need. If our body cells are ailing—as they must be in disease—the chances are excellent that it is because they are being inadequately provisioned. The list of the things that these cells may need include not only all the amino acids and all the minerals, plus trace elements, but about fifteen vitamins, and probably many other co-enzymes, nutrilites and metabolites."

Many drugs, including numerous ones which are obtainable without a prescription, can upset chemical balance and create additional stress. For instance, oral contraceptives, which many women use, interfere with the availability of vitamins B_6, B_{12}, folic acid, vitamin C, and magnesium. The ability to cope with stress diminishes with age. We are born with a certain amount of stress reserve. When we are young, we may not show the evidence of stress as when we do after we have spent or dissipated our stress reserve. As we age and accumulate stress, we reach a stage when we show symptoms. Eventually we develop a peptic ulcer, heart problems, skin disease, or other illnesses. The body does not distinguish between physical, chemical, or emotional stress. So, if we want to feel better, we must get rid of stress.

Good Health Habits

Five health habits which reduce stress and disease are:

1. Elimination of smoking
2. Elimination of alcoholic beverages or very moderate use
3. Normalization of body weight to within ten percent of ideal weight
4. Reduction of fat, salt and sugar consumption, and
5. Adequate physical exercise.

These health habits would reduce our four

hundred billion dollar annual health expense significantly.

Good nutrition should include a good water supply. Most municipal water is contaminated with pollutants and carcinogens. The American Medical Association is aware of the impact of drinking water on human health. To enhance public awareness, it has published a book titled *Drinking Water and Human Health*—which should be read by all concerned individuals.

Proper exercise is very essential to reduce stress and improve health. There are several types of exercise that are beneficial to a good stress-reduction program. These include walking, stationary bicycling, trampolining, and swimming. Exercise should be "aerobic," which means it needs to move oxygen through the cardiovascular system.

A good criterion to insure the aerobic state is to monitor the pulse rate. During exercise, it should be elevated to approximately 180 beats per minute minus the age of the exerciser in years. For a fifty-year-old person, the rate should be 130. Aerobic exercising should eventually be built up to fifteen continuous minutes and at least four days a week.

Aerobic exercising balances cellular chemistry by increasing the number of mitochondria within our cells. These vital structures burn food more efficiently to produce greater energy.

Before a person starts an exercising program, he

or she should consult with a doctor.

Balancing Mental Chemistry

First and foremost, we must have a positive attitude, since without it, we can accomplish nothing in life. We must have a belief in ourselves. We must accept the idea that we are capable of learning new ways, new lifestyles, and new attitudes. Since birth we learned to tie our shoes, feed ourselves, master a language, and many other things. Some of the things we learned are not conducive to good health. We learned through repetition. And we can learn new attitudes through repetition. But we cannot learn optimally unless we master the art of relaxation.

How To Relax

We can relax only when we focus our attention on a thought that isn't stressful. One way is to sit comfortably on a chair with spine straight, feet on the floor and hands resting on the knees. Now close the eyes and breathe easily. Relax the muscles one by one, from the feet all the way up to the scalp. In practicing relaxation, learn to focus full attention on a single word or phrase or on the act of breathing. Concentration is important in bringing on the relaxation response. Mentally repeat "peace" while breathing in and "peace" while breathing out.

Practice this relaxation exercise for at least ten minutes twice a day.

Among many other benefits, relaxation may normalize blood pressure and pulse rate, lower insulin requirement, and reduce the production of catecholamine secretion. It puts us in a state of homeostasis.

Harmonize Body Feelings

Our thinking determines how our bodies feel. Whether we feel good or bad, is a result of the thinking that has taken place over the years. We can alter that state by several techniques. One of the best techniques is "Energy Visualization" which is taught by Biogenics, founded by C. Norman Shealy, M.D., Ph.D., an internationally recognized physician specializing in stress management.

After practicing the relaxation technique for a few minutes, do the "Energy Visualization" exercise by imagining that the electrical energy is circulating all over the body. Visualize electrical energy going up the spine from the back and then coming down from the front. Realize that everything that happens in the body is electrical. This energy creates magnetism, which promotes optimal relaxation and healing.

Balancing Emotions

We can experience only two emotions: fear and love. All other emotions spring forth from these two. Fear is the most powerful stressor. It causes spasm and blocks the nervous system. Love radiates joy and happiness and promotes healing. Emotions are states of mind; they are determined by our mental interpretation of what happens in our inner or outer worlds. Epictetus (1st century A.D.) stated, "I am upset, not by events, but rather by the way I view them."

We can learn to control thinking and, therefore, our way of viewing events. When we undertake this mental process, we will have started a work of self-integration and discovery. St. Paul made reference to this work when he wrote, "...but be ye transformed by the renewing of your mind." (Roman 12:2)

This alchemical transmutation is not accomplished by violence or condemnation but by a persistent and patient work of substitution. The Nazarene expressed this concept by, "But I say unto you, that ye resist not evil." (Matthew 5:39). We must replace fear and all the negative emotions derived from it with love and the positive emotions which constitute its many beautiful facets.

The Kingdom Within

After we balance our bodies and emotions, we are

ready for spiritual attunement, which is the real purpose of life. Ralph Waldo Emerson stated, "What lies behind us and what lies before us are tiny matters compared to what lies within us. Christ taught, "...behold, the kingdom of God is within you." (Luke 17:21). How do we find this spiritual highway to the Infinite? All philosophers, mystics, sages, and saints of all religions tell us that we can commune with our higher self and God by means of meditation.

Meditation

Meditation is the science of spiritual realization. Most people would want to meditate if they understood its value and experienced its many beneficial effects. The French mystic Constant Chevillon called meditation "the ladder of Jacob"— which directs man to ascend again to God.

Many centuries before the birth of Christ, Persians, Greeks, Egyptians and Jews taught meditation. The Psalmist proclaims, "Be still, and know that I am God."(Psalm 46:10) Hermes of ancient Egypt preached, "O people of the earth, men born and made of the elements, but with the spirit of the Divine within you, rise from your sleep of ignorance! Be sober and thoughtful. Realize that your home is not in the earth but in the Light. Repent, and change your minds. Prepare yourselves to climb through the Seven Rings and blend your Souls with the Eternal Light."

Meditation is a mental and spiritual practice where we still the mind and learn to concentrate on God. Plato (428-347 B.C.) defined it as "the ardent turning of the soul towards the Divine." It is the mystical marriage of the soul that seeks and needs real happiness that it can only find by merging with the Creator.

No matter what our religion is, we can experience the reality of the spiritual world and learn to walk and talk with God. We don't need to climb the summit of the Himalayas or withdraw to the Judean desert for, "Behold, the kingdom of God is within you." It is our duty to be in the world and serve our fellow man according to our call and talent, but we need to divorce ourselves from that state of delusion that has lured us to ignorance and spiritual oblivion. Meditation is the road that brings us—prodigal sons and daughters, spiritual beings trapped in houses made of clay—back to the royal palace of our Father to enjoy the ever-new bliss and joy. The heavenly banquet is always ready whenever we wish to partake.

When we partake of this divine manna, we can taste a peace that cannot be conveyed in words. It can only be experienced. We understand then the words of the Nazarene—who said, "Seek ye first the kingdom of God, and all the other things will be added to you." We discover our true nature and establish a new relationship with God—who is true love and the Essence of our own being. We are a part of Him since we are Divine. And we are unable to find lasting happiness in anything material. Francis Thompson expressed this idea when he wrote, "Naught shelters thee, who wilt not shelter me." Until we attain contentment in God, we will not win contentment from anything else in this life.

This is the holistic approach to the stress of life. We can all use it. It is derived from both science and religion. And as Albert Einstein once declared, "Science without religion is lame, and religion without science is blind."

MAUREEN G. MULVANEY, P.M.A.
M.G.M. & Associates
8118 North 38th Avenue
Phoenix, AZ 85051
(602) 841-9398

Maureen G. Mulvaney

After struggling through a difficult delivery, numerous complications and a brush with death, she burst into this world with a grin on her face. Her parents, Marie and Paul, were overjoyed that this little being so positively wanted to be born. She should bear a name that denoted her style at birth so they named her Maureen G. Mulvaney...M.G.M...A BIG PRODUCTION!

M.G.M. then heard the click of the clapper-board and call for ACTION! With her positive mental attitude, enthusiasm for life and endless energy she sprang into action. MGM acquired a B.A. in Special Education and a Master's in Counseling Psychology from Boston University. MGM tried various roles in life to give her a rounded and rich source of experiences for her speaking and writing: College Instructor, Elementary and High School Teacher, Traveling Public Relations Executive, Federal Government Psychologist, Radio Account Executive & Announcer, Author, and Professional Speaker and Consultant.

MGM's audiences have acknowledged her outstanding achievements in speaking and counseling with numerous awards to include Who's Who in Human Services and National Woman of the Year. MGM has received rave reviews for the hundreds of seminars and workshops she has conducted throughout the United States and Europe, speaking on various subjects such as Stress Management and Saneness Training for businesses, educational institutions, sales staffs, government agencies and community groups.

MGM's audiences applaud her positive practical speeches, leading people to happier and more productive lives.

MGM critics say, "She's one in a million, Catch her act."

15

Slam the Door on Dis-Stress
by Maureen G. Mulvaney

"Belief creates the actual Fact"
—William James

In the midst of a busy southern college quadrangle, I lay motionless. Before slipping into unconsciousness, I glimpsed the petal of a magnolia blossom suddenly drop to the ground, as I had, without warning.

I awoke to the shrill sound of an ambulance and a blinding red light. Before I could register my protest, they strapped me in the stretcher and whisked me off to the hospital.

"Get an IV in her arm stat, this kid is completely dehydrated! Is she one of the students from campus?"

"No, I understand she is a traveling secretary for one of the national sororities. She travels around to different colleges as a public relations person, trouble shooter and leadership trainer. Her friend said for about two weeks she has been feeling tired, throwing up, has pain in her stomach and is losing weight."

"Nurse, where am I?"

"At the hospital, you'll be OK."

The pain in my stomach was intense. I knew I had not been feeling well for some time but surely it would all go away soon. My thoughts began to race.... There just is no time to be sick. I have lectures to prepare, news releases to work on, students who expect a leader to teach them how to lead and an afternoon plane to catch to Michigan. "OK, Maureen G. Mulvaney, your mother named you M.G.M. because she wanted you to possess Irish charm, the gift of blarney—eloquent speech—and performing skills. Put on an act right now and convince this genteel southern doctor to release you at once."

After arming me with a prescription for pain and antibiotics, the doctor gave me a stern lecture.

My Irish charm was successfully persuasive. He released me. The IV juices that had been sent through my veins produced the right amount of energy which I needed to walk out the door, pack my bags, and dash to the airport headed for Michigan.

I was famished by the time I arrived at the airport but remembered that lately everything I ate came back up so I wisely chose to have a cup of tea instead of my usual Polish sausage.

Although I had traveled for almost two years, I had not learned the art of traveling light. As I made my trek down the corridor to the plane my energy began to wane. My hands were shaking, I could hardly drag myself and belongings any further. The stewardess took one look at my pale face and emaciated appearance and asked if I were feeling well. I replied indignantly, "I feel fine" as I remembered a man I had seen taken from a plane because he was ill. I had deadlines to meet and nothing was going to stop me.

Plane rides were usually a welcome respite, but not this one. My head began to pound, my stomach was doing loop the loops worse than the plane. I was beginning to feel faint. The stewardess, thinking I was afraid of flying, related numerous stories of how safe the airways were. My normal reaction would have been to laugh with gusto but all I could do was muster a weak grin.

Then came the pain. At first it was a dull pain in my gut which rapidly turned into an all consuming ripping pain. I had known this pain for some time, but it seemed to be getting worse. My panicky thoughts began…"What will the people meeting you think? You're the leader, You're supposed to be bubbling, happy and full of energy. Isn't that why you're the only one ever selected to travel for two years, instead of the usual one year contract? Perfect traveling secretaries never get sick."

Aha, the pills the darling doctor gave me. Instant relief would be mine if I could find them quickly. I knew that I would feel no pain or anything else if I could just take a pill.

"Final Destination—
All Passengers Must Disembark"

A big banner, "WELCOME MAUREEN," plenty of smiles and enthusiasm greeted me as I disembarked. Even though they had seen my picture in the national magazine they did not recognize this gaunt person before them. I waved to them and thank heaven they rushed to relieve me of my luggage. My movement was slow and my perky personality was subdued but they had never known me before so perhaps they just thought I was tired.

The pill was kicking-in, so there was no pain.

My highest priority was food. My hunger

overcame my sensible thoughts and I devoured a Big Mac, fries and milk shake. The entire meal took less than 10 minutes to inhale. I had more important things to do besides eat.

No sooner had we arrived at the dorm when that familiar queasy feeling hit. I rushed into the dorm and headed for the bathroom. I hugged the commode for almost 20 minutes, longer than it had taken me to eat the food. When I finished depositing my lunch, breakfast and anything else I had eaten into the toilet I was horrified to find that I had no energy. I had to crawl out of the stall over to the sink to pull myself up.

Something was definitely wrong with me but I had work to do, people to please and deadlines to meet. I just couldn't be sick now.

Four days later I woke to find myself hospitalized again. I heard the familiar lines..."Dehydrated, IV's stat." National headquarters gave directives that I was to be placed on the next plane home so that I could recoup. The hospital released me and sent me on my way with more medication and new energy via the IVs.

By now I only weighed 94 pounds. I stopped by a 5 and Dime Store on the way to the airport and bought suspenders to hold up my pants. I figured with a heavy sweater thrown over the top no one would know how thin I had become.

My dear mother met the plane. She took one

look and was aghast. I caught sight of myself in a full length mirror and didn't recognize myself. My normal body shape which had always been a slightly athletic 128 pounds was gone and replaced with a mere skeleton. My arms and legs had dwindled and I looked anarexic. My full face was now drawn, tired and pale. My energy level which had always been high was now below zero. I could hardly walk and what was worse I could hardly talk.

Mother immediately rushed me to the hospital. That is where I stayed through Thanksgiving, Christmas, and the New Year. The days turned into weeks, weeks into months, and the months into years while I went in and out of the hospital. The doctors discovered hyper-thyroidism, jaundice, back to back infections, tumors and a host of other problems and complications that seemed endless.

One day while in the hospital recovering from major surgery the thought went through my head...Participate in illness and you stay ill, participate in wellness and you get well. I had taken literally thousands of pills, had hundreds of tests and IVs and gone through numerous major and minor surgeries. That was enough.

Without telling anyone, I put on my make-up, dressed myself, packed my belongings, waved good-bye to the nurses and walked out, slamming the door to my hospital room.

I Slammed the Door to Illness and Dis-Stress and Said Hello to Health and Eu-stress

All through my illness I continued to hear: "Stress did this to you. It was that stressful job." At first I was convinced that stress couldn't make me sick, that was just something that happened to me. I had no control over illness. Then the scientific side of me came out and I began to wonder...was it stress? Can we control illness? What if we can? I began to research these questions. Here is the knowledge I gained after robbing myself of precious years of my life by giving myself illness and dis-stress.

Dis-Stress vs. Eu-Stress

"People are not disturbed by things, but by the views which they take of them" —**Epictetus**

What is stress? I thought it must be my job, my schedule, expectations of others, college students or the airlines. Those are just what we call stressors, the multitude of daily occurrences that call upon us to adapt. There is plenty of evidence to support the fact that as long as we continue to live on planet earth we will be surrounded by stressors. So stress is not your job, your boss, your spouse or the "things" in your life, but actually the perception, belief or view you have of the stressors in your life. Epictetus made it quite clear when he said, "People are not disturbed by things, but by the views which they take of them." You may constantly be surrounded by stressors but your view of those stressors causes the stress.

My college students often say things like, "Stress is bad for you." My reply is, "Thank heaven for stress. It is the dynamic force that gets me into action every day. If there was no stress or belief that it is important for me to wake up and have a purpose for each day then there is a possibility that I would never get out of bed."

I also point out that if they didn't have some stress they would not come to class or study for tests. If they have too much stress then they come into class to take the test and go blank. There has to be a balance unique to each individual.

Hans Selye pointed out, there are two kinds of stress: **EU**-stress, the good kind, that gets you busy coping; and **DYS** or **DIS**-stress, the bad kind, when you can't cope. Then you burn up energy in frustration, anger, hate and other negative emotions and often become immobilized.

EU-stress and Dis-stress

As you read, differentiate between EU-stress and DIS-stress.

Driver A gets in her car each morning and accepts the fact that traffic is a normal occurrence in her life in the city. She decides before leaving her driveway whether she will listen to a meditation tape, easy listening or a superb motivational tape by Maureen G. Mulvaney. She knows that not everyone is courteous or skilled at driving so she will drive with a sense of awareness about her surroundings. She takes driving time as her private instruction time and enjoys herself.

Driver B gets in his car and starts telling himself, "It's going to be one of those days." By the time he gets to the corner just a block away he is already angry. He pulls into the flow of traffic honking his horn and waving his hands giving several other drivers the international "sign of poor taste." He rants and raves every time he is stopped by those red lights. He drives on the bumper of the car in front of him and switches lanes when they don't go fast enough. By the time he gets to work he already is drained and barks at his secretary who immediately whispers to her friend, "It's the traffic that gets him."

EU-stress or Dis-stress?

Would you tell which was which? Of course you can, Driver B is in lots of DIS-stress. It couldn't be the traffic that causes his distress because driver A would have reacted the very same way. Stress is the view we take of things. Driver A chose to use a possibly stressful situation as a learning situation. She turned her DIS-stress into EU-stress by changing her thoughts, which in turn created positive feelings and behaviors. Driver B chose to have upsetting thoughts which produced negative emotions and behaviors that were nonproductive.

Thoughts, beliefs, or our views produce our feelings and behaviors.

My daily goal, as I hope yours will be, is to turn all my DIS-stress into EU-stress by changing my thoughts, which will create new feelings and positive behaviors. To change my thoughts it would be wise to be aware of which thoughts are causing me DIS-stress.

MUSTology

A should is a should,
A must is a must;
Beware of them both,
Before they turn you to dust.   **—M.G.M.**

When I couldn't find a word that exactly described distressing, diseased thoughts I made it up—MUSTology—the art of letting MUSTS, SHOULDS, AND COULD HAVE's control our lives. Most of the MUSTizing that we do was learned through spaced repetition.

We did not intentionally set out to learn these musts but through repeated experiences we internalized them. They became over-learned and therefore automatic. An example of spaced repetition would be, "Plop plop fizz fizz"...(what comes to mind?) "Oh, what a relief it is." You did not intentionally learn this but through repeated experience it went in. Another example would be cursive writing. When learning to write you consciously thought about each letter...to make the capital D start at the top, go down and make a loop-de-loop, swing around and make Santa Claus Belly, swing up and connect it to the top and loop-de-loop off. When writing Capital D now you do so automatically. Constant repetition produced a habit. Basically, that is what we do with our thoughts, feelings and behaviors.

While growing up, constant and repeated exposure to the following beliefs produced learned MUSTS: "If you can't do it right then don't do it at all"—you learned I MUST do things perfectly: "That's just the way I am"—People MUST stay the same all their life; "Don't air the family's dirty laundry"—YOU MUST keep up appearances and impress and please others.

MUSTizing was, and is, learned, so with awareness and practice it can be replaced with new learning. Here is the process I used to change my mustizing or stinkin' thinkin':

1. Be aware of your mustizing thoughts.
2. Accept the fact that you can change.
3. Switch from automatic to manual; begin to consciously examine your thoughts, feelings,

and behaviors.

4. Gain new information.

5. Practice, practice, practice new thoughts, feelings and behaviors at least 21 times so they become habit.

Albert Ellis, famed psychologist and founder of Rational Emotive Therapy, isolated MUSTisms common to us all. Following are the MUSTisms that I endorsed daily and new information I used to change my stinkin' thinkin'.

I MUST NEVER HAVE PHYSICAL OR EMOTIONAL PAIN. I SHOULD PANIC IF I DO.

"I am ill because my mind is in a rut, and refuses to leave."

—Karen Giardino

I honestly believed that my body was like my car. No matter how I abused it, what kind of fuel I put in or how I maintained it, it should always function at peak performance. If it began to break down and give me pain I panicked by wanting an instant solution. Usually, I masked my physical pain with prescribed medications, blaming others and denying it's existence.

Then I discovered that pain is an indicator, our own built in warning system. Doctors Paul and Margaret Brand studied people who had contracted leprosy. The loss of digits and gashes and tears in the skin were once thought to be part of the disease. While studying the disease they discovered the active agent *bacillus leprae* actually kills the nerve endings. The delicate sense of touch no longer exists for these people—no pain sensations. You and I would stop turning a key when we met with resistant pressure whereas the person with leprocy would continue to turn the key and damage the flesh. With further study the doctors unveiled that while the lepers slept they often were being assaulted by rodents that gnawed on the flesh and caused the loss of digits. With no pain sensations they were unaware of the rodents. Although we often wish to live without pain, I think this graphically reminds us that *pain is a gift to people that don't have it.*

New Information for Change

1. **Realize** that pain is both a warning system and protective mechanism.
2. **Teach** yourself to discover the triggers and reason for your pain. I asked myself HOW DID I GIVE MYSELF THIS PAIN? I did a self-assessment and discovered my pain came from most of my mustisms. By mustizing on a daily basis—trying to be perfect, trying to be loved by everyone, and trying to be purposeful every minute of the day—I wore myself down. My

negative stinkin' thinkin' caused negative chemical reactions in my body that actually weakened my immune system and made me very susceptible to any and all diseases.

Experts estimate that approximately 90 percent of all disease is stress related. WHY WAS IT USEFUL TO ME TO BE SICK? I lacked the assertive skills to communicate to my employers that I had too much work. Instead I allowed my body to do it for me. Who could blame me because I happened to get sick? One must never quit, but I could resign graciously and with honor by being ill. Of course, I did not become ill consciously. But, if I do not pay attention to warning signs it could happen again. HOW CAN I TAKE ILLNESS AWAY? I became aware of my thoughts, accepted that I could get well, switched from automatic to manual, gathered new information and practiced healthy thoughts and habits.

3. **Take responsibility** for your health. Wellness is the lifestyle you design. Choose healthy eating habits, be aware that everything you do, think, feel, and believe has an impact on your state of health. Choose healthy thoughts, laugh more, channel your energies to achieve a balance between the areas of your life. Learn to relax and choose to act and be well.

*I MUST HAVE LOVE AND APPROVAL FROM ALL
PEOPLE IN MY LIFE.*

> *"Those who seek to please everyone, please no one."*
>
> **—Marie Landry Mulvaney**

I came about this one quite naturally. When I was a child I learned quickly that if I talked about myself someone would instantly say, "You shouldn't toot your own horn or people will think you egotistical, conceited and self-centered." If I couldn't say how good I was I guess I should wait till others told me their opinion. The opinions of others became important. I started to internalize these opinions as my own self-concept. If they said something nice I felt all puffed up like a little turkey and if they said something unkind, I got my feelings hurt. Does any of this sound familiar?

New Information for Change

1. **Be aware** how often you falsely attribute your feelings to other people or external events. Keep a log.

    Monday: 9:00 a.m. Blamed my anger on Mom's nagging
    11:20 a.m. Accused Mike of hurting my feelings.

    Each day at the same time go over the entries in your log. Correct the thoughts by taking responsibility for your own thoughts, feelings and behaviors.

"Mom's nagging can't make me angry. I make myself angry when I think Mom does not approve of my behavior. I would like Mom's approval but I know that we will not always hold the same opinion about everything. We come from different generations and value systems. I will accept her for what she is and not upset myself again!"

"Mike can't hurt my feelings. I let my feelings get hurt when Mike didn't stop by to see me last night. I expected him to read my mind and know that I wanted to see him. I didn't actually invite him over. Next time I'll call him and let him know how I feel."

2. **You are unique.** No one else has your thoughts or feelings. Use verbal communications instead of mental telepathy with significant people in your life.

3. **Differentiate between fact and opinion.** Fact can be proved: Geraldine Ferraro ran for Vice President of the USA in 1984. Belief, perception or opinion cannot: good mothers don't work; red hair is prettier than blonde.

4. **Filter all feedback.** Determine if a comment is fact or opinion. Feedback that is accurate, accept. Say "Thank you." Give yourself an invisible pat on the back. Feedback that is not accurate, decline. Say "Thank you." Dump it out. Filter, filter, filter by switching from automatic

to manual. Example: If someone says, "Gee, what a lousy speech," determine if that is opinion. Then ask, in a non-threatening manner, "Could you be more specific?" ask them to tell you exactly what they did not like. If they communicate accurate feedback, perhaps you spoke too rapidly, then you say, "Thank you for the feedback." Put SPEAK SLOWLY on your list of things you want to change for the better. You do not register hurt feelings because it is factual information that will help you to improve. If the feedback is not accurate for you then you say, "Thank you for the feedback" and don't accept it. Or say, 'Just to keep things in proper perspective, could you tell me two things you did like about my speech?" A little humor always helps.

5. **Tolerance of different opinions leads to growth.** Me' dear mother used to tell this story about my grandfather. When Granddad was a middle aged man his hair started to turn grey. He was courting two women at the time. One was younger than he and the other was advanced in years. Every time he took the younger one out, she was ashamed of being seen with someone older so she pulled out his grey hair. Every time he took the older woman out, she was ashamed of being seen with someone younger and she pulled out his black hair. By the time my

grandmother came along and rescued him he was completely bald.

The moral of the story: *Those that seek to please everyone please no one.*

I MUST BE PERFECT AT EVERYTHING I DO.

"A man must have his faults."

—Gaius Petronius

The dictionary defines perfection as flawless. Isn't it silly that for years I sought perfection in all areas of my life without being aware that it DOES NOT EXIST. Perhaps, in heaven God made angels without flaws. But If I were to look around on earth at humans I would clearly find that humans are not perfect. They make mistakes. Often on a daily basis. You lock your keys in the car, forget to enter a check in your register. You have acne, one nostril is smaller than the other and a multitude of other imperfections

New Information for Change

1. **Accept the fact** that all human beings, by their very nature, are imperfect. Collect data to prove this to yourself.

2. **It is human** to have faults and imperfections but it is inhumane to condemn yourself and others for having them.

3. **Accept the things** you cannot change and

change the things you cannot accept. For years I tried to bleach my freckles off. It did not work. I now accept them as beauty marks. I could not change the freckles but I could change my thoughts about those freckles.

4. **To insist** that you and others in your life be perfect is a fantasy. It will lead to disappointment, resentment and frustration. Instead of striving for perfection, which seldom exists, strive to do things well and competently.

5. **Aim to get pleasure** from all the activities you do. Enjoy each activity regardless of the end result. Each morning as you flip on the bedroom light flip on the thought that today you will gain pleasure from all your activities.

Open New Doors

"Our life is what our thoughts make it."

—**Marcus Aurelius**

Slamming the door on DIS-stress is symbolic of letting go of the old negative destructive patterns of your life. Opening the door to new patterns of living is accepting the responsibility for your own life. Choose to take back control of all your thoughts, feelings and behaviors. Opening the door to wellness is accepting your commitment to participate and defend the integrity of your own body.

Opening the door to EU-stress is accepting that

although there are many things we cannot control in our lives, we can control how we react to them. Choose to open new doors by being aware of mustizing thoughts, accepting change, switching from automatic to manual, gaining new information and practicing until it becomes a habit.

> *Slam the door on negative, diseased, and destructive thoughts.*
> *Open the door to new feelings of love, understanding and happiness.*

> *Slam the door on anger, hate and resentment,*
> *Open the door to new behaviors of risking, trusting and taking responsibility.*

> *Slam the door on yelling, non-assertiveness and aggression,*
> *Open the door to new habits of compromise, negotiation and assertiveness.*

> *Slam the door on Dis-stress,*
> *Open the door to Life.*

—Maureen G. Mulvaney

CLINT MAUN
Maun-Lemke
8031 West Center Road
Suite 215
Omaha, NE 68124
Bus. (402) 391-5540 • Res. (712) 624-8082

Clint Maun

Clint Maun is the creator of the nationally acclaimed process, "Smooth Operations," a practical approach to leadership today. A professional speaker and consultant, Clint captivates his audiences and truly inspires them to positive action with his boundless enthusiasm, sense of humor, and down-to-earth ideas. Thousands of individuals and businesses across the country are now "Celebrating Smooth" as a result of implementing Clint's ideas. He obtained his ideas from his extensive research and 15 years experience in human resource development, line management, and business consulting. Clint provides practical assistance with action-oriented discussion of challenges, techniques, and solutions which individuals can immediately utilize in setting the foundation for "Achieving Smooth Operations."

Clint Maun has completed undergraduate and graduate work in clinical/industrial psychology. He is also a licensed health care administrator and member of the National Speakers Association. His past positions have included Chief Operations Officer for Freshman Systems, Inc., Director of Corporate Training for First Data Resources, Inc., Director of Staff Development for Glenwood State Hospital-School, and Past President of the Nebraska Chapter of the American Society of Training and Development.

16

Are You A Victim of "P.D.S."?
by Clint Maun

*"We are as happy as we give ourself
permission to be."*
—Abraham Lincoln

E very role we find ourselves in should be considered a professional involvement. Some people treat involvement in a professional manner, many do not. Your role could be a professional parent, student, employee, manager, or friend. People get involved in professional relationships but don't realize the end result. I have found that a great number of individuals end up with what I call "P.D.S." or "Professional Death Syndrome."

"P.D.S." is a cancer-like stress that spirals throughout their involvement in a specific role. The individual finds himself in several situations while in one role, where there is extreme discomfort. In most situations, we find ourselves stuck "between a rock and a hard spot." Many times, we find out about stress conditions when it is too late. Then we seek out methods for improvement. This sometimes produces even greater stress in this *professional* role.

People experience "P.D.S." for the following reasons:

1. They are recovering pleaseaholics.
2. They sit on the fence in conflict situations.
3. They try to be a mediating psychotherapist with other human beings.

Symptoms of the Pleaseaholic

A great number of human beings like to please other individuals. These people spend their day trying not to upset the apple cart. They go out of their way to continually help others. As a result, they fail to obtain the most important relationship in their life with another human being, the relationship of mutual respect. You must have mutual respect in your relationships, as well as being liked. If you are liked by everyone but not respected, you will be used and abused. It is at this time that the pleaseaholic tendencies enter. If no one likes you, you have a personality flaw. You must take positive steps to immediately correct it. However, there will be those on this planet that will not like you in every situation. People who have a spiraling increase of "P.D.S." fail to recognize the significant difference between being respected and being liked.

King on the Mountain

A great many individuals have had programming throughout their lives which influence their ending up with "Professional Death Syndrome." Example: a number of men have a real problem. They believe they are "God's gift to the universe." They are programmed to think they are all things to all people. They spend all day long solving problems, zapping down the answers in Zeus-like fashion. They sit in their white flowing robes, on top of the mountain. This syndrome started a long time ago in caveman days when we sent the male out to beat saber-toothed tigers on the head and to drag in the raw meat for the rest of the cave people. Then we programmed men throughout generations to express a stereotyped, macho role. Therefore, many men spend all day long solving problems at work, then go home and try to solve all the problems at home. This causes them excess worrying or even smoking and/or drinking. They believe that they alone should have all the answers. A number of men never know how to stop and smell the roses, or to let others share responsibility.

As a man, I have experienced this kind of lifelong programming. It has caused problems in my professional roles. I have played "Father-Knows-Best" all day long. I used to work 80 hour work weeks, strapping two pagers around my neck in case one went out. "How could they reach me if I wasn't accessible?" Soon, I had to have a phone in my car so I could keep in constant contact with the organizations where I was responsible. How could I ever take vacations? "They might not be able to contact me." I took phone calls late into the night. After I went to meetings, I called back to see how things were going. I went home, hollered at the kids, kicked the dog (we had a bruised dog in those days.) Then I drank too much and ate too much and spent all my time worrying about problems. I know how P.D.S. works, particularly in my management, parenting, and spouse role. I have to fight it every day of my life.

The Yes Syndrome

A great number of women, on the other hand, have a different problem. They have been taught to play mother since birth. Just as men have been taught to play "Father-Knows-Best," women have been pro-grammed to own everybody else's problems. They listen and act on remarks like, "Honey, where is my red shirt?" "Mom, where are my action figures?" (Each sold separately). Some women spend all day long solving everyone's problems at work. Then they go home and solve everybody's problems around home, next door, or at school. They never take time for themselves. The definition of a smooth day for these women is to make it to late night. Then they put on a pair of dirty pink bunny slippers, a holey nightgown, and watch the weather on TV. What a definition of a smooth day! I suggest that these women need to be able to realize that their "P.D.S." levels would greatly reduce if they took time to smell the roses. If only they could quit taking on everyone's problems in a motherly fashion.

Avoid Sitting on the Fence

Have you known people who sit on the fence in situations where they know they should take immediate action? They don't want to cause a conflict. Example: an individual is hit with a request for an immediate "snap" decision. The answer is either yes or no. These questioners have learned to catch you when they are likely to get the most favorable response. They say things like, "It's Monday morning, he has so much on his mind he won't be listening;" or "It's Friday afternoon, she is trying to get out of here." One of my favorites, "He is in a good mood today, let's go talk to him." In these situations the boss is always put between a rock and a hard spot. You are faced with making a decision that will ultimately produce inconsistency. When you are faced with a yes or no decision and you have no knowledge, no time, no examples, no information, or any reason to reply, try this for a quick answer: You should respond with some form of the word no. If you turn it around later and say yes, people will like you and respect you. If you say yes to start with, but have to turn it into no later, people will hold your vacillation against you for a long period of time. When snap decisions cause a great amount of fence sitting behavior, they increase the probability of "P.D.S." in a specific role.

You can say no in a number of different ways that will allow people to respect your decision and still give you a method of changing your mind later. Try responding with:

1. Not right now;
2. Let me look into it;
3. Get back to me with some more information;
4. I'll let you know by tomorrow afternoon;
5. I'm not going to make a decision on that until I check into it.

These responses allow you to get off the fence,

but keep movement going in that particular situation. Also, these answers allow you to make better decisions in the long run and not get caught with a no-win decision.

The Psychotherapist Trap

In the third situation, some people spend their day involved in head games with other individuals. They believe they must understand everything that is occurring with those around them. They want to see the potential moods, thoughts, ideas, and motivation of everyone else. Alas, this is almost impossible. It is nip and tuck to be able to understand your own behavior, let alone everyone else's actions. If you are honest, specific, and consistent with others, you have a better chance of success in dealing with them, thereby keeping the "P.D.S." levels at a minimum. If you get involved in head games, you will get "beat up." For instance:

Your child hasn't cleaned his room. You say to him, "Tommy, why didn't you clean your room?" Of course, you already know the reason Tommy didn't clean his room. He never cleans his room. He says, "The room is clean enough. It doesn't make any difference. It is my room. It is behind closed doors." He has many excuses that are normal for children.

You get back the exact response you asked for, an excuse. It could be legitimate. However, that won't make a difference. It will still be an excuse. The conscious mind is set up to justify every action that you take and keep you doing the same things that you have always done. When you ask the question, "Why didn't you clean your room?" You are now thinking of another series of questions and answers. You go back and forth, never getting to the bottom line of the problem. The room is not cleaned. What can be done to get the room cleaned? What are the contingencies if the room is not cleaned? It is extremely important to state your position in an honest, specific, and consistent way. Avoid the why, what if, how come, and so forth. These only lead to head games. In the professional role you are involved in, you will not be able to come out a winner. In fact, it will usually increase your stress levels and cause a great amount of discomfort in your relationships.

Research on P.D.S.

Research on what I've somewhat humorously defined as "P.D.S." has been completed by the American Medical Association in the past 10 years. They found that if you never get comfortable in your roles in life, the stress will cause a stroke which has the potential to kill you. Stress starts with taking all the work problems home. It brings on ulcers, backaches, and migraines. Then it develops into cancer of the colon. From there, it creeps back up into blood pressure problems and pulsating temples. It leads to marital problems, family problems, kid problems, and social withdrawal. From there, stress spirals on into possible mental health problems where the people in "designer white jackets" come and take you away. Finally, stress goes into the chronic stages of cerebral hemorrhage, heart attack, and stroke. I have watched many human beings work their way up to that stress level of life, and eventually, stroke out. The reason these maladies occur is because the people never became comfortable in their role, whatever their role might be.

If you allow the entire world to place its problems on you, you will never have time to work on the precious things that are the most important to you.

Handling the B.M.G.

Successful people avoid "P.D.S." by understanding that they must first take care of themselves before they can take care of anyone else. Successful people understand that it is not caring to take on everyone's problems. They learn how to avoid being a pleaseaholic, how to avoid sitting on the fence, and how to avoid head games. Successful people avoid "P.D.S." by understanding that the only learning growth which takes place in life is the opportunity for people to solve their own problems. When you take away people's ability to solve their own problems, you turn them into Ph.D.'s in problem finding. They then have second grade educations in problem solving. Problem finders spend all day long looking for problems to give to you, because that is what they believe they are supposed to do. They never find anything right, never have anything good to say, and constantly critique every situation. I find problem finders continue this attitude throughout life because they were never challenged to find solutions to the problems they encounter. I define problem finders as "B.M.G.s" (bitchers, moaners and groaners). The "B.M.G.s" continue to have a Ph.D. in problem finding because that is how they receive their rewards. They can literally destroy your day within the first 10 minutes by convincing you there is no hope. The sky has fallen; Chicken Little is right! The prophecy of doom is occurring right now. Problem finders have a dramatic effect on your own brain programming and increase your level of "P.D.S."

"Never Take Anyone Else's Problems Without Their Recommendations for Solutions."

This one sentence has done more for my life than anything else that I have ever read or heard. It helped me get off the fence, quit playing head games, and avoid being a pleaseaholic. I have practiced this philosophy for nearly twelve years now and have been able to help so many people, including myself, because of this principle.

It does not matter if it is your boss, employees, spouse, kids, friends, volunteers, or whomever. You can't win a poker game when you lay your cards on the table and put all your chips out. The other players keep their cards up against their chests with no chips on the table. If you take others' problems without allowing them to think of solutions, rest assured they will bring you more problems very soon. The world needs people with Ph.D.'s in problem-solving, not second grade educations. If you surround yourself with people who have the problem-solving philosophy of life, you will provide a tremendous amount of success for yourself. Their input will allow you to take the appropriate time necessary to produce successful activities. Your own "P.D.S." levels will decrease dramatically. As a result, true learning for all individuals will take place.

What happens if you take small children who have the potential of being super stars, who are brilliant and who have a lot of capability, then put these children in an environment where they are never allowed to fail? If they are always picked up after, have shoes tied for them, are allowed to quit whenever they want to, their noses wiped for them—then look out. Those children will be unable to cope with life's problems. But children with learning disabilities, speech defects, physical problems, or children that have to start slowly and learn to solve their own problems, will eventually catch up to the problem-finders easily and surpass them. In fact, most successful business people have failed once or twice in their lives. They fail on the way to succeeding.

Effective Vs. Efficient

Successful people spend the time necessary on activities that are important for them. It's impossible to care for anyone else if you don't care for yourself first. You must be able to have a priority-plan of activities which will allow you to be effective during each day. Your list does not have to include everyone else's priorities, problems, or concerns. Look at your own activities for a day, week, or month. If you find that everything on the list is related to other individuals' problems, concerns, or activities, you can not find success in your own life. In fact, you will find yourself with a high level of "P.D.S."

It is extremely important to understand the difference between effective and efficient. Effective means getting the most important thing done. That's called working smarter, not harder. Efficient means getting more things done faster, quicker, longer, harder, better, more profitably, etc. You must be effective before you are efficient. It does not make any difference how many irons you have in the fire. What counts is how many irons you can handle. Are you handling the most important irons in your fire? Anyone can have a bad day, week or month and not get the most important things done. However, I challenge you to take a look at an entire lifetime where the most important things were not accomplished. Not getting anywhere will result in a tremendous amount of "P.D.S."

Stop and look at your day. See if your most important things are getting done. Ask yourself these questions at the end of the month, "Am I getting the number 1's, 2's, and 3's accomplished throughout the month? Are they slipping by?" Every day of your life list what is the most important thing for you to get accomplished. Then list what you have to do to get those goals accomplished. You must also understand how other people's problems, concerns, activities, or situations will impact upon your top priority. Do not let them paralyze you.

Successful people find appropriate balance in their life. They realize they must accomplish the important things on their priority list if they are going to ever be able to help anyone else achieve their activities or goals in their lives. Success is a Do-It-Yourself Project.

Smelling the Roses

"P.D.S." or "Professional Death Syndrome," is a complex stress situation which occurs over time in our roles no matter what part we play. To be able to reduce the "P.D.S." levels, we must understand that we have to be effective, not efficient, in our personal top priorities. Accept the principle of never taking anyone else's problem without their strength-building recommendation for a solution. Get off the fence, handle snap decisions in a consistent method, avoid head games, and realize that it is more important to be respected, than to be liked. When these principles come into your life, you will be able to see the "P.D.S." levels of stress decrease. Your personal success will bloom on a daily basis.

START SMELLING THE ROSES AND FIGHT "P.D.S." TODAY!

MARLA McWILLIAMS
Time Ltd
P.O. Box 1061
Guasti, CA 91743
(714) 947-4325

Marla McWilliams

Marla McWilliams feels that time is the most valuable asset anyone can have as no amount of money or power can buy time.

Marla is the founder of two successful businesses, Marla's Fine Jewelry, 14K Gold and diamond sales, and Time Ltd, a consulting firm.

Marla believes that each individual houses a tremendous amount of energy within them and she focuses on releasing that energy. She has always felt that a person could excell in anything they desire and she strives to show people that they are unique, special and creative individuals.

"Success is no more than the achievement of a goal," Marla states, and she helps people to develop and achieve their goals. She has always felt that successful people were not "born" successful, but they simply realized that they, like everyone, had special talents to offer and they utilized them.

Marla attempts to bring out these positive talents in everyone she encounters. She recognizes an employee's untapped potential and works with them to bring out personal satisfaction and motivation. In addition, a more productive and successful company results.

Soon after she received her BS in Business Administration, Marketing Management, she began giving seminars/lectures and consulting on effective time management. Her tape, "A New Perspective on Time" has aided many professionals seeking an answer to their limited time and unlimited responsibilities. Ms. McWilliams notes that corporations everywhere are realizing the importance of continued employee education. Therefore, she has developed an extensive training program in the area of Time, Success and Stress Management.

Marla is currently working on completing her Masters Degree in Psychology at California State University San Bernardino.

17

Time and Stress Management—
A New Perspective on Time
by Marla McWilliams

"If you look back, you will stay back,
If you look ahead, you will move ahead!"
—Marla McWilliams

Time...What does it mean to you? Does it conjure up negative thoughts of meeting deadlines, missing appointments and just a general feeling of stress? Does time control you, or do you control time? I'd like to give you some simple techniques that should enable you to control your time and the demands made upon you. I will not only discuss functions and techniques of effective Time Management, but also a new attitude towards time—this is my New Perspective on Time.

You and I both have the same amount of time...we have the same amount of time as movie stars, doctors, lawyers and two year olds. Certainly we have more *responsibilities* than the two-year-olds. But why do we say we don't have as much time as we used to? That's what we are going to examine, ways in dealing with our all too busy lives and the many responsibilities within them. Without managing your time, precious hours can be wasted. The average person wastes over an hour a day by not handling situations and priorities properly, constant interruptions or looking for those misplaced notes or lost car keys and endless other time wasters. Here is a frightening statistic. One hour per day of wasted time totals six full weeks per year!! Do you know what you can accomplish in six weeks? The list is too long to mention all of the dreams that could become reality within six weeks time.

This chapter is full of wonderful ideas to give yourself more time and in essense freedom, but you will not become a Time Management expert on your first try—it will take review and DISCIPLINE in order for you to pick up these new GOOD habits. And you certainly won't become a Time Management expert unless you decide for yourself that you will *apply* these techniques and allow yourself to control your life and time, and not let it control you.

The old saying..."Nothing good comes easy" is true in regards to breaking bad habits and developing new positive habits. Remember there is NO SHORTCUT when investing in oneself. I think that you probably bought this book in hopes of relieving stress in your life. Through properly managing your time, you can be on your way to alleviating stress in your life. This is only possible when you apply these techniques. Many of the ideas I give you may seem to be basic, simple, common sense ideas—they are— so is taking out the trash, but how OFTEN is that neglected, so just because these things seem easy to you, do NOT discount them, give them a try!! It certainly can't hurt, and you will probably find that you are enjoying life more and finding you have more available time, or at least that you are getting more things done in the same time.

Speed Writing

I am sure you have heard of speed reading, I'd like to introduce you to SPEED WRITING, yes learning to write faster. I abbreviate almost everything. In fact I do it so much now that I no longer know how to spell...that I will leave up to my secretary. And for you secretaries, never fear, if you learn to abbreviate too well and lose your knack to spell, there's always the dictionary and word processor spelling programs. Let me give you a few examples of speed writing abbreviations that you can start to utilize in your daily note writing. The first one is the letter "U," that is short for *you*...the number "2" for *to* and *two*...the number "4" for the word *for*...always use the "and sign" (&)...one that I often use is the three letters "wcb," that stands for *will call back*... everyone knows "asap" (*as soon as possible*), now if some of these seem silly and hard to remember, just think about asap. It has been adopted by business and is widely accepted and used. You can make up some of your own. Many companys have their own particular "buzz" words, you can use initials instead of the complete word. I often write "TL" for my company's name, Time Ltd. Here's a good one, "yr" instead of *your*, "pls" instead of *please*. The word *before* can be written as "b/4." There are numerous combinations and don't be afraid to make up your own, not many of the preceeding abbreviations are official, so feel free to create and save yourself lots of time! At first it might be awkward and your co-workers may not know what you are saying. Either give them a little legend or send an intercompany memo showing the new *standard* abbreviations...you may find that everyone likes the idea...once they get used to it, of course.

Paper Flow Management

Do you receive a lot of interoffice mail and respond by dictating yet another interoffice memo? That looks real nice and impressive but it is a waste of time. Jot down a neat response in writing in the corner of the letter and return it to the sender. This way you don't take the time to dictate, copy, distribute and file ANOTHER interoffice memo; it is handled directly and the person receiving it doesn't need to waste time reading "IN REFERENCE TO YOUR INTEROFFICE MEMO #43294, dated January 30, regarding SUCH AND SUCH..." The receiver can clearly see that you are responding to the letter that you returned with your message on it. And if it is of some importance, you may make a copy of the letter and file it in your follow-up file. If you are not sure what I mean by a follow-up file, let me tell you about it. A follow-up file is probably the most essential tool for good paper flow management in and on your desk. It is made up of 43 separate file folders that you keep in your desk file drawer or in some kind of holder on or near your desk. Each folder is numbered from 1 to 31 and there are 12 others with January through December on them. Into these folders you can put everything from bills to birthday cards to memos that you sent out and are awaiting a response. You simply file the item under the appropriate number of the day you want to have it called back up. Each day you pull the folder for that day and there are a number of items for you to handle...sometimes you will find the item has already been handled and you can trash it. Other times you may want to postpone action for another week so you simply file it for a week away. This is much better than having to pick it up every day for two or three weeks and then when the day comes that it is needed it's buried under a pile of other papers and forgotten. The follow-up file eliminates piles forever and makes files.

Always remember the five P's PROPER PLANNING PREVENTS POOR PERFORMANCE. Plan NOW to make a follow-up system for your desk.

Proper Communication Can Save Time

Do you recall the last frustrating time you called a large corporation and were transferred from one department to the next? Getting upset and raising your voice never really gets you anywhere. However, if you try your best to "keep your cool" and treat the person on the other line with the utmost patience and kindness, it is surprising what you can accomplish. If people feel they are being harshly shoved to do something, they'll resist But if they're gently persuaded, they'll often be won over. This doesn't mean you need to run around being obsequious; it does mean that if you respect people they will respect you.

Another phase of communication that is in the realm of time management is the incredible waste of time I see in business wherein two or three or more people are arguing about who caused a certain problem...WHO CARES WHO CAUSED THE PROBLEM!! Let's find out what the options are at hand in solving this problem, forget about who did what and let's solve the problem and get on with business. In short, GET TO THE BOTTOM LINE... Now this doesn't mean we need to be harsh to one another. Remember that modern science is still trying to produce a tranquilizer more effective than a few kind words. I realize it is not always easy to be nice to everyone, and don't become frustrated when you find it hard, just remember that patience is merely the art of concealing one's impatience. If everyone treated people a little nicer I think that the world would become a lot more productive.

Quotes to Live By

True success and happiness that you can come closer to with my new perspective on time is not a matter of good fortune or worldly possessions. It's a mental attitude. It comes from appreciating what we have, instead of being miserable about what we don't have. It's so simple yet so hard for the human mind to comprehend.

Henry Kaiser said, "I make progress by having people around me who are smarter than I am—and listening to them. And I assume that EVERYONE is smarter about SOMETHING than I am. "That too, is good advice. If you want to learn, don't be afraid to ask questions...it's those people who want to pretend they know everything that are afraid to seem ignorant by asking questions. Eleanor Roosevelt said that "NO ONE CAN MAKE YOU FEEL INFERIOR WITHOUT YOUR CONSENT." Those people that refuse to be curious and ask questions never learn anything and go thru life PRETENDING to know it all. They are only hurting themselves.

Some people pursue success and happiness, while others create it. That should tell you something. You can create your own success and happiness, no one is going to do it for you. Celeste Holm said, "IF YOU DO SOMETHING NEW EVERY DAY AND LEARN SOMETHING NEW EVERY DAY, YOU WON'T WASTE YOUR TIME HERE ON EARTH." Another good one comes from J.B. Priestley who said, "I HAVE ALWAYS BEEN DELIGHTED AT THE PROSPECT OF A NEW DAY, A FRESH TRY, ONE MORE START, WITH PERHAPS A BIT OF MAGIC WAITING SOME-WHERE BEHIND THE MORNING."

How nice that is, how refreshing. I like to use a lot of quotes because to me they are motivating. They make me reflect on my own thoughts and let me realize that I am the master of my own destiny, which leads me back to the functions of time and stress management.

80/20 rule (Whales & Guppies)

An Italian economist in the 16th Century named Pareto noted that 80% of Italy's wealth came from 20% of the population. It was similarly found that the 80/20 rule applies in most every area. 80% of your business comes from 20% of your best customers, 80% of personnel problems come from 20% of your employees, on the other hand, 80% of the work is done by only 20% of those hard-working employees, and humorously enough 80% of the beer is consumed by 20% of the population. How does the 80/20 rule apply to time management? 80% of what you do reaps you only 20% of your success, sales or results. On the other hand 20% of what you do reaps you 80% of your success, sales or results. What are those activities that will result in 80% of your rewards? Find out what they are and concentrate mainly on those activities. Don't worry about the other 80%. I refer to those 80% unnecessary activities as "guppies," and those important 20% as "whales." For instance, if you fill your day with activities such as straightening your desk, filing, reorganizing your address book, etc. etc., you are doing nothing more than fishing for guppies, giving yourself a false sense of accomplishment, when you should really be working on harpooning a whale. You should work on that project that is going to reap you the most benefit. Most people spend their time fishing for guppies rather than trying to harpoon a whale because it is easier and because they can come home at the end of the day with a bucket full of guppies. Believe me, in the long run, it will be to your advantage to bring home that whale. You may have to work on it a little bit each day and you may not even be able to catch one for a whole week. Wouldn't you say that pound for pound, your whale at the end of the week is better than your neighbor's five buckets full of guppies?

Next time you make a list of things to do for the day, and find you can't possibly do all of the items, look them over and categorize them within the two categories—are they guppies or are they whales? How can you tell? Look at each one and ask yourself, "What are the consequences if this project does not get done?" If you will lose your job, it's definitely a whale,   if it can wait until tomorrow and no one will be affected, it is a guppy. According to the 80/20 rule, you will find that 20% of your list will contain "whales" and 80% will contain "guppies." Your job is to categorize them into whales and guppies and then focus on the whales. Work on the whales one step at a time, not looking to complete the project, but just to complete the step you are currently working on and before you know it you will find that your important projects are getting done.

Delegation

Delegate some of those "guppies" to others. Delegation does not necessarily have to be downward. In fact, you may not have an assistant to delegate to. You can delegate upwardly and laterally. An example of upward delegation might be wherein you have four or five important pending projects and the boss walks in with yet another "important RUSH project." You suddenly feel inundated with work and don't know where to start. I have been in this position myself many times and I would simply keep a running list of the projects that were assigned to me. I would put a star by the one I was currently working on. Add to the list the new project, sit down with your boss, hand he/she the list and say, "Here are the projects assigned to me, which ones should I work on now and which ones can be postponed?" This way you are putting the ball in his/her court. This may raise a few eyebrows, however, you are certainly showing an interest in your position and the work that needs to be done. Your boss can only thank you for this, and you will not have unfinished projects hanging over your head. This is not a way to get out of work, only a way to work on the most important projects. Remember, without hard work, you will not succeed. Nothing good in life comes easy.

Interruptions

Most managers are interrupted once every four to eight minutes. Add that to normal management duties and the manager doesn't do much more than get interrupted. There are many ways that you can eliminate excess interruptions. However, none of them will be effective until you realize and accept your NEED for interruptions!! Sound strange? It's true. What if you went to work tomorrow only to find that the phone didn't ring and no one said "hello" and no one asked your opinion? You would be very depressed and also question the stability of your position! The answer to eliminating excess interruptions, therefore, lies within yourself. You must ADMIT that you ENJOY interruptions at times, and therefore, schedule a certain amount of time during the day that you WILL allow interruptions and another time that you will avoid them. Here are a few ways to eliminate the interruptions during those times you choose to avoid interruptions:

1. Put a brief case on your guest chair (intruder can't sit down)
2. Stand to greet intruder and remain standing— they feel uncomfortable

3. Look at your watch
4. Close your door and leave a note saying when you will be available
5. Schedule a different lunch hour from others and work during theirs
6. Face desk away from flow of traffic and away from the door.

Remember, the key to solving your problems with interruptions is in YOUR HANDS!

Five Minutes Is a Long Time

One of my favorite professors during college, Joseph A. Dolan, always told his students, *"Five Minutes Is a Long Time."* This is so true. What do you do when you have 5 minutes to spare? Do you think about all your pending projects that will take you at least 2 hours to complete? Five minutes is enough time to make a rough outline of an upcoming project, or to schedule tomorrow's activities or to return an important phone call. Too many of us discount the amount of things that can be accomplished in just FIVE MINUTES! Next time you are planning to go someplace and you have five minutes to spare, tell yourself *FIVE MINUTES IS A LONG TIME.* Then pick up the beginning of a project and work on it. You will be amazed at the many things you will be able to begin and later accomplish within these small sections of five minutes. Too many people try to set aside "blocks" of time to work on projects, only to find those "blocks" of time never arrive. Keeping this in mind, you can accomplish much more by working on projects one step at a time. Next time you find you have a few extra minutes, tell yourself FIVE MINUTES IS A LONG TIME and USE IT!

Learn to say NO, nicely

Do you find yourself saying "yes" to everyone that asks a favor of you? If you do, you are like many other "nice guys" and you know what they say about "nice guys"...they finish last! Nice guys finish last because they are doing everything for everyone else, with no time for themselves or their own projects. Our time is limited yet we have an *unlimited* amount of demands on our time from husbands, wives, children, coworkers, bosses and others. You must explain to these people that you will be happy to take care of their request on another day, and give them a day. They will learn to work around your schedule and will certainly respect you in the long run.

Time Wasters (Don't WASTE in Line!)

Do you find your stomach knotting up while waiting in lines? Don't look at these moments as wasted time, look at them as a GIFT OF TIME. You had to be in that place either way, so pull out that project that you SHOULD be carrying with you at all times and make an outline, or schedule next week in your appointment book, set goals, do something! Remember what Joseph A. Dolan told his students, *Five Minutes Is a Long Time!!* This won't work if you are empty handed. Always remember to carry something with you *wherever* you go and you won't be frustrated. Even if that "something" is a novel you've been reading, don't be caught with extra time and nothing to do. I've even gone as far as carrying projects with me on dinner dates, you *never* know when something will come up and your partner must leave or cancel. At least your night or "waiting time" won't be wasted, you will have accomplished the work you brought along! I know this sounds a touch on the neurotic side, but think of it, you'll have the person who stood you up to thank for the timely completion of an upcoming project!

Do you take your deposit to the bank each week and wait in line to personally hand it to the teller? Many people are beginning to realize the convenience of banking by mail, automated teller machines and the simple night drop. However, many people feel that with the millions of people and relatively few banks, they are destined to stand in line. This is not true. Banking by mail is a safe and simple procedure. Even safer yet, is having your company deposit your check directly into your account. This way your check is in the bank on payday and you can get extra cash at the super-market when you pick up groceries. This is a great time saver, and you should realize and respect the value of your time instead of wasting an hour every week at the bank! Yes, it is an hour, by the time you prepare to leave, get in the car, drive to the bank, out of the car, into the bank, into the line, etc. etc. etc. Reconsider your banking methods, and if you insist on waiting in line, bring a project with you.

Did you know that you can buy stamps through the Post Office by mail? There is no shipping or handling charge. Simply request 5 or 6 mailing envelopes from your local Postmaster. That should save you another hour per week/month of standing in line.

Telephone Time Wasters

When you call a client, associate or friend to talk business, do you ask, "How's it going?" This is an open-ended question that you do not want to ask. Why? Because he/she will tell you how it's going, all about their vacation, marriage, divorce, kids, friends and lovers. You do not have time for this. Instead, rephrase your opening question. Say, "Good morning John, do you have a moment to discuss the Cannon project?" This way you get right down to business immediately. This can save up to 3 minutes and with 10 to 20 calls a day, you can save up to one hour a day with proper phone management alone! Always have a list of the items you would like to discuss with the person on the other end. I tell this to executives and they tell me, "Oh, I'm not going to forget what I am talking about with my associate." Later, they tell me they forgot one pertinent item and had to take the time to recontact that person. How many times have you hung up the phone and realized there was one other thing you meant to mention. Keep a section in your Appointment book for calls, have the person that you need to call and their phone number, and also the different items that need to be discussed.

Now there is another time management problem that can be *stressful*, and that is getting *off* of the phone. One of the most effective ways is to simply "sum up" what you have been discussing, "OK, John, I will take care of developing the plans and the lay-out and meet with you Friday in your office, I'll let *you* get back to work now." Always tell the person that you will let them get back to work, not that you are busy. Make others feel important. Effective telephone time management is much like limiting interruptions, you must take the initiative to speak out, be assertive, and let the other party know that you respect their time.

Goals

If you aim at nothing, you will hit nothing. If you

look back, you will go back. If you look ahead, you will move ahead. Many people take six months to plan a one week vacation and yet never take one moment to set a one year goal. General Douglas MacArthur, the man who more than any other helped us win World War II, might never have had power and fame. When he applied for admission at West Point, he was turned down. Not once, but twice. He tried a third time and was accepted and marched right down into the history books. He was determined. He set a goal and didn't let anything get in the way.

In setting goals, you must be specific. You needn't be afraid to commit yourself to the goal by writing it down. It is simply a guide for you to follow. Every successful person and company has a written ONE YEAR and FIVE YEAR plan. Just because they are in writing does not mean you must do them. Many companies don't accomplish their plans, and they certainly don't consider themselves failures because of it. However, they often exceed their goals and objectives. Without the charted goal in writing, they would not know what to aim for. In working on your goals, you need only to work on them one small step at a time, so long as you work on them a little each day.

I'd like to conclude with a story about a little 10 year old girl who had a goal. She saw a stuffed snake in the toy store window. She really wanted that snake. She figured there were three ways for her to have the snake. #1, she could ask her parents to give her the $25. However, she knew they weren't in the financial position to do so; #2, she could walk into the store and take it, but she knew that wasn't right; #3, she could set a goal to buy the snake and find ways to earn money. She liked this alternative, so she sat down with pen and paper and wrote in big letters at the top of the page, *I WANT THE SNAKE AT THE TOY STORE.* Below that she wrote down certain activities that would bring her closer to her goal. She noted that she needed to advertise her services to the neighbors—grass cutting and yard-work (she wasn't afraid to get dirty!), babysitting and pet care. Soon people responded and she was working a little each day. Even if she didn't have a specific job one day, she would spend time promoting her business. This, she knew, brought her that much closer to her goal. After weeks of working just a little each day, she earned the money to purchase the stuffed snake. She ran down to the toy store and bought it...and guess what? I still have "Snakey" today, and a lot of other goals I set out to accomplish because I believed in the goal and I believed in myself. You, too, can do whatever you set your mind to . Get out the pen and paper and start setting some goals. Good luck, and don't forget...the harder you work the luckier you get!

He that will not command his thoughts . . .
Will lose the command of his actions.

—**Thomas Wilson**

JOE D. BATTEN
Batten, Batten, Hudson & Swab, Inc.
820 Keo Way
Des Moines, IA 50309
Bus. (515) 244-3176 • Res. (515) 285-7088

Joe Batten
In addition to his numerous honors in the field of management, Joe Batten is known throughout the world as the DEAN OF MANAGEMENT TRAINERS.

He is the founder and Chairman of the Board of Batten, Batten, Hudson & Swab, Inc., Des Moines, Iowa, a 28-year-old human resource firm engaged in creative management research, consulting, film production, and educational services. Joe is a renowned consultant, philosopher, speaker, trainer, film maker, and author. He is known world-wide as the author of Tough-Minded Management and such films as Keep Reaching, and Ask For The Order. He has spoken over 2,000 times on motivation, selling, and management. He is a charter member of the National Speakers Association Hall of Fame (CPAE).

Joe Batten is a renowned consultant and speaker in the United States and abroad. He has trained thousands in management, sales and human relationship skills. His teachings are acclaimed as the prototype for tomorrow's management. His philosophy advocates the development of the "Whole Person" and he and his colleagues have been heavily involved in counseling and speaking on "Whole Person Wellness" and stress management. He is generally considered to be the principal pioneer in the establishment of management philosophies basic beliefs and values, as the basis of corporate cultures/climates. His book, Tough-Minded Management is and has been the leadership Bible for several heads of state including some emerging African nations. He actively serves as a mentor on HOW TO DEVELOP A WINNING ATTITUDE with major athletic coaches.

He has written numerous articles for national publications and has appeared on network television and radio programs as well as local television and radio. As an author he has received wide acknowledgement from organizations throughout the world.

18

Make Tension An Asset...
The Music of Taut Strings
by Joe Batten

"Men grow when inspired by a high purpose, when contemplating vast horizons."

—Alex Carrel

It's mid-afternoon and the executive has lines of strain around his mouth and between his eyebrows. "Sure, I can use some better management know-how, who can't?...What I *really* need though is a lot more knowledge about how to manage *me!* I feel so hyper sometimes, you can't believe it." Such a person is the *recipient* for tensions & stress.

For over almost three decades my consulting colleagues at Batten, Batten, Hudson & Swab, Inc. and I have encountered many variations of this in many companies, times and places. We believe there is nothing more urgent in the organizations of the future than to learn, design, develop and practice an updated paradigm and strategy of *stress management*.

First, we must sharply revamp many stale stereotypes about the *nature* of stress.

Second, we must develop living and interactive styles for the generation and focusing of stress for renewal, enrichment and accomplishment.

The wide diffusion of light can be pleasant and, yes, enlightening. But, enlightenment without focus and action may not accomplish much. My favorite example is the laser. When light is sufficiently concentrated and focused it becomes a laser beam that can penetrate as much as twelve inches of steel.

So, energy is to be cherished and used. There lies the path of creativity, productivity and JOY. I'm referring to those blessed people who have mastered and focused their tensions into a "laser beam" of *out*-flowing energy, rather than the sad, wan people who seem to prepare for years to take the ultimate walk into the twilight. The latter seem to constantly court *in*-flowing tensions by seeking expedient, defensive and dim patterns of "tranquility."

The time to challenge these pervasive and suffocating stereotypes is *now*.

Are you the bland leading the bland?—or—the passive pursuing the pusillanimous? I profoundly hope you are neither. Rather, it is my hope that you *dare to live passionately!* There is a mass flight taking place in our society. A flight from stress and tension. There is one towering thing wrong with this. To wit, bad tension and stress are bad for you, *but* good tension and stress are absolutely crucial to a life of excellence; a life of growth, achievement, faith, hope, love, and JOY. Viability and positive stress are not only indivisible; they mean virtually the same thing.

Our tensions can be involutional. They can *implode* with sickening and abrasive impact or they can *explode* with productivity, zest, and JOY. One of the appalling facts of modern life is that the "tranquilizer" industry is a multi-billion dollar business. All too often we confuse happiness with tranquility. And yet—the ultimate condition of total tranquility is *rigor mortis*—and—who's in a hurry for that?

Let's rejoice and exult in the fact that we have emotions, tensions, and stress. Life would be meaningless and vegetable-like if we did not. *Nothing* can be accomplished without energy—physical, mental and spiritual.

Let us be *transmitters* rather than *receiving sets* for

our tensions. Let's dare to feel as good and *transmit* as much energy toward constructive goals and dreams as our imagination can produce. Such transmitters grow *stronger*. Such receivers grow *weaker*. Remember, a tough mind and a tender heart are one. They have no relationship to hardness and rigidity.

Do you dare to feel as good as you can possibly feel? Will you shun the habits of *dis*tress and target the habits of *meta*stress? From negative to positive— from getting to giving—from compression to extension—from grey sickness to vibrancy and buoyancy?

Live, Love and Laugh

It can be very damaging and naive to try to overlook the fact that we have emotions, to try and bury them and maintain an aloof, glacial and bland exterior to the entire world. A recent study seemed to show a strong relationship between degenerative, nervous diseases and responsible executive and professional jobs. One manager said to me, "I'll never be caught by tension, I'm going to stay unruffled, I won't let anybody create any tension in me, I'll surround myself with an environment that is calm and unruffled." A few months after this statement this man *had developed an ulcer!* He was locking tensions up *in* himself. He was not letting the normal flow of emotions express themselves and escape him through wholesome, stimulating, goal-oriented *work*. He was building up internally a hot, seething furnace of emotions and the tissues inside his vital organs suffered because of this. Something had to give. What happens if a tea kettle is sealed and left on the heat? So this manager had made of tension a very negative and destructive thing. Subsequently he was counseled that if he continued to build up these tensions and lock them in and offer this bland controlled face at all times to the world he would certainly shorten his life. He was urged to Live, Love and Laugh, to stretch, reach and strive. He was counseled and developed insight into the *two* kinds of tension in life. Tension is essential and very important to the good life. The Almighty never intended for a person to live the life of a vegetable without surging, racing emotions; and emotions cause a tenseness of tissue, a tenseness of mind and brain, thus the actual meaning of the word tense is tension. But as I say, there are two kinds. Virtually any kind of building material is only as strong and good as its *tensile* strength.

The Amateur and the Pro

Let me illustrate this by describing the amateur and the pro. *Amateur* speakers, for instance, may very well have delivered 200 or 300 speeches and still be amateurs. What makes them amateurs? When they stand up in the group they have a tendency to think about themselves, to wonder what the audience is thinking of them. They wonder if they are properly groomed, they wonder if their hair is unmussed, they wonder if they look alert, poised and intelligent. They wonder if people are going to snicker at them, they wonder if the audience is going to be bored, they wonder if they are going to be hostile. Their emotions are *coming in on them* and such implosive emotions can literally consume them, tighten them up, cause heart attacks, nervous breakdowns and all of the related degenerative diseases.

On the other hand, *professional* speakers can be pros after only 30 or 40 speeches if they visualize their role in front of the audience as being to *give* them something to use to make their lives better, to make them more efficient, to make their entire existence more meaningful... to *honor* their audiences. Thus they see that their only justification for taking up the time of a group of people is to *give* them something. If they are up there simply to get, the pleasure of having plodded through a presentation so that they can chalk this up as another professional or business credit, that's all it will amount to. And it will be a hollow attention producing effort indeed, because the true pro gets up in front of the group and he or she probably has even more tension than the amateur, but this tension is flowing *out* and reaching out and enveloping, affecting, and energizing the audience.

Take Constructive Action

Speakers are only one example. This applies in every phase of living. The wife who decides that she will endure every little indignity that a gross or boorish husband may inflict on her and the family, will build up a nice batch of tension internally and develop a lot of constrictive complications. On the other hand she may elect to express these tensions in various ways, by scrubbing the floor extra hard, by walking or working out, or by working extra hard and, perhaps, this will help her. The man who decides that he will bottle up every source of tension that his wife creates ultimately reaches a point where he is liable to desert the family, drop dead, or physically hurt her in some way. There is no substitute for letting the emotions come out and be directed in terms of constructive action, wholesome physical exercise, and meaningful or even inconsequential talking. The secret—to a great extent—in minimizing destructive tensions in effective family life is to "talk it out." These are three simple little words but they hold a very powerful key to draining off destructive tensions and turning them into constructive conversation, enlightenment and serenity. Chemically induced *tranquility?* NO! *Serenity* induced by a healthy and vigorous lifestyle, YES!

Tension—Motivating or Killing?

We have said that tension can be very productive, that it can be positive, that it can be good. And this is particularly true when each individual knows the motives that will guide their life from here on. Then they have a goal to point toward, they have a direction in which to fuse and focus their energy. We have from time to time used the old saw "the shortest distance between two points is a straight line." This is equally true in making constructive use of tension. When we have purpose to our days, our weekends, our jobs and in the course and direction of our family living, then we can let loose great amounts of outgoing, ebullient tension and make this focused energy achieve some very worthwhile things. If we decide to lock it up within us we must be aware of the fact that we are virtually sentencing ourselves to ill health and to certain negative and destructive reactions. This is not to rule out the value and essential nature of self-discipline. It has been defined as self-training which strengthens, molds and develops. So, if we pour our tensions into action patterns, into words, into expressions, into daily habits which build, strengthen and develop, we need have no fear of tension as an enemy, but on the other hand, we can readily recognize it and feel good about it as a true asset. Healthy and properly done meditation is the reverse of the tight inner-directed anxieties discussed here. Excellent meditation, rather, *releases* one. Ergo, "let go and let God."

Fear—Foundation for Disaster

Perhaps the greatest single source of unhappiness in the world today is *fear;* a dread, ethereal, evanescent thing called fear. Fear is a fog hovering over the world soaking in and dampening us as we move through life, and it is all so unnecessary. This is not to say that fear is easily eradicated, but there are definite principles and guideposts which will point the way if properly understood and applied. To discuss tough-minded performance in this competitive world without treating fear would be to dodge a vital issue. Fears can multiply rapidly if we let them, but fears are destructive largely because of the ignorance of the people involved, and this statement in no way excludes highly educated people. Vast numbers of people have not had the opportunity to discover what can be done in a truly productive climate to eradicate fear.

People develop fears for a number of reasons. Among the stumbling blocks to letting oneself go and ridding oneself of fear is fear of futility, of superiors and subordinates, fear of success, fear of pressure, fear of being labeled as timid, fear of failure, thus becoming a "rigid perfectionist"—habits which are repetitive and which compound negative patterns and attitudes which are based only on the past and the status quo. One aid in the eradication of fear is so simple that one is apt to dismiss it cynically and say, "I tried it and it didn't work." But for the person who has discipline and determination and a questing mind and spirit, a complete reading of the New Testament will provide much enlightenment and do much to eradicate fear. Fear cannot flourish in an environment of faith, hope, and love just as depression cannot coexist with gratitude.

The Good News

Zero in particularly on the Gospels, the "good news," and read them again and again—tieing in every truth there with the other truths and the specific techniques you find in other chapters in this greatest of all books. Bit by bit you begin to wash away the legacy of fear that you may have built up in your childhood. You may have been told a number of things which your parents genuinely believed, but which are no longer applicable. Concepts which propound fear of God instead of love of God, which teach a sad, grim approach to Christianity rather than an enlightened, optimistic, buoyant approach. One way you can clear this up in your own mind is to make a thorough study of this greatest of all sources of basic truths...the greatest handbook of mental health in existence.

Jacques Maritain, the Christian Existentialist,

has said:

> When he (man) obeys the law as a friend
> of the law because the Spirit of God
> renders him one in spirit and love with
> the principle of the law, and does of his
> own accord that which the law com-
> mands, he is no longer under the law, it is
> his own love, now sovereign and
> sovereignly free, his love of his God and
> his All, which causes him to obey the law
> that has now become his law, the personal
> call by which the word of Him he loves
> reaches him. This is a law in regard to
> which he is no longer a *self* to be identified
> with *everyman*. He is *this man* himself, this
> man answering in his own name, to
> whom the law speaks in his pure solitude
> with God.

Here he is saying (existentially) that man's love
of God *can* enable him to transcend fear by giving
much of himself to others if the true definition of
God is, "God is Love."

It is also very important to recognize that many
of the people who generate in us certain fearful
reactions are people who desire our compassion and
our help much more than our fear. Until we look
behind the behavior of the domineering boss, the
blusterer, the bully, the sarcastic master of the

perfect squelch (and recognize that this is almost always motivated by insecurity or *fear* on his part) we can do very little to eradicate our own fear of him. So let's recognize that all anti-social and irascible behavior is prompted primarily by fear on the part of the individual who manifests it, and recognize that we have a worthwhile challenge in front of us to help this person get over their fears, to shift from negative to positive, to shift from what they are *against* to what they are *for*, and in the very process we very clearly begin to shape up an attitude and a daily pattern of courage which renders fear an increasingly negligible roadblock to our future success. "Life is too short to waste precious moments in fear of nothing." Doctor Gerald Jampolsky has wisely said, "Love is the absence of fear."

Are They Really Out to Get You?

Doesn't that sound ominous? Are they really out to *get you?* There is, of course, a particular kind of psychosis called paranoia where the individual has the deep-seated feeling that others are out to persecute them. This can only be treated adequately by a competent professional psychiatrist. It is well for the relatively normal, relatively well-adjusted person however to recognize that you're not really "that important." *Nobody's really out to get you.* You can build this up in your mind to a point where it truly

becomes a ghost, where it truly becomes a per-
secuting straw man.

For instance, let's take a look at the shy person.
If you have a tendency to withdraw from a
confrontation with your boss, if you have a tendency
to avoid (through a series of well contrived excuses)
certain social engagements, in short—all kinds of
affairs that take you into active contact with a lot of
people and you say with an apologetic and sometimes rather proud and martyred smile, "I guess I'm
just shy, I'm bashful, always have been and I guess I
always will be," my temptation would be to say to
you privately but with considerable sincerity and
feeling, "What makes you think you're that
important? Who do you think you are?" Because, the
basis of shyness, of so called bashfulness, is almost
always an exaggerated feeling that others are going
to be looking at you, analyzing you, out to get you,
being concerned with you, ready to focus on your
weaknesses, and the bald fact is *it just ain't so.* In
reality,it is our feelings of inadequacy strangely
enough that cause us to imagine we are always
being scrutinized that closely. *Implosive* stress thrives
on feelings of inadequacy. Healthy *explosive* stress
thrives on an ever growing awareness of one's
strengths.

The only way people really care enough about
you to give you a lot of consistent attention is when
you have shown a real interest in *them,* when you

learn to ask concerned caring questions and have indicated that you have some interest in focusing on their strengths and *giving* them something. This will build a real interest in you on their part, but certainly the usual passive withdrawal type of thing which we call shyness and bashfulness is usually simply a comfortable set of crutches to enable you to wallow defensively in your self preoccupation without getting too unhappy because *nobody's out to get you.* The only person who can get you is *you!!*

One sure-fire way to increase and perpetuate such feelings of inadequacy is to continue to flee down the labyrinthine corridors of your mind and scrupulously avoid confronting your possibilities and strengths.

This is the stuff of negative stress.

The Business of Living a Long Time

Walter Pitkin has these cynical things to say in his otherwise hope-full book *Life Begins at Forty* (Simon and Schuster): "If life begins at forty, then most of us have only fifteen or sixteen years to live. This was hurled at me by one sincere dispenser of gloom, who went on to cite (with deadly accuracy) statistics showing that most Americans die in their mid-fifties.

"After thirty-seven, Americans die off fast. Their kidneys, hearts, and blood vessels give way, as a rule. By fifty-five, the death rate is shocking. If, having abused themselves until their fortieth birthdays, they are seized with the typical panic of oncoming middle age and try to begin living, they may succeed; but they will probably pass from the scene in their late fifties; for the deeper damage to body and spirit has been done."

"If you wish to begin living after forty and to keep on living beyond threescore and ten, you must start planning at ten. This is a platitude of such green antiquity that I am ashamed to echo it here; but it must enter our records. Start right, and forty will be high noon. You could live to be eighty, hale and hearty—barring accidents and bad ancestors."

A lesson to be extracted from Mr. Pitkin's comments is that, whatever your age, the time to begin building a healthier mind, body and spirit is NOW.

How about this for a challenge? The Mayo Clinic after years of research states that the best life must consist of four balanced parts: Work, Love, Play and Worship. Destroy the balance and you invite disease, worry and *dis*tress. Develop the balance and you can have a life that builds and enriches.

The Constructive Tension of Humor

In recent years a number of studies have been made of the kind of people we often refer to affectionately as the "sprightly oldster." The man or woman who is in their 80's and 90's, sometimes past 100, who seems to be spare and spry and bright-eyed, who seems to spread some good will and good feeling wherever they go, is often plagued with the question, "What do you think is your great secret?" Well, of course, many of these people have looked back with a twinkle in their eye and said, "Because I smoke 14 cigars a day or because I never had a sober day in my life" or some such thing, and many times don't give you a definite answer and...here lies one of the keys. These people have learned to develop a resilient, buoyant, *humorous* reaction to life, and this is one of the basic secrets.

Humor is one of life's most therapeutic elixirs. Can a belly laugh and *dis*tress co-exist? Sound sociological, anthropological and psychiatric research has been conducted and has isolated three principal things in these "oldsters." They are: they learned fairly early in life to work; that much involvement in *work,* commitment to *work,* can be fun, pleasant, every bit as pleasant if not more so, than play itself. They never quit learning and changing. Never!! They continue to read, they continue to ask questions, they continue to want to travel, they continue to query about the "why" of the world, the society, the culture around them. They are *out*going individuals. They do not regard young people as their enemies but rather as great sources of delight and renewal. And last but certainly not least, they learned to *make tension an asset* by turning it into humor. A loud and genuine belly-laugh is a form of tension, but it is a form of very helpful, healthful, replenishing, and constructive tension. So here are some simply stated, but key building blocks in the foundation of a long and happy life. In summary they loved to work, stayed mentally curious, and had a sense of humor. *They lived passionately!* Research into the lifting and healing power of humor suggests that it is virtually a new mental health frontier.

I first met J. Paul Getty, the late billionaire, in 1968 when he was 75. One of the most memorable things he told me was that he loved to dance and considered himself excellent at doing the "Twist." My chat with Mr. Getty will be more fully chronicled in some future article, however, I'd like to share some impressions of—and some remarks by— the man who was often described as "the richest man in the *world.*" Most people who have read about him have some very erroneous notions. For some reason it has been assumed that earning money was his one consuming passion and that he was not a joyful, healthy, and *whole* person.

Nothing could be further from the truth!! He radiated positivism, fitness, and happiness. His interests were indeed broad and eclectic. In his delightful book, *The Golden Age,* he places much emphasis on the need for a healthy, growing, and ever-changing mind, body and spirit.

I believe it is significant that the six chapters dealing with such subjects as:

A Fiscal Primer

Pointers for Practical Planning

Closer Focus on the Future

Next Rungs on the Investment Ladder

As the Investor Becomes More Sophisticated, and

The Alchemy That Turns Retirement Into a Golden Age

were preceded by *twelve* chapters on how to prepare oneself broadly and deeply for full functioning as a person—how to savor the flavor of each passing NOW. This performer closes *The Golden Age* with these words:

"I am—and have been—convinced that it is when the human being reaches middle age that he really has the experience and ability to savor life, to qualify as and *be* a connoisseur of the art of living.

Getty knew that *every* age can be a golden age if one truly applies these tough-minded peak performance principles.

He prescribed this equation:

Physical health + psychological preparation + activities and interests gratifying human relationships - pernicious myths and misconceptions × an individual's energy and enthusiasm = the negation of age and triumphant 'connoisseurship of life' after retirement." He was a master of positive stress management!

You *can*—

Discover your possibilities.

Fulfill your potential.

Actualize your dreams.

Keep reaching and expect the best.

Lead by example.

Create your expective blueprint.

Build on your strengths.

Become what you *think*.

Become what you *say*.

Become what you expect.

Dare to live passionately.

**Will you do it? The choice is *yours!*

The mind is its own place, and in itself
Can make a Heav'n of Hell, a Hell of Heav'n.

—Milton

TERRY HOPWOOD
Success Center
14547 Titus Street
Panorama City, CA 91402
(818) 989-2923

Terry Hopwood

Terry Hopwood, Director of the Success Center in Panorama City, California is a hypnotherapist registered with the Hypnotists Examining Council. She has 17 years professional experience in her field, beginning at age 15. Terry started her training in this subject when, at age 13, her father (also a hypnotist) caught her hypnotizing the neighborhood kids!

Terry developed the Seven Keys to Self Actualization, a systematic program of personal growth which enables her students/clients to achieve their fullest potential physically, mentally and emotionally. She does not believe in solving others' problems for them—she gives them the tools to find their own solutions.

Terry graduated cum laude from Cal State University at Northridge with a B.A. in Psychology. She also studied four years at the Hypnosis Motivation Institute, the Emile Franchel School of Living Science, and the Hypnotism Training Center.

In addition to her work in private practice, and supervising the Center, she is in great demand as a forceful, interesting speaker throughout Southern California. She lectures and gives seminars on Habit Control (Stop Smoking, Lose Weight, etc.), Intimacy Without Jealousy, Bloom Where You're Planted, Growing With Your Company, Memory/Learning Enhancement, Sales Motivation, From Stress to Success, and Business/Personal Success Through Self Hypnosis.

19

From Stress to Success
by Terry Hopwood

*"Problems are challenges, and if there
are no challenges, there are no
opportunities!"*
—M.R. Kopmeyer

S tress is the tension in life that can come from
excitement, worry, pressure, or simply the fast pace
of our modern world.

Anyone functioning in this world experiences
stress on a fairly regular basis. Complete elimination

of stress is not our goal here. An institutionalized person unable to care for himself receives bed, board, and basic needs without effort. His stress-free life probably doesn't attract you.

A corpse has no worries, either.

You are ALIVE IN THE WORLD. That's why you're reading something designed for personal growth. Your life will never be entirely stress-free.

Are you going to allow the stress of daily life to result in headaches, ulcers, or a nervous breakdown? Many people in modern society do, and the percentage is increasing. Others under equal stress, however, use that stress to stimulate and motivate them. They have learned to react to potentially stressful situations with physical relaxation, emotional control, and mental problem solving behavior.

Who are these lucky people? Well, some of them simply had the good sense to select perfect parents who never gave them any emotional problems. Such "good sense" is rare to non-existent in the real world. Actually, most such people have *learned* to react in this adaptive fashion by using such disciplines as yoga, meditation, guided imagery, or one of the other myriad names for self-hypnosis.

Don't shudder. I am not talking about stage nonsense or horror movie melodrama. I am talking about a mental technique as old as magic, as effective as faith-healing, and as scientifically provable as drugless anesthesia in today's most modern hospitals.

Does all of this sound like a contradiction in terms? Magic and faith-healing may be dirty words in scientific circles today, but their effectiveness in curing everything from (hysterical) blindness to catatonic psychosis has been well documented over thousands of years. Did witch doctors & faith healers have some special power? Does a hypnotist use "the evil eye" to get results?

Hardly. It is our own minds which have the power to relieve stress, let go of phobias, and motivate us in the direction of success, mental, physical, and emotional. How?

Regression

Hypnotic age regression is the process of mentally/emotionally returning to an earlier time in one's life. You go back to each incident in your life which led to the present problem, whether that be fear of snakes (dogs, people, success) or an addiction to cigarettes. You rewrite each such incident in a way which leads to the deletion of that problem in your life.

Generally, such a rewrite must be limited to one's attitude toward the events which actually occurred rather than changing the incident itself—particularly the actions of others. If your first grade teacher called you stupid and you reacted by believing it and doing poorly in school (and life) thereafter, you would relive it mentally, so that you react to the teacher's comment by resolving to show him how truly intelligent and capable you are. Please note that Einstein's biography opens with his math teacher's exclamation. "That stupid child!" 'Nuf said.

Anxiety Attack

One of our clients (we'll call him Tom) had a severe stammering problem. He couldn't get out a single sentence without repeating himself on almost every word. Each time he opened his mouth to speak, an anxiety would "clutch at his heart" and cause him to stutter. There are two ways to deal with such a problem—eliminate the anxiety and/or change the person's reaction to it. We did both.

The necessity to speak is a response to environmental demands at home or at work—situational demands. Whether you want the salt passed or you're after that million dollar account, *you've got to ask for it.* There is a chance of not being granted your request which might be defined as rejection, that scariest of happenings. Before you ask, however, the potential reaction of the environment to your request has not happened. The feared response doesn't exist *except in your mind.* Envisioning acceptance rather than a rejection in his mind made that image as much a part of reality as his earlier negative projection. Tom relaxed and his stuttering decreased.

Did he ever experience real rejection? An actual refusal to give him what he wanted? Surely. The world was not created for our convenience and doesn't always or even usually cooperate fully with our desires. Through the positive imagery of self-hypnosis, Tom was able to mentally rehearse his *effective* handling of such lack of cooperation. He learned to use the energy he had formerly put into anxiety/stuttering for persuasion of others and inner positive motivation. He now used each actual refusal as a learning experience which would help him to better handle similar situations in order to get what he wanted in the future. Tom still doesn't bat a thousand on getting a positive response every time, but at $100,000 a year, this successful business owner is getting enough yeses to make him feel pretty damned good about himself and his life.

Tom did not eliminate stress. As a successful business owner, he probably encounters more potentially stressful situations than he did as someone else's 9 to 5 employee. It is his way of dealing with such situations which has changed internally and externally. He turned stress to success by programming his personal computer, his sub-conscious mind, to react to such situations as stimulating challenges spurring him to use creative problem solving methods to bring from his environment the most positive possible results for him.

The school teacher whose class is full of noisy, uncooperative students, can radiate nervousness which his charges detect and take advantage of, nervousness which perhaps even triggers tensions and increased behavior problems in those students. Or he can choose to react with dynamic personal magnetism to channel the energies of these young hellions into fascinating learning experiences and innovative projects. The writer whose personal problems or marital difficulties are putting him under stress can allow the tension to stifle his creativity until it destroys his career, or he can choose to write out his difficulties in a comic monologue or dramatic theatrical presentation. Whether it's "Take my wife, please!" or "Camelot," this is one way of channeling potentially destructive energies into life stimulating success.

The key is recognizing that outside events have no direct effect on you—the same event can sometimes make you angry, other times resigned or determined. Through the proper mental disciplines, you can take command of these seemingly inexplicable variations and choose your reactions to outside events. Turn your stress into success. I have developed an organized, effective way to do just that: The Seven Keys to Self-Actualization.

Self hypnosis has proven to be an effective tool

for resolving problems such as nervousness, over-eating, smoking, low self confidence, and learning/memory difficulties. While continuing this valid use of self-hypnosis in problem solving, the SEVEN KEYS TO SELF-ACTUALIZATION also encourage self discovery, expansion of personal boundaries and the learning of new skills. It is a systematic program of personal growth which will enable you to achieve your fullest potential mentally, physically, and emotionally.

Bronze Key

The basic use of autosuggestion and self-hypnosis.

This is the first of the seven keys and acts as a basis for all the others. Due to the necessity of learning the basic skills presented here in order to practice the techniques taught in the other keys, this is the one required before any of the others may be learned. The rest of the keys may be taken in any order after completion of this one.

This key consists of four forty-five minute sessions, as do most of the others, though there is some flexibility to this. Each of the Bronze sessions imparts a basic skill leading to mental, physical, and emotional integration—goal achievement through personal growth.

The first session is an introduction to progressive relaxation—a total release of physical tension starting from the toes all the way to the top of the head. Though it is the voice of the hypnotist which produces this during the session in the office, the client is given a formula for self-hypnosis while in the hypnotic state. At home he will be able to use it for both relaxation and to enter a state of greater suggestibility to himself.

This state can be used to accomplish almost anything a hypnotist could do, once the client learns the techniques needed to accomplish each goal. These techniques are best learned in private sessions customized to the individual needs of the client. Group sessions, tapes, or a good book on the subject come next. For our purposes here, I will simply share with you a method of entering a relaxed state in which your mind will be open to the positive, health and success promoting suggestions you wish to give yourself.

Lie or sit in a comfortable position—body untwisted, legs uncrossed, hands open, etc. Begin to relax by saying to yourself: "I am relaxing my feet completely, ankles letting go—relaxing, calves of my legs so relaxed," etc., all the way to your scalp. Then take five deep breaths and say to yourself, "Deep, deep asleep." Having completed this, you will be in a (probably light) state of self-hypnosis. In that state you can use many of the suggestions I will be mentioning in subsequent pages.

During these first four sessions you will relieve

stress by learning better control of your environment, simplifying decision-making processes and taking control of your own emotions. If you are a student, your tensions will be greatly relieved by learning to really enjoy your studies, remember the essence of what you read and hear, and take tests in a relaxed, effective way. Really enjoying is probably most important here, as much tension is caused by putting off studying and resenting it so much that you actually fight your own efforts to learn. Anything you enjoy flows more easily than something you hate and will certainly not be put off to the last minute. As an added benefit, by developing the will to learn (a hunger for knowledge as strong in your mind as the hunger for food is in your body), you will have a method of gaining for yourself anything that can be taught—how to be a carpenter, actor, doctor, lawyer, how to make a million dollars or be a better mother. All these can be learned from books, tapes, classes. And what you will love doing may bring you excitement, but not the kind of tension which gives you ulcers or a nervous breakdown.

The Bronze Key also offers stress reduction through allowing you to make personally satisfying decisions, by determining if there is a conflict between your conscious and sub-conscious (hidden, deeper) desires, resolving that conflict, and allowing your complete mind to move in one direction. Take a moment and press your palms together. Press hard. Getting anywhere? No? Right. And it's taking quite a bit of effort to do it. That's frustrating and nothing is more negatively stressful than frustration. The same thing happens when you try to study because you know you have a test tomorrow, while your gaze keeps drifting out the window. You consciously want to pass the test, while subconsciously wanting to go to the beach. You accomplish neither. Through hypnosis you find out what your subconscious mind wants through ideo-motor response—your right finger (if you are right-handed) automatically jumping up for "yes" while your left finger jumps for "no." You can then convince your subconscious mind to accept a compromise such as beach later (without guilt) for studying now. The whole process is greatly simplified here, of course. A seminar is available on mediation between conscious and sub-conscious desires, through the Success Center.

Environmental control is achieved in part by vividly imagining your ideal room, the room which represents the life-style you wish to lead, suggesting that you will do everything in your power— mentally, physically, and emotionally to make it a reality. The room, of course, will change over time as your goals change. The same techniques can be applied to any life goal by envisioning the desired reality on a screen in your room. Draw it into your life by using the above suggestion.

Finally, emotional awareness, control, and expression is the ultimate answer to stress. By inducing each emotion—sadness, happiness, anger, love, fear, and insecurity—analyzing its physical and mental effects, then releasing it by neutralizing each physical and mental symptom one by one, it is possible to eliminate unproductive stress reaction from any emotion. The following Bronze Sample Suggestions may also be used to eliminate negative stress and enhance the positive.

> *I feel a deep hunger for knowledge, a hunger in my mind as strong as any hunger in my body. This hunger remains with me, and grows stronger with each passing day until it is as strong as I wish it to be. I will feed this hunger each and every day through reading, listening, learning, and gathering information in every way that I can.*
>
> *I will create a room in my mind that expresses the life style I wish to lead.*
>
> *When I experience the emotion of sadness I use it to help understand myself better. When it ceases to be productive, I release it. I release it by releasing each physical and mental symptom, one by one.*
>
> *The emotion of happiness is part of my Natural State, part of the state I'll be in most of the time, part of the state to which I'll return after the more intense emotions have passed. The ability*

to give and receive love is part of my Natural State.

In my Natural State I am calm, confident, competent.

The Bronze Key is the most important, as it is the one which teaches the basic skills which will be used in all other sessions. It is the only one I will cover in detail.

Copper Key:
Memory Enhancement.

This key enables you to get into direct contact with your subconscious memory source. Everything you've ever seen, heard, read, or experienced has been recorded on your subconscious mind. It can be removed only through such physical means as brain injury or stroke. Any other kind of "forgetting" is merely the burying of information on some level of mind not reachable in an ordinary conscious state. Through hypnosis you can program your subconscious computer to automatically make such information available at conscious need—names, faces, history lessons, teacher's lectures or yesterday's market quotes will appear clearly and accurately whenever you feel the need. Have you ever felt the frustration of trying to recall something you really needed and can almost get at? This key can almost completely eliminate that problem and its accompanying stress.

Photographic memory, speed-reading, and the ability to record a teacher's lecture in your mind are all part of this key.

Sample suggestions in the Copper Key are:

I see the question and the answer comes.

I hear the question and the answer comes.

I need to know and I do know.

I see the face and I know the name.

I hear the name and I see the face.

The faster I read the more I remember, the faster I read the more I understand.

Silver Key:
Creativity

This key is actually many keys since it is different for writers, actors, speakers, singers, artists, interior decorators, etc. Specific sets of four sessions have been developed for each of these and many others.

Working out tensions by creative self-expression is as productive as it is traditional. Camelot's "What Do the Simple Folk Do to help them escape when they're blue? They whistle,...dance,...sing..." is probably historically accurate. Musicians often work out frustrations on their instruments, sometimes creating their greatest masterpieces in the process— witness Greig's *Peer Gynt*. This comes under the heading of using stress in a positive way. We mortals may not create the work of a Greig from our upsets, but we can certainly learn to work them out in similar fashion. And, who knows what hidden talents lie in our beings?

The Silver Key can be geared towards improving the student's ability to write a creative essay/speech, instilling a habit pattern of creative expression rather than nervous fidgeting or physical distress, or removing writer's (or artist's) block and allowing the subject to call on inspiration at will.

This last is extremely important for tension reduction. An individual who is used to dealing with his problems in a creative way and suddenly can't is like a pressure cooker ready to explode. Those tensions have to go somewhere and, deprived of their usual outlet, the blocked creator can become anything from depressed to psychotic. A regression removes the block. The next couple of sessions keep it from returning.

Naturally, many people take this key simply to improve their abilities in the creative pursuit of their choice, rather than due to any block. The sessions are geared to the needs and abilities of the individual, whether that be someone with the talent of a Mozart or the child trying to learn to play a violin. Complete seminars are available in each special talent this Key enhances.

Sample suggestions in the Silver Key are:
I need to create.

I need to create and I need to share that creativity with others (by selling my art work, getting speaking engagements, etc.)

Gold Key:
Body Awareness and Control.

This Key includes deep body awareness and control of physical functioning, from producing anesthesia to improving athletic ability.

Through this key it is possible to control one's blood pressure by suggesting dilation or constriction of blood vessels. I love the reaction that gets from nurses trying to take my blood pressure!

The Gold Key enables the client to bring previously autonomic bodily functions under conscious control. All physical effects of stress fall into this category and can be eliminated in this way.

One technique for achieving this is to take a "fantastic voyage" through your own body mentally and determine what changes must be made and how to accomplish them.

The highly stressful condition of physical pain can be completely controlled by hypnotic suggestion.

On a lighter topic, the athlete under stress to play well can relieve it by playing better than ever before as he relaxes. Whatever the mind imagines, the body will do.

One girl came to me for help in releasing her

fears of skiing before her boyfriend began teaching her. She envisioned herself skiing beautifully, gracefully. She imagined it so vividly that by the time she got out on the slopes with her boyfriend, she was better than he was!

The Gold Key can help relieve the stresses of childbirth, giving the mother the ability to eliminate pain while maintaining both consciousness of the experience and capability to cooperate with the doctor or midwife (pushing, etc).

The most popular use of the Gold Key is in changing the body's metabolism so as to lose weight more easily. This is done strictly through suggestion with none of the dangerous drugs sometimes used by desperate dieters. The body now cooperates with them in weight loss, from making the best use of exercise to appetite control. It takes a lot of the stress out of this experience, as does the regression which removes any emotional blocks to weight loss.

Sample suggestions in the Gold Key are:

Whatever my mind can conceive, my body will do.

My body metabolism adjusts itself for the quickest safe weight loss.

I react to emotional stress with physical relaxation and problem solving behavior.

Platinum Key:
Psychic Development

This key includes past life regression, telepathy,

astral projection, precognition, and a variety of other psychic abilities. Most people take this regression to explore the unknown, but frequently find that regaining past skills and knowledge has practical value. One student who originally came in to improve an inadequate beginning speaker's style regained the skill he had had as an ancient Greek statesman. From getting a "D" at mid-semester, this student finished with an "A" plus a degree of Honor in the National Forensic League. Did he really relive a previous life or was this knowledge simply buried in subconscious experiences of this life? A researcher might be concerned about this. All I care about as a therapist is that it worked.

This student greatly reduced his tensions about public speaking—today he is a lawyer. In other cases I've used the past life regression specifically for stress reduction, treating past life experiences just as we do those of this life in regular regressions. It works.

I won't go into the development of psychic abilities here except to say that I believe everyone has them to one degree or another and can learn to use them effectively through methods such as this key.

Diamond Key:
Success

This Key begins by removing all blocks to your

personal and/or business success through a success regression. You go back to each incident in your life in which your reactions caused you to accept and expect failure instead of striving for success. You relive these incidents in your Natural State. Many students have started on the road to school and job mediocrity or worse based on their reaction to a thoughtless word. Through hypnotic regression, each such incident can be relived in a positive way. The negative evaluation of an authority figure—teacher, parent, etc.—is transformed from a prophesy of failure which our acceptance makes a reality into a challenge to succeed. Time and again the regression reveals a single negative experience which triggered all the rest. We rewrite each one of them through the years until the transformation becomes automatic and the client's self-image shines forth with the joy of expected, achieved, success.

The next couple of sessions are aimed at the development of specific techniques for accomplishing each client's individual goals or those of the particular group being addressed. A salesman, Ken, for example, learned to be a dynamic closer. He would see a customer's need, determine whether his product would best fit that need, and, if so, radiate his intense belief in the need for his product so strongly that the customer would believe it too, and BUY. We also changed cold calls from a dreaded task to an exciting challenge he could look forward to and do more effectively than ever before. His commissions tripled in the period of a year.

On a more personal level, Bob, who had never been able to establish a successful relationship, had a regression geared towards removing the barriers to loving and being loved. Rewriting his reaction to being rejected by an early girl-friend involved experiencing that rejection as a learning opportunity to improve future relationships, while his own self-esteem remained intact. His skill sessions allowed him to mentally rehearse his behavior in the positive, fulfilling relationship he was now ready for. Bob, who had never kept a relationship together for more than six weeks, has now been married five years and is the proud father of two children.

Failure is stressful and draining. The salesman who loses a deal by radiating nervousness and using poor communication techniques probably uses up more energy than does the positive person whose enthusiasm for his product is so contagious that his customer can't wait to buy it. Let go of failure images. Even if failure happens, use it as a learning experience.

Helping Key

Nurses, doctors, dentists, parents, counselors, hypnotherapists, and anyone who helps others will benefit from this key. It includes increasing empathy, improving communication techniques, and enhancing particular skills of use to the "helper" in his own line of work. Helpers frequently run into stresses leading to "burnout." Converting such reactions to positive ways of responding to the needs of others, while not neglecting your own needs, is achieved through a regression under this key. Psychic diagnosis and healing can also be covered here—many nurses are discovering benefits in "the healing touch." Most importantly, the Helping Key teaches you to help others turn **STRESS TO SUCCESS.**

DR. BLAINE N. LEE
Skills for Living
555 South State
Orem, UT 84058
(801) 423-1212

Dr. Blaine N. Lee

Dr. Lee believes you were born to succeed in your career and in your life.

In 1983, Dr. Lee founded Skills for Living, a professional consulting company which offers seminars, workshops and private coaching for CEOs and top level corporate management. Specialties include: strategic planning, product and market analysis, stress management, personal and human resource development and sales management training.

Dr. Lee is President of Speakers Who Change Lives, A Professional Speaker's Bureau which trains, coaches, books and markets professional speakers. He has coached beginners to become professionals who earn over one million dollars per year. Executive Plaza, his professional toll free answering service, offers office and fulfillment of orders for speakers and other businesses with national clienteles.

Dr. Lee has worked with hundreds of teenagers, parents and school districts throughout the United States as the Education Director for Provo Canyon School, a residential high school for teenagers who had not been successful in public schools. He teaches the principles of personal change, psychology and leadership seminars and is a faculty member at Texas Lutheran College, Utah Valley Community College, the United States Air Force Academy and Brigham Young University.

Dr. Lee, a National Speakers Association professional has written numerous books, college texts and articles sharing his belief that each person has divine, unlimited potential. He was designated an Outstanding Young Man of America in 1978 and again in 1985.

Dr. Blaine Lee has committed his life to being a LifeCoach, for those who desire excellence in their personal and professional lives. He and his wife Shawny live near Salem, Utah, where they are the proud "coaches" of eight children— seven sons and one daughter.

20

A Stress Primer
by Dr. Blaine Lee

*"The only difference between a diamond
and a lump of coal is that the diamond
had a little more pressure put on it."*
—Anonymous

A billboard in my hometown reads "STRESS? We
Can Help." Below the words is a six foot long candle
which is lit and burning at both ends. The advertise-
ment is sponsored by the Mental Health Division of
the county hospital. Stress and stress management

have indeed become commonplace issues in the world today.

As I am writing this, I feel pressure. This chapter was due at the publisher's last week. There is a stack of unpaid bills on the desk next to my word processor. I hear my wife in the other room talking with one of our sons about his grades. Our youngest is crying upstairs. The phone is ringing. Another son is bouncing his basketball waiting for a ride to the gym. It is not easy parenting eight children. I am the professional—I am supposed to have all the answers. I am supposed to be a master at the juggling routine required of a modern parent. As I am thinking about my family I hear a loud ringing. Within a few seconds I realize it is our fire alarm. The house! It's on fire!

I charge out of my office and see the smoke. My heart leaps in my chest and I have trouble breathing. And then I see...it is only our fireplace, pouring smoke into the family room because of a downdraft in the chimney. I return to the fire alarm and deactivate it. Sitting back at the word processor, my mind is racing and I have difficulty concentrating. I am experiencing stress.

What Is Stress, Anyway?

When I am teaching stress management seminars, attendees sometimes describe their stress as though it were a tangible thing. "I have too much stress," they complain. Or they talk about the stress they feel because of a particular person or event or circumstance. "My new job is just too stressful..."

Stress is a description of our perceptions about and reaction to something. Stress is not some tangible thing lurking out in the world, waiting to get us. But its effects certainly are tangible.

There are many potentially stressful things in life, but whether or not they actually create stress is dependent on two things—when they occur and what they mean to us. It is often our perception of those events that determines whether they are stressful to us. For example, is a raincloud stressful? Perhaps so, if you have a Springtime wedding reception about to begin in your backyard. Perhaps not, if you are stranded in a rubber raft in the ocean, about to die of thirst. How about getting a raise? That could be stressful if it means uprooting your family and moving across the country. To someone who desperately needs the money, however, it might be a reason for celebrating. The difference has nothing to do with rainclouds or raises—the difference is in us.

I call anything external or internal that can have an effect on us a Stressor. Stressors may or may not cause stress, depending on what the event means to us. The death of a spouse or loved one is probably the greatest stressor possible for most people. Other personal traumas and tragedies have a similar effect. Getting a new job or a promotion can also be stressful. Getting a traffic ticket, remembering a missed appointment, even celebrating a holiday like Christmas can be stressful. Stressors often come with a change of some kind in our routine; death, trouble with a boss, being fired, jail detention, sexual difficulties—all can signal stress.

How Much Is Too Much?

Most people feel they have some capacity for dealing with stress. They know when they are having a "hard day" or "easy day," for example. But it is hard to measure the stress. It may be helpful to think about stress in imaginary "stress units." Suppose that the amount of energy or personal resources it took just to function from day to day could be measured and calculated in these "stress units." Although days vary, just suppose that an average day took 100 stress units. Now any day that was "easy" on you might only take 75 units. That left 25 units for a reserve.

But sooner or later you have a day that is just awful. It is so bad that it takes 150 units. If you have built up some reserves, you may experience discomfort but you survive the day. If you have few reserves, or a number of hard days in a row, you may "overdraw your account." Emotional bankruptcy occurs when you have more demands placed on you than you can handle. Rage, nervous breakdowns, flying off the handle, even suicide can result when you exceed your capacity.

There are two direct solutions, both of which require a change in your lifestyle. The first is to build up reserves so that your capacity to handle stress is increased. The second is to take specific action to reduce the stressors in your life so that you almost never have a "150 unit day." Effective stress management requires that you either increase your capacity or reduce life's demands on you, or both.

In this chapter I share specific steps you can take today to manage your stress by changing the quality of your life. Effective stress management can be summed up in one word—lifestyle.

Is Stress Bad?

Many people believe stress is bad and should be eliminated. But is it? Research with athletes has shown that a certain amount of stress is essential for peak performance. There is an edge in a winning performance that comes from the pressure. Some weightlifters live by the motto, "No pain—no gain." I believe this statement is at least partially true. Especially in muscle development, an optimum amount of weight or resistance promotes the fastest growth. Without resistance or pressure, no strength develops. Too little pressure and performance diminishes. But with too much pressure, performance drops again. With optimum pressure performance peaks.

This phenomenon seems to be true in our lives as well as our bodies. Volunteer organizations often live by the dictum, "Ask a busy person to do it—they know how to find the time to get things done." With some pressure, such as a deadline, or a budget limit, or the critical observation of a competitor, we tend to do better. So stress, in the right proportions, may not always be bad.

But stress in strong doses can destroy you. High blood pressure, heart problems, ulcers—all are the result of excessive stress and a high-risk lifestyle.

Thresholds—A Matter of Timing

We all have different stress thresholds. What that means is that some have great capacity to deal with stress and others can be destroyed by the slightest thing.

A college coed winces to wake up to a blemish on her cheek the day of the prom; a wealthy friend sees his million dollar corporate mountain retreat buried by an avalanche one week after it is finished; a mother with small children contracts terminal cancer—which is the most stressful? Sometimes it seems that the smaller items, inconveniences and nuisances in our lives cause us the most trouble. The wealthy man had insurance and the means to replace his building. The mother had a loving husband, supportive family and religious faith to strengthen her through her difficult trial. But the teenager's blemish? It just might push her to the brink.

When I was teaching college I would administer a stress test to each class each semester. I would continually be amazed that some people who were carrying very heavy personal loads sometimes functioned much better than others who really had very little to complain about in their lives. Each student's threshold, or the point at which the stress became "too much," was quite different.

It is helpful to distinguish between contributing and precipitating stressors. Once you understand them, you are well on the road to having increased control over your performance and your life. Everyone has the capacity to handle some difficulties. But when that capacity is exhausted, then the smallest event can trigger an emotional and psychological overload. The final "straw that broke the camel's back" is a precipitating cause. It pushed you over the brink, although by itself, or under normal circumstances, it would not have been difficult to deal with.

I first learned about stress management when I was a teenager growing up in Southern California.

I got the lead! Me, the male lead in the senior class

play! I could hardly wait for track practice to finish so I could hurry home to tell my family. Bursting with excitement, I rushed into the house. My mother took one look at me and shouted, "Son, lie down on the floor."

"What? Mom, wait 'till you hear what's happened!"

"Lie down . . . right now."

"Mom—"

"Don't talk . . . don't move . . . just let go and relax. I'll be back in five minutes," she said as she went into the kitchen.

I stretched my 6 foot frame on the living room floor and waited, puzzled. Gradually, my heart slowed, my breathing evened out, and I started to relax. I began to wonder, "What was the rush all about?"

A few minutes later, my mother came back into the room with a grin on her face. "Feel better, don't you?" Yawning, I nodded.

"How did you know I needed that?"

"It's hard to be in a hurry when you are relaxed . . ." she answered.

She was right, and I had just completed my first lesson in stress management.

Years later I would conduct stress and performance training for thousands throughout the country. But what I learned from a wise mother still provides the foundation for everything I know about increasing capacity for dealing with stress. You cannot be uptight and relaxed at the same time. Your body just can't do it. So if you can learn how to relax, when you are under pressure you can change your response pattern by relaxing on cue.

The Plimsoll Line

During the war, the British Navy had difficulty determining how heavy a cargo to load on each ship. Too light a cargo would be poor economics; too heavy a cargo would jeopardize the safety of the ship and the lives of the crew. An overloaded ship had insufficient bouyancy and when storms arose at sea, the ship might be lost. A Navy officer by the name of Plimsoll finally came up with a simple way to solve the problem. He ordered his ship into drydock. Then he had maintenance crews paint a line on the side of the ship at a preset distance from the bottom of the keel. When the ship was placed back in the water, the line became a guide for determining how heavy the ship was. As the cargo was brought aboard, the ship would gradually lower further and further into the water. When the painted line was level with the water, the loading stopped. To go further would be dangerous.

I have advised many clients that they needed to determine where their "Plimsoll line" was. Knowing this threshold, you can take action to stay in control of your life.

Similar to the Plimsoll line, all of us need to know when we have taken on too much. We then must say no. For many people, this is difficult to do. They feel that they are betraying or letting down others when they do not accept every job and task that comes along. An insight that may be helpful is to think about the many things saying "No" makes possible. That is, when we say "No" to some things, that gives us the freedom and right to say "Yes" to others. There is great freedom in that awareness.

Executive Monkeys

Some years ago, a scientist investigating the effect of pain on stress conducted an interesting experiment. He placed two monkey cages side by side. Each cage had a metal grid on the bottom. A wire was connected to each grid so that a mild electric current could be applied. When the current was turned on, it went to both cages at the same time. One monkey was then put in each cage. Periodically, the monkeys got a shock which was unpleasant but not harmful. The scientist moved the switch near one cage, so that one monkey could turn the electricity off if the shock became painful. When the monkey turned the switch off, the shock stopped in both cages.

When the electricity was on, both monkeys jumped. After awhile, however, the monkey who could reach the switch started acting funny. He would jump up and down, run around the cage, scratch all over and squeal—even when there was no current. The other monkey acted normal and would play except when the current was on. The scientist was puzzled because both monkeys were experiencing the same amount of "pain." Why would one monkey act different?

The answer came as a surprise. Medical examination showed that one of the monkeys actually developed ulcers during the experiment! Can you guesss which one? Many people guess that the monkey who was a "victim," and could do nothing about the shocks, would suffer greater stress.

Actually, it was the other monkey, who came to be known as the "Executive Monkey," who had the highest stress. The executive monkey appeared worried about turning off the switch, even when it wasn't on. He would touch the switch many times each hour and demonstrate erratic behavior before and after the shock.

One of the conclusions of the experiment was that it is not the difficulty of the hardships we experience that is so tough on us, but it is our anticipation and concern for them that is so hard. The more we can detach from difficult situations, thoughts and events, the better we are able to cope with them. Are there "switches" in your life that you are struggling to control?

Learning to Relax

One of the best ways to develop emotional reserves is to learn a variety of relaxation techniques. There are many types of relaxation. You can take control of your body and your mind, if you know how.

Biofeedback techniques are ways of learning to tune in to your body by receiving biological feedback. Biofeedback can help you increase the times and ways you relax. There are very sophisticated as well as relatively simple devices which can be used to signal the mind that the body is relaxing. Meditation has a similar effect of clearing the head and body. For many people, prayer has a relaxing effect, if it is sincere and heartfelt, regardless of any specific religious affiliation. Listening to great classical music, being in the out-of-doors, viewing beautiful works of art—these work for many. Being in the mountains, or watching ocean waves works for others. The specific stimulus doesn't seem to be as important as the nature of the experience.

Once you have learned to relax in one setting, you can transfer those feelings and responses to other situations. Then when you feel uptight, recall and/or recreate those feelings and responses and the anxiety response disappears. Remember, you cannot be uptight and relaxed at the same time. It is impossible. That gives *you* the final vote in determining whether to be happy or miserable.

How to Say "No"

Economics students are taught the principle of "opportunity cost." This is a simple concept which demonstrates that with limited resources a choice to do something is a simultaneous choice to not do many other things. Suppose you have $5. What could you do with it? Spend it. Invest it. Go to a movie. Donate it to a charity. Give it away. Buy penny stocks. But whatever you choose to do with the money makes the other choices disappear. Spending or investing the money in one way is the price you pay to not being able to use that time in other ways. Most people find that it is easier to reduce stressors than to increase capacity.

By saying "No" to some things, you are then free to say "Yes" to other things which are more important to you. Be motivated by the possibility of saying "yes" rather than being discouraged by the many things you will be saying "No" to. Saying "No" may mean the loss of a job, loss of a spouse, loss of an opportunity. *But the "Yesses" that are left will be a delight.*

Our Father, when we long for life without difficulties, remind us that oaks grow strong in contrary winds and diamonds are made under pressure. With stout hearts may we see in every calamity an opportunity, and not give way to the pessimist that sees in every opportunity a calamity.

—Senate prayer by Chaplain **Peter Marshall**

PATRICIA R. WELLING
Patricia R. Welling & Associates
8931 Appleknoll Lane
Cincinnati, OH 45236
(513) 984-3039

Patricia Welling

Patricia Welling is a nationally recognized professional speaker, consultant, seminar leader, sales trainer, and communication specialist in the education, health care, industrial and financial markets. She is on the faculty of Fred Pryor Seminars, Inc. and annually conducts over one hundred fifty seminars nationwide. Her presentations include "How to Manage the Office Staff," "Professional Development for the Senior Level Secretary," "How to Work with People," and "Professional Skills for the Woman Achiever."

Ms. Welling maintains a private consulting and training business with corporations such as Procter and Gamble, Blue Cross, Blue Shield, ARA Services, Council on Aging, Citizens State Bank, Indiana Bell, and Cincinnati Board of Realtors. In 1983 she completed an eight-month contract with Avon Products, Inc, implementing two-day professional development seminars for their managers.

As a certified managing consultant with Performax Systems International, Ms. Welling shares her concept of the development of the "Whole Person" in working extensively with sales training motivation and management communications programs. These programs and seminars focus on increasing the effectiveness of persuasive communication skills. Her use of self-discovery learning instruments opens the door to greater understanding of self and others to build and maintain self-esteem.

Patricia Welling is a member of the American Society of Training and Development and served on the Board of Directors of the Ohio Speakers Forum, 1983-1985. As a member she addressed the National Speakers Annual Convention in Chicago in 1982 and in Washington, D.C. 1985.

Patricia Welling resides in Cincinnati, Ohio, with her husband and four children.

21

Crisis: The Birth of a Career
by Patricia Welling

*"There is no man but that I may learn
something from him, and in that I am
his pupil."*
—Walt Whitman

"You have to feel it to create it."
—Patricia Welling

CANCER—Does it mean sickness? Does it mean change? Does it mean focusing on your needs? It is a critical incident which generates a significant emotional event. Then there are choices to make.

How do I go about dealing with the changes that will occur because of the reality that a member of my family has cancer?

Crisis #1: Don's Career

On July 15, 1982 at eleven o'clock in the morning, I received a phone call from my husband, Don, with the poignant words, "Patti, you won't believe it; I don't have a job." After twelve years of loyalty with an international firm, many awards and promotion to branch manager, Don Welling was faced with that much-asked question, "Is this all there is?"

For me, as a wife and mother of four children, this was a critical incident, a significant emotional event. On the phone, motionless as I listened to the pain in the voice of the man I loved, I made a vow to myself. I call this a mental affirmation. The voice inside of me said loudly and clearly, regardless of the outcome for Don, the family's standard of living and income will increase. I didn't know how. That was unimportant. I simply knew that it would be.

As the days passed, the family experienced unanswered questions, many expressed and un-expressed feelings—much ambiguity. Where would Don get another comparable position? Would he work for himself? How would I step up my speaking and consulting business? What about the mortgage, car and utility payments, the cost of education for four children? How long would the money last? As we delved deeper and deeper into the profit-sharing, the questions mounted.

A Ray of Hope

Then, as if by some miracle, I received a phone call in January of 1983 from Bill Rezmerski, now the president of Performax Systems International, Inc. His call was to ask me if I was interested in an eight-month contract working with Avon Products, Inc., as a trainer implementing A.C.T. (Avon Career Training) for their managers. Any one of us in business for ourselves knows how rare it is to get such a call with no previous initiation. My answer, of course, was affirmative. It was during this same time period that Don joined PS Group, a full-line dealership in office furnishings and signage, as a manufacturer's representative. And so, both of us self-employed, we set out to weather our financial crisis.

Little did we realize that the change in the dynamics of our family structure was powerful enough to be a contributing factor in the next life-altering event. It was as if the critical incident of 1982 was an antecedent in preparation for what manifested itself on April 29, 1985. One of the most dreaded, detested words in the English language, sometimes called "the big one," had struck home...

CANCER.

As Don's career crisis was just starting to mellow out, another jolt was whirled upon him. After being hit with a racquetball in the upper left thigh in the latter part of the winter of '85, a soft billowy mass appeared in that area. Don, maintaining perfect health all of his life, thought he had a hematoma. He found it totally appropriate to have his brother, a surgeon, schedule outpatient surgery for him on April 29, 1985. On that early Monday morning in Good Samaritan Hospital in Cincinnati, Ohio, Dr. Richard E. Welling operated on his brother, Don.

Crisis #2: Don's Health

The anguish on Richard's face is a vivid memory as I recall our meeting in the hallway immediately following the surgery. Slowly shaking his head from side to side, with tears rolling down his cheeks, he told me the news. "Patti, this is serious. In all of my years in surgery, I have hardly seen anything like it." After embracing each other, we slowly walked into a conference room where we could make our plans. How do we tell Don? What do we say? When? What are the next steps? What about the children? His parents? Where do we go from here? And, of course, are you sure it is *cancer*? Is it possible that it is not? Dick scheduled an appointment for Don and me the following afternoon at 3 p.m. with Dr. James Hall, an oncologist. At this meeting Don would be officially told the prognosis and the further recommended treatment.

Being an outpatient, Don left the hospital that same Monday afternoon of the surgery, only to return the following day to hear the fateful news. As 3 p.m. approached, the expressions on the faces of those involved in the meeting were extremely glum. I saw not a ray of hope anywhere. And as I reflect now, I believe that is what I regret the most. I regret the fact that, regardless of the statistics, the severity of the condition, very little optimism was expressed in any form—body language, words. In a grave manner, Don was told. It was suggested that if at all possible Don be admitted to the National Cancer Institute (NCI), National Institutes of Health (NIH) in Bethesda, Maryland, where they were utilizing the most advanced methods of treatment for this type of cancer. They thought that Don had senovial sarcoma, one of the rarest forms of cancer. Of course, this would be confirmed by additional pathology reports, as would the grade of malignancy (the degree of severity based on a scale of 1-4).

After the grim news, we were left alone to deal with our pain. Don looked rather stunned and pale as he uttered the words to me, "Patti, I have cancer, I have cancer—how can this be? I have hardly been sick a day in my life. This just can't be, What are we going to do?" I was very quiet, listening. This is unusual for me, being a speaker. What could I say to any human being—let alone my own husband—that just found out they had the worst illness known to mankind? I do recall saying that I thought it best that Don consider going through the additional treatment they suggested, at the same time investigating other methods of treatment less aggressive. Somehow additional cutting, burning and poisoning of the human specimen seemed atrocious to me, being health-conscious and prevention-oriented.

As we quietly removed ourselves from the small room, Don's brother met us in the hallway. He offered to go home with Don and help him inform the children. My wonderful, loving, caring parents, Ethel and Elmer Romes, were with the children. As Don and Dick approached our house, the children were all gathered together out on the deck. At that time their ages were Marisa, 15; David, 11; Elizabeth, 8; and Emily, 5; four beautiful children all totally in love with their father. My parents came outside to join the group and Dick proceeded. My mother said it was handled eloquently by Dick, and the children took it quite well. She said it was a very poignant moment when Marisa threw her arms around her father, sobbing, "I love you, Dad. I love you."

Regretably, I had to wait until 10 p.m. to share the pain with my family. Fortunately or unfortunately, I am in a business where there is a bottom-line premise that "The Show Goes On"—regardless. In most of my seminars I define "professional"...a person who is able to do what needs to be done even if they don't feel like doing it. At 7 p.m. that very evening I was the only speaker at a women's career symposium. I had to be there. Yes, I have to practice the words I share with my participants. I did have a few moments to pick up my associate, Jane Paris, who assists me in my business. On the way to the symposium, it was therapeutic to share with Jane the current significant emotional event we were experiencing. I have always found that ventilating—verbally expressing with or without tears to a significant other—to be extremely important in the healing process.

As the days passed and the family was adjusting to the reality of the situation, word was received that Don could be scheduled on May 21st at NIH for the second surgery. After much investigation of alternative methods, including a macrobiotic diet and a private consultation with a macrobiotic counselor, the 21st was set.

Crisis #2 Escalates

It was early evening on May 15 when I entered the Ramada Inn on Wisconsin Avenue in Bethesda, Maryland, to join Don. He was required to be at the

NIH several days prior to surgery to be checked thoroughly for acceptance into the protocol best suited for his specific case. I had just arrived by public limousine from Richmond, Virginia, after presenting a six-hour seminar, which ironically had been scheduled in this close proximity to Bethesda for months.

As Don welcomed me into our new "temporary abode," he said, "Patti, I think you better sit down." He then gave me an account of his day. He said after several tests and scans, a team of three surgeons were looking over his left leg, scrutinizing the afflicted area, when a fourth surgeon arrived. Don said he was well over six feet and, in a deep powerful voice asked, "Did your brother tell you anything about further treatment?" Don replied that his brother had told him about additional surgery, radiation and chemotherapy. As the new person in the room towered over Don, lying on an observation table, he asked again, "Did your brother say anything about amputation?" Don, reeling from the shock, uttered a negative response. With that the "Big Guy" walked out of the room and the rest of the group followed momentarily.

We had to live with the ambiguity of their proposed treatment until 5:30 p.m., Monday, May 20, the afternoon before surgery. Preceding this private consultation with Dr. Chang, the head surgeon over Don's case, a most unique experience occurred.

Don was presented center stage, spotlighted, amphitheater style, on a roll-in bed, garbed only in a hospital gown, to all of the NIH staff personnel involved in his case. They had just reviewed in unison all of the pertinent data affecting his medical history. Now they wanted to hear the story again, first-hand from Don. There were approximately forty persons gathered, firing questions at him in succession. At the conclusion Dr. Chang asked Don if there was anything else he would like to add. Don replied, "Yes, I am a young man, forty-one years old, active, athletic. I play golf, racquetball and coach my son's sports teams. Please decide to spare my leg and do limb salvage surgery. I need my leg. Please..." As I sat in awe in a corner of that stage, I felt privileged to have witnessed the most touching, heartfelt, articulate speech of my life in that of Don Welling's plea for his leg.

The Verdict...

It was a fifty-fifty vote of the "select group" to do limb salvage surgery. Dr. Chang in final analysis called the shot—Limb Salvage Surgery. Dick had just arrived to be present for the edict and was privy to some details of surgery, scheduled for the following day. One hitch—a spot on a top right rib was looking possibly "suspicious." A team of chest surgeons would remove that small piece of rib simultaneously.

After four long hours, excellent news was released. The surgery went better than expected and all negative margins were found. The rib looked like scar tissue from an old injury. The pathology report would have to confirm that. Dick and I, sighing breaths of relief, went into Intensive Care to see Don.

Don recovered from surgery remarkably well and was told to go home and heal a couple or more weeks and return for the "rest" of his treatment. This consisted of being an out patient for thirty-five radiation treatments to the thigh and five chemotherapy treatments, one every four weeks. Homeward bound we were.

Crisis #3: Family Adjustments

Homecoming

During the interval of treatment in Bethesda, the home fires were kept blazing by our parents. Mom and Dad Romes stayed at our house with the children, and Don's parents, Henry and Rosalia Welling were there daily to fill any need. Their love and support brought all of us courage to adjust to our new reality.

As the joy of the homecoming subsided, there were many decisions to be made, many questions to be answered. My greatest concern was renting a house nearby the hospital so that we could be with Don during his treatment. Much energy was invested in letting others know of my need for a temporary location in the Washington, D.C. area. Most discouraged the idea, saying it would be impossible for such a short period of time, five to six weeks.

Believing in the power of affirmations, I only listened to those who encouraged me. One of my encouragers and mentor, Bill McGrane, mentioned our family's plight to an acquaintance at a seminar. On the spot Minnie Spiller said, "I have a summer residence in Linden, Virginia, about sixty miles from the NIH. They are welcome to use it." I called immediately to confirm it. We were getting closer.

Another encourager, Doris Diethrich, from the Nuclear Medicine Branch at the NIH, was successful in locating a house within five miles of the hospital for the required time frame. Don and I had to use our utmost persuasive skills, as this elderly couple vowed never to rent to people with children. Of course we only had four. We did it! They even assisted us in acquiring temporary membership in their Swim Club.

We utilized both houses during that summer, maximizing all that our capital city had to offer. It was a bittersweet summer, mixing the joy with the pain, the tears with the laughter.

Due to chemotherapy, Don was losing some hair. Maintaining our sense of humor was crucial to all of us at this time. One evening as our family was dining in a restaurant, I recall receiving extremely poor service and Don, after speaking to the manager, was walking toward our family seated in a booth when Elizabeth, age eight, exclaimed, "Here comes 'Mohawk'" to which David, age twelve, replied in equal exuberance, "Oh no, he looks more like 'Bald Eagle' now." Emily, age five, always getting into the act, retorted, "Oh no, sillies, it's just Daddy with hair like a baby's." A visit to the wig store where we all modeled every wig in stock was also fun.

Crisis #4: My Career

How did I handle the distress of:
- Don's job loss in 1982?
- Becoming a major breadwinner in 1983?
- Conducting over 100 seminars and speaking dates nationwide in 1984?
- Cancer of spouse in 1985?
- 150 speaking, seminar and consulting dates nationwide in 1985?
- Balancing a family and career 1982-1985?

I had the choice to be immobilized or get moving. Here's what I did:
- Experienced family vacations regardless of

economic circumstances
- Went out to dinner with the whole family
- Attended school and sports events together
- Included children as participants in local seminars
- Scheduled family meetings every Sunday evening
- Kept the lines of communication open during Don's illness
- Allowed myself personal quiet time daily
- Set aside time daily for music appreciation and relaxation
- Kept contact with close friends
- Gave myself positive affirmations frequently
- Spent time with each child one-on-one
- Reacted spontaneously when opportunities presented themselves; i.e. taking daughter Marisa to Paris
- Attended to personal grooming habits, nutrition, and exercise
- Invested daily in my lifelong learning programs; i.e. books, tapes, seminars
- Committed myself spiritually to God

Previously to 1982, I was a wife and mother, and perpetual seminar attendee working parttime at becoming an excellent speaker, consultant, and seminar leader. As a communication specialist, investment dressing consultant and former fashion model, I did have several individual and corporate clients, but certainly not enough to pay the bills.

The Time Had Come

Being a survivor of the fittest, an idealist, and an eternal optimist, the time had come for Patricia to stop "playing" at her work and rise to the occasion. It was then that Avon called.

Based on a conversation in August of 1983 with John Schuster of the Fred Pryor Seminars Faculty in describing the successful outcome of the Avon career training, John said, "I think I'll tell Fred Pryor about you." The rest is history.

I have been on the staff of Fred Pryor Seminars since November of 1983; income from presenting over 200 seminars has buffered much of the distress of our financial situation. During our crisis the entire Fred Pryor staff was most supportive and helpful. They flew me out of Washington National Airport and coordinated their schedule to fit mine.

What Really Counts the Most in Life

During this entire time from 1982 to 1986 I became aware that the highest priority of life is to focus on the ideal for yourself, family, and career. As a result of all of the crises and stress, I designed a career concept that creates greater impact because of the antecedents discovered during this time.

Identify what it is you want to be complete, to be whole for your *ideal* in all phases of your life. Initiate action toward it. Most people do not do this. That is the reason they are not getting the outcomes they want. Whatever they are getting is exactly what they feel they deserve. I do this exercise: Draw several areas of life in pie shaped wedges in a circle in direct proportion to the amount of time spent on them. Seven areas might include physical, mental, spiritual, social, career, financial, family. Then rearrange the pie wedges in proportion to the size you would like them to be.

Do something every single day about what it is you have identified as being your ideal. Be determined and have a definite, precise way of going about it. Watch the outcome to make sure it is exactly what you want to repeat. Ask for your missing piece. Find a mentor to get a perspective on the inconsistencies and balance in your life.

Energy you channel toward your ideal also gives you a level of self-esteem. This perpetuates your desire to do it, even when there is distress, possibly causing you to want to give up and not continue. Test your energy level frequently. How is it? How would you like it to be? Your level of self-esteem determines where you focus your energy.

Attitudes are the way you think. They are a major part of the filters in communication process. In my crises the way I thought was very important because what I thought about gave me my perception of my reality, catapulting me into action.

Love is to be present to the moment, living each moment as if it were the last. It is to accept, to appreciate, to enjoy, to delight, to contemplate. I know my capacity to love based on how present I am to each person in every moment. Saint Bernard quotes, "Love seeks no cause beyond itself and no limit; it is its own fruit, its own enjoyment. I love because I love, I live in order that I may love."

Acceptance

Once I accepted the reality of my crises, opportunities emerged for my growth and the growth of my family. Don's courage and strength inspired all of us at this time.

In the beginning you may have wondered about the word *cancer* and how I immediately left you hanging. When people hear the word cancer, very often they feel anger, fear, rage, disgust, frustration, and a sense of hopelessness. The moment I heard it I immediately looked for the solution.

The Chinese symbol for crisis is opportunity. It

is an opportunity for action. Every step of the way was to get the family moving in the direction of healing.

Now, in looking back over the last four years from 1982 to 1986 I see that the crises became the opportunity which triggered the birth of my career.

In retrospect I can look back now and appreciate that the feedback I received from my seminar participants is a direct result of my decision to take charge of the family income while my husband was creating a new business and recovering from his illness. The intensity of my desire for competence and excellence gave me the freedom to release more of my potential. I totally believe that our family unit remained intact because of the way I chose to be free of distress. Our children became self-sufficient. They learned to deal with reality. They accepted responsibility and we fulfilled our commitment to them as parents by preparing them for life.

> *Calmness is the rarest quality in human life. It is the poise of a great nature in harmony with itself and its ideals. It is the moral atmosphere of a life self-reliant and self-controlled.*
>
> *Calmness is singleness of purpose, absolute conviction and conscious power ready to be focused in an instant to meet any crisis.*
>
> —*from* The Majesty of Calmness
> *by* **William George Jordan**

If a child lives with approval, he learns to like himself.
—Dorothy Law Nolte

H.I. "SONNY" BLOCH
The Action Line Group
1410 15th Street, NW
Washington, D.C. 20005
(202)483-2314

H.I. "Sonny" Bloch

When ABC NIGHTLINE anchorman Ted Koppel and PBS LATE NIGHT AMERICA anchorman Dennis Wholey wanted a nationally known real estate expert to appear on their programs, they went to H. I. "Sonny" Bloch, host of the national television series REAL ESTATE ACTION LINE.

"Sonny" Bloch is known for his expertise in the fields of real estate and building. During his 22 years as a developer, he built 36 communities throughout the eastern United States.

In 1979, Mr. Bloch began a new career as a broadcast journalist with the first real estate two-way talk radio show REAL ESTATE ACTION LINE. This quickly led to a thirty-minute television program of the same name, and a series of television and radio programs including two nationally syndicated shows about animals on PBS and commercial television. He can also be heard on the Associated Press Wide World Network live, coast to coast, each Sunday. Sonny's weekly cumulative audience numbers in the millions in the United States, southern Canada and the Pacific Islands, as well as New York City where he is heard live on WMCA nightly.

Mr. Bloch fulfills over 50 speaking engagements on topics including real estate, sales motivation, animals, communications, entrepreneurism, and working with the press. In addition to his own syndicated real estate column he is a contributing columnist to industry publications, and has received awards from the American Society of Appraisers, American Land Development Association, National Center for Financial Education, and The Humane Society of the United States.

22

The Pet Prescription Works For Stress Relief
by H.I. "Sonny" Bloch

"I have been prescribing pets for my stress patients for years."
—Dr. Arnold Fox
Physician and Author of the best seller
The Beverly Hills Medical Diet

If a friend or stranger tells me that they are feeling stressed from divorce, the loss of a loved one, poor health, financial problems or anything else, I always recommend the PET PRESCRIPTION. Try pets for stress; it works!

The next time that you are feeling down, go to the nearest humane shelter and pet a puppy or a kitten. You'll find that the stress relief is instantaneous. If you are not a dog or cat person, why not get a fish, a bird or even a horse as a pet? They all work for me to reduce that stress in my life and now science agrees.

Mad Scientists or Practical Practitioners?

Stress is a very debilitating, painful, and costly medical condition. We go to psychiatrists and psychologists; we take pills; we take vacations; we get divorces; we pray. We do many things to relieve stress because in addition to being a very painful, expensive medical condition, it can also be life threatening, causing heart attacks, high blood pressure, and depression.

The scientific community has finally admitted that pets have a *measurable* beneficial and positive physiological effect on our bodies. Several university studies have shown that persons with high blood pressure can actually lower their blood pressure by petting an animal.

We have known for centuries that man and beast can live together as friends and neighbors, whether by choice or by chance. Upon examination of the stories in the Bible and the works of Plato, Shakespeare, and some of the other great writers of the world up to the present time, it is very clear that animals have played a very important role in the lives of humans throughout the centuries. The cave man who domesticated the wolf and other small animals must have felt the same tranquility that we feel today as we sit in front of the fireplace stroking our favorite pet.

It is nice to know, therefore, that in this highly technological, scientific world that we live in today, there are people who realize the importance and value of animals in our lives. Dr. Arnold Fox is one of these people, a medical doctor who actually writes prescriptions for his patients under much stress, instructing them to go to their local humane shelter and adopt a pet. He knows from experience that an animal will share their lives and help relieve their stress.

In one case, Dr. Fox prescribed a horse for a particular patient. At the end of the year, the Internal Revenue Service challenged the man because he had listed the cost of purchasing and maintaining the horse as a medical expense. In the end, Dr. Fox and his patient prevailed and the IRS let the man deduct seventy-five percent of the costs incurred from his income tax.

We Kill 15 Million Pets Each Year!

There are approximately fifteen million animals in the humane society shelters who are euthanized each year for lack of anyone to adopt them. There are over fifty million cases of stress reported every year. If thirty percent of those stress patients would try adopting a pet from the animal shelters, we could put an end to the needless deaths of fifteen million animals every year and make millions of people a lot happier in the process.

Love is one of the greatest stress relievers that exists on Earth. Love, however, can also be a great cause of stress. While loving a human being can be very satisfying, loving a pet is not quite as emotionally dangerous. Those of us that have shared our lives with animals would unanimously echo the fact that the love of dog, cat, or bird is uncritical. Your pet will love you and ask nothing in return but food, water, shelter and love.

As the host of two nationally syndicated television series dealing with the world of animals, one on public broadcasting stations and the other on commercial television, I have had the unique opportunity to go into the animal world as an observer. I would like to share with you some first-hand experiences concerning the relationship between man and animals.

Observations of a Television Host

I received a call from my producer one day asking me to meet the television crew at a children's hospital in Washington, D.C. I arrived at the hospital and was shown into a room where there were people with brain damage, cerebral palsy, and other debilitating, mind altering diseases placed in various sections of the room in wheelchairs or if they were unable to sit up, lying on cots. These children did not react to me, the crew, or the staff who were caring for them. The only reaction I could see in them was the involuntary movement caused by their illnesses. The Humane Society in the area has a program set up to bring cats and dogs into the hospital for the children to see and to touch. The moment the animals arrived the children immediately came to life, they laughed and smiled. I asked one of the nurses if this was the usual reaction and she said that yes, these children who are normally in a hopeless catatonic state perk up whenever the pets arrive. What a wonderful testimony for the PET PRESCRIPTION.

The PET Prescription for the Elderly

The largest growing segment of America's population today is the fifty and over age group, and a large portion of these people are in the seventy and over age bracket. Unfortunately, many of these older Americans are confined to nursing homes and medical facilities or are confined to their homes. There is a national program which reaches out to these people called "Pets as Therapy." With this program, volunteers go to the animal shelters and bring cats, dogs, birds, and other small animals to elderly people in nursing homes or in their homes. For shut-ins and elderly people who could not take care of a pet on their own, this is a wonderful program.

When we took our cameras into a nursing home to do a story for our "Pet Action Line" show, we discovered the elderly people anxiously awaiting the arrival of the animals. Residents of the homes who had previously been sitting around with unhappy, bored faces, quickly came to life as the sounds of the approaching animals grew more noticeable. The immediate reaction of these people to the animals was extremely touching and brought tears to the eyes of the crew. I found it difficult to speak as I choked back tears while interviewing one ninety-two year old woman. She said, "I only live for these days when I have the opportunity to play with the dogs and cats." The only problem is getting enough pets to the senior citizens who so anxiously await their visits.

Some life care facilities are now making arrangements for animals to live within the homes. I feel this is an excellent way to solve two serious problems; one, the overcrowding of our animal shelters and two, the loneliness and despair of the elderly.

The PET PRESCRIPTION: Get A Bird

The Maryland Gerontological Association in the City of Rockville, Maryland, with Coordinator of Support Service, Lorraine Schack-Critzer, has put together a program called "Lend a Pet," a program which improves the quality of life of the elderly by providing them with a companion pet on a loan basis. The philosophy of the Lend a Pet program is not for the person to adopt the pet but to borrow it instead. The Association's experience has shown them that elderly people are afraid of making a commitment to a pet for fear of what would happen to it if they should pass away before their pet did. In addition, many older people lack the confidence in their own facilities and doubt whether they would be able to care for an animal on their own.

The program has been very successful, showing that a person who has spent a lifetime loving and caring for others makes an excellent pet owner. In their retirement years, with all of their free time and love to share, a winning situation is created for both senior citizen and animal. Also, research has shown that the life span of an elderly person who has a pet to care for, to interact with, and to love is markedly lengthened. The project places birds and fish with elderly people who are not in life care facilities but are confined to their homes. The local pet store donates animals who have been returned to the store. All animals are initially screened and are taken to the area's senior citizen center where people can come and select a pet. An expert in pet care is on hand to instruct the elderly on the proper care of the animal they select and then the animal is taken to the senior citizen's home to let them "try it out." After several visits are conducted in the home to check the relationship between the animal and the senior citizen, they are given a one month's supply of everything the animal needs. For example, in the case of a bird, the cage, food, gravel, and vitamins would be supplied. After an initial one month trial period, if the senior citizen would like to keep the pet, they can either continue to receive supplies from the center or purchase the food and supplies on their own. Local 4-H club members, Girl Scouts, and Boy Scouts who have been trained in the care of these animals by the pet care expert make regular visits to the senior citizen's home to insure that both pet and pet loaner are happy with the arrangement and are doing fine. This is truly a wonderful example of people-to-people and pet-to-people relationships at work in a truly positive manner. THE PET PRESCRIPTION WORKS!

Research done by the City of Rockville shows that:

- The most popular animal for loan is the parakeet.
- *Ninety percent* of the people borrowing animals keep them and care for them very well.

- The program provides an outlet for the elderly to keep a pet when it normally would be impossible to do so.
- Eating habits improve when the elderly person has a pet since they no longer have to eat alone.
- The pet fills the home nest left empty after the loss of a loved one.
- The recipients have responded to the program with descriptions of their new pet as "devoted friend," "family member," and "entertainment" as these senior citizens can now share their love with an animal.

YOU CAN GET INVOLVED! if you are interested in starting a "Lend a Pet" program in your local senior citizen organization.

The PET PRESCRIPTION On Camera

The lights are hot and beads of sweat are appearing on the forehead of my guest, Nelly, an eighty-two year old woman who is holding in her hands a tiny blue parakeet named Butch. As we speak Nelly caresses Butch and Butch lovingly touches Nelly's lips with his beak the way parakeets do to show their affection to the person they love.

Question: How long have you known Butch?
Answer: About three years.
Question: What was your life like before you met Butch?

Answer: I had trouble sleeping, I had trouble eating, I was always crying because I was so lonely. I have lived alone in this house since my husband passed away.

Question: What is your life like since you adopted Butch?

Answer: We go to bed each night. I say goodnight to him, put the cover over his cage, and then go to sleep myself, knowing that in the morning he will sing to wake me up. I look forward to mealtime now because we eat together, each with our own food. I sometimes let him out of the cage and he eats with me at the table. Sometimes, he even shares part of my breakfast with me. When I leave he says goodbye to me and when I return he says hello. I recommend to anyone who lives alone that they should go to the local humane shelter and adopt an animal to share their life with them. Butch gives me love and asks no questions. All I have to do is look forward to the time that I spend with him. All my life I took care of my husband and my children and now, each and every day, I can look forward to taking care of Butch. I now have a reason to live!

This is typical of the interviews that I have done time and time again with people who, prior to adopting their pet, felt that life was not worth living.

The PET PRESCRIPTION: Stress Cure for Latchkey Children

Dr. Lynette Long, well known for her book *Pets Are*

Wonderful Companions is the world's leading authority on latchkey children, children who must come home to an empty house every day since both of their parents are at work. The situation has been shown to cause a great deal of stress that leaves, in many cases, lifelong scars on the child. Dr. Long feels if the latchkey child comes home to a pet, much of that stress can be reduced. Of course, the animal and the child will also develop a close bond of love and responsibility towards each other.

Dr. Long has treated many children with severe problems caused by the fact that they are alone from the time that they get home from school until the time their parents arrive home from work. If the parents of latchkey children go to the animal shelter and adopt a pet, the life of an animal will be saved and a child will be happier and much more at ease. A dog, especially a large dog, is an excellent companion for a child alone in a house and would serve as good protection against intruders, giving the parents and the child peace of mind.

A Very Large PET PRESCRIPTION: Get A Horse!

Horses are fun, horses are expensive, horses take an enormous amount of time. But did you know that horses are used to eliminate stress in patients with cerebral palsy and other disabilities; the stress caused by the lack of physical activity and frustration of not being able to do the same things that other people can do, who have not had the misfortune of being disabled.

Therapeutic riding is probably one of the most interesting stories that I have ever covered during my last one hundred shows about animals. There is a riding center at Rock Creek Park in Washington, D.C. which has therapeutic riding sessions. The gentleman who initiated the program has a nerve disorder and he began to ride to counteract some of the physical symptoms of his medical problems. Seeing the obvious benefit of horseback riding in his own situation, he decided to start a program where others could reap the same benefits.

The day that we were filming the show, one young man went, before our very eyes, from a terrified, screaming, helpless individual to a self-confident rider astride a 1,200 pound animal, clapping, smiling, and raising his hands above his head like a Roman warrior who had just won the greatest battle of his life.

Riding therapeutically helps these individuals to develop eye-hand coordination, relieves stress, and gives the person a sense of accomplishment. It also enables them to do better in school as well as starting them on their journey into everyday life. Today, we are placing more disabled people into the workforce and this type of program is a great way to show them that they can, in fact, accomplish feats that they once thought were impossible. I refer to this as the VERY LARGE PET PRESCRIPTION.

My Personal PET PRESCRIPTION

You would have to describe me as a dog and horse person as far as the animal world is concerned. About fifteen years ago, I was going through a very difficult time in my life and was fortunate enough to meet a very beautiful quarterhorse named Dunny Goodbar. He and I became very close friends. I cared for him on a daily basis and spent hours riding through the woods, gathering my thoughts and relieving my stress. If you have the time and resources, I strongly recommend this experience to you. During the dark part of my life, when I thought my life was falling apart, I don't know what I would have done without Dunny. I am now thanking him publicly as I have done many times privately. He will always have a special "smile" place in my heart. He served me well and I care for him with all of the love that a human being can give to his animal friend.

From my earliest childhood memories, I remember that we always had pets, everything from dogs and cats to birds and horses. Those animals have proven to me over and over, that a life without animals is an empty and lonely one.

The PET PRESCRIPTION
For the Hard of Hearing or the Deaf

All of us have seen a blind person stopping at a red light on a street corner, coached by his or her dog to go across the street when the light turns green. How many times has a dog saved a person who can not see? Did you know that we now have hearing ear dogs? There are hearing dog programs opening up all over the nation and aside from the extreme cases where a hearing ear dog must warn a person about a fire in the house, there are day-to-day occurrences that hearing people take for granted, that put a hearing ear dog into service for a deaf person. For example, an alarm goes off and the hearing dog wakes you by licking your face. There are trainers that will train these dogs to let you know when the phone is ringing, when someone is at the door, when something is burning in the oven, or when a water faucet is dripping. In one case, a deaf person was also a quadriplegic and her Irish Setter was trained to bring her things as she needed them. Another woman who I interviewed had a dog trained to let her know when her baby was crying, when the tea kettle was whistling, when she dropped her keys on the pavement, and even when an ambulance was approaching so that she could pull over while driving. Besides the fact that the dogs become an extension and a faithful partner in the owner's everyday life, they relieve stress by letting the owner know that they are not helpless, that their dog is there to assist them twenty-four hours a day.

There are thousands of dogs being placed each year through organizations such as the Handy Dogs program in Tucson, Arizona and the Red Acre Farm Hearing Dog Center in Stow, Massachusetts. My personal congratulations and applause goes to the hearing dogs and their trainers who have broken the sound barrier for many deaf people in the country. Now we must continue to spread the word about these wonderful programs. This is a PET PRESCRIPTION that should be mandatory for anyone who wishes to live a full life but cannot hear. It is definitely a situation that benefits both the owner and the dog, an animal finds a home and a human gains a new life.

Pet As Therapy Is Gaining International Momentum

Some of our research done recently has shown that THE PET PRESCRIPTION is gaining worldwide momentum. Scotland, Australia, England, and even Japan are following America's lead by bringing pets into facilities for the elderly as well as into schools and hospitals for children.

Self-Prescribe the PET PRESCRIPTION

Whether you are the President of the United States of America, a lonely senior citizen in South Florida, a corporate executive in New York City, or a lumberjack in Oregon, the PET PRESCRIPTION can work for you.

Don't wait for your doctor to write the prescription. Take advantage of the millions of pets out there looking for a home.

**Bring a pet in the door
and stress will fly out of the window!**

JERI KOPPLEMAN, B.E., C.S.P.
Ragpickers—S.M.I.L.E. Workshops
11025 N. 35th Street
Phoenix, AZ 85028
Bus. (602) 996-1719 • Res. (602) 953-3051

Jeri Koppleman

Jeri Koppleman has experienced miracles in her life. Through goal-setting and positive thinking, she has been able to turn her own negative life and the lives of many others into happy, productive, positive and extremely successful ones.

Jeri grew up in Madison, Wisconsin, received a B.E. there and went on to teach for 15 years. Eager to continue improving herself, she turned toward lectures, workshops and self-improvement books and classes. A second degree led to a consulting firm, a very successful clothing store, and a course on self-confidence and goal-setting which she wrote and used in her elementary school classes.

Discouraged at not being able to teach her course as she wanted to, Jeri left the public schools. After the death of her husband, she moved to Phoenix, where she has set goal after goal and achieved each one.

Jeri and her new husband, Steve Mertes, accomplished what very few people have done. Through various real estate training courses, and using no money of their own, they accumulated nearly $4,000,000 worth of property in the Phoenix area in just 2½ years.

This feat led to a new type of consulting business for them, teaching others how to legally shelter their income from tax-paying, and how to achieve a more desirable lifestyle.

Jeri has appeared on two national television documentaries, including Lifestyles of the Rich and Famous, *and is the current president of the* Phoenix Millionaire's Club.

23

Focus Your Energy— for Stress or Success
by Jeri Koppleman

"Where the attention goes, the energy flows."

—Foster Hibbard

"Could he have known?"

I sat in a state of shock when the doctor answered my question. "No," he informed me gravely. "It would have been impossible for your husband to have known he had cancer even six months ago, much less three years ago. He has a very rare and fast growing type of cancer. If he'd had this cancer more than six months, he would be dead by now."

How then, the thought raced through my mind, could he possibly have told me, almost three years ago, that he would not live past the age of forty? Was it possible that he had predicted, perhaps even planned, his own death? Right down to the very disease that would cause it? Do we set our own life goals—negative OR positive?

The events that followed altered my life and those of my two daughters as nothing else could have. It took me many months after his death to even begin to put together all the pieces of the puzzle. I had heard that stress could cause cancer. I had also heard that people who were not happy with their jobs had a shorter life expectancy than those engaged in doing what they truly enjoyed.

In those succeeding months, when I was completely reorganizing my life and virtually starting over, I had little time or desire to reflect on the past; however, in more recent months, after considerable thought and research, I feel I have come up with some of the answers.

Our life together began in one of the night classes I was taking at the local college. I was in my first semester of classes, taking six credits and working at a full-time secretarial job. He had just dropped out of another college where he had been failing his engineering courses. Now he was beginning again in business administration, also working a full-time job. His real dream, like mine, had been to become a teacher. He really wanted to teach high-school history; he was a whiz at names, dates and events and obsolutely LOVED it.

A Counselor Changed His Life

During his senior year of high school, just before he graduated, a counselor had told him, "History teachers are a dime a dozen," and advised him to forget that field and go into something else like engineering or business administration. So he'd given up his desire to become a teacher—given up the only subject he ever really enjoyed, and enrolled in engineering. It proved to be more than he could handle, especially without the proper math background. After one year, he was failing. He decided to change majors and go in the other direction the counselor had convinced him was "right for him."

Now George never was cut out to be in that field, although he didn't realize it fully until several years out of college. After two unsuccessful job experiences, he was well on his way to getting an ulcer.

By this time, I had graduated with very high honors, obtained an excellent teaching position in a public elementary school, and was beginning to move up the pay scale as quickly as a teacher could back in the sixties. I had three months off every summer with excellent hours and fringe benefits. I was happy with my career and pleased with the way my life was progressing.

The longer I taught, the more George wished he, too, was teaching. So much so, that he finally made the decision he should have made years before to become a teacher. That meant two more years of school and entering the job market when teaching positions were rapidly getting fewer and farther between. He ended up "subbing" his first year and then landed a position in a technical institute. Still not in his beloved field of history, he had to settle for teaching business administration courses.

His Ego Made Him a Workaholic

At the time, I had no idea why he felt it necessary to work a second job, but he was apparently driven to earn at least as much as I was earning. The pay was slightly lower at the technical institute than in the public schools, and being a first year teacher, while I had experienced five pay raises, didn't help his ego.

His second job, the same mechanic's position he had held on a part-time basis since high school, took about thirty hours per week of his time in addition to his full-time teaching position. This meant he worked most of the weekend, every weekend, in addition to many evenings. Sunday was the only day that the entire fleet of trucks was in the garage, so he had to put in long hours that day, eliminating the possibility of attending church with me. In fact, we were able to find little time to spend together at all. When he was home, he liked to work on old cars he collected, or watch football on television. As a result, everything that we accomplished during our marriage was caused by MY desires, and MY energy.

Did I Push Him Out of His Comfort Zone?

I didn't realize it until much later, but it is possible I was continually pushing him out of his comfort zone. I was not content to remain in our first apartment, as he obviously was, but longed for a house, and then yet a larger house. I THOUGHT I was working for the good of us both and our life together, but I didn't realize how deep his convictions were.

Had the truth been known, he would have preferred a wife who didn't work at all; so to have a wife with a better job and more ambition than he had must have been almost unbearable for him. His own father had died at a young age, leaving his mother to work full time while raising him. Could he have resented the fact that she was not around when he was growing up? Especially in an age when

VERY FEW women worked outside of the home? He was NOT the type of person to reveal his feelings about these things, and I doubt that he ever did let anyone know. After carefully analyzing everything that happened, however, it is the only logical conclusion to which I can come.

To make matters worse, I took an interior design course and began a consulting business during my free summer months to keep myself busy and earn extra money. This eventually led me into the apparel business and the opening of a unique clothing store. I subsequently designed a 4000 square foot home, which I subcontracted myself and furnished with lovely handcrafted and imported items from all over the world. I was still teaching full-time and managing the other two businesses simultaneously, and quite successfully, with the help of a friend.

I now realize that George did NOT want me to succeed in those endeavors. The better I looked, the worse he felt. He continually blasted my efforts and put down my ideas, hoping to discourage me. Each time I succeeded, he scoffed and assured me that something would surely go wrong soon.

Perhaps his negativity came from the loss of his father at such an early age. Perhaps it was from his mother's absence when all of his friends' mothers were at home. It may have stemmed from my successes. Wherever it came from, it was surely there. His mother called it "bull-headedness" and was sure it had been inherited from his grandfather.

Fortunately, my own negative background began changing for the better in the first college class I took as a full-time student after we were married. I had grown up tall and spindly, with a set of the worst buck-teeth you can imagine. I was not an achiever in school, being both extremely shy and awkward. In fact, I cannot to this day imagine anyone ANYWHERE with a worse self-image than I had. I considered myself an average student, if that, and was "Wallflower #1" when it came to the dances in high-school.

A simple piece of paper changed my life. I was fortunate enough to have a professor, the first day of classes, who gave us an IQ test and let us see the results. Since he had allowed us to check our own tests, I was sure, upon seeing the results, that I must have cheated. He informed us that this test was for our own information, just because he knew we had never been told the results in previous years.

WHAT A SHOCK! For the first time in my life, I realized that I was not just "average," at least not in intelligence. I made up my mind that day to begin living up to my potential—and that is exactly what I did. I graduated from college with very high honors, in just three years, while working a full-time job. I became very goal-oriented, but even then, I didn't fully understand the TREMENDOUS impact of the words YOU CAN BE ANYTHING YOU WANT TO BE! I always set my sights a little higher than the norm, and I always got EXACTLY what I aimed for. It took a tragedy in my life to show me that I just hadn't been aiming high enough.

Comfortable With the "Status-Quo"

About the time I opened up my clothing store, I began to realize that my husband and I really had very little in common. I was very goal-oriented, obviously an achiever, while he was what I now refer to as "comfortable with the status-quo." It was also about this time that I began to notice, as did my parents and many of our friends, his ever-increasing alcohol consumption. It began with a six-pack or two while working on a race car with a friend, then turned into a martini or two every night after work.

In retrospect, I see a man lost in a world where values were changing quickly; where women could not only make their own decision to have a career, but to be successful and achieve things unheard of only a decade before. He, in turn, like thousands of others, had begun working at a job with which he was not happy, feeling totally unsuccessful and unfulfilled. After finally getting into the career he wanted, he was overshadowed by a wife who was already way ahead of him.

After eleven years of a "tolerable" marriage, we began our family. Our daughters were eighteen months apart, and the oldest had just turned two when I first heard his remarkable prediction. The day before her seventh birthday, after two long years of cancer treatments, he was gone. He died before he reached his 41st birthday.

The rebuilding of my life, after losing my home and virtually everything I had, is quite another story. My incredible rise to fame and fortune in a new home 2000 miles distant, my fantastic new husband, and the reshaping of my children after their devastating experiences, is much too voluminous to include here. I am currently writing a book which will encompass it all. At this time, however, I would like to explore the question that has been haunting me for many years...

How Could This Have Happened?

Does our society, in fact, program us to accept less in life than that which we need to make us happy? Do our schools discourage us from dreaming and becoming successful in the fields we enjoy? Do they try to mold us to fit into the current job market where we will, doubtless, experience discontent and lack of satisfaction?

Having been an elementary school teacher for fifteen years, I can look back and analyze those years, as well as my own years as a student in our public school system. I am not at all happy with what I see, nor can I ever be satisfied until I can find a way to change it.

I see that our schools, from elementary to the higher institutions, are not doing the job for which they are intended. These conclusions come not just from my own observations and experience, but from the comments of other teachers (many of whom have left the profession, as I did) and from college administrators and job placement people. They all agree that the vast majority of young people are embarking on their "chosen" careers without the self-confidence, the dreams and the goal-setting necessary to succeed in that career. Most of them do not BELIEVE they can do well, attain a desirable life-style and make outstanding contributions in THEIR field. They have had their dreams crushed so many times that they have quit dreaming. And most are entering a career to which they have been molded, rather than molding the career to fit THEM.

Our schools are succeeding in teaching our citizens to "fit in," but not to stand out; to get by, but not to succeed. Our colleges teach generalized knowledge, of little use in the accumulation of wealth. As a rule, our teachers specialize on TEACHING knowledge, but not how to organize or USE knowledge. Knowledge is only POTENTIAL power; it first needs to be organized. We must begin to deal more with practice and less with theories.

Every Second is a New Chance

It is little wonder that so many adults today are coming to workshops, such as the one we have developed, to get their spirits lifted and learn how to change their lives. Our S.M.I.L.E workshop (Success Motivation and Improved Lifestyle Education) evolved out of what we perceived to be a need on the part of the people we met to establish a plan for their life, a goal, and to consciously work toward that goal. Our system is an extremely unique, self-reward system that really works for all who use it.

Over the years, I had been reading every self-help book I could squeeze into my busy schedule. I had attended a few workshops on the subject as well.

During my career as a teacher, I had developed a "mini-unit" based on some of this material. It was aimed at building self-confidence and raising the self-esteem of my students. Due to the very highly structured nature of our curriculum, I was told that I could not teach this unit because it was "Not a part of the curriculum." There was not time during the school year to squeeze it in without taking out something "more important." Being the rebel that I was, I continued to work it into my classes until I had a parent complain to my principal. Their child had informed them that he had learned that he was probably picking up negativity at home. As it is when things are taken out of context, this bit of misinformation from one parent had the effect of a minority group lobbying in congress.

My principal looked over the materials I was teaching and agreed that they were valuable; however, public opinion is a hearty opponent. There are very conclusive studies that prove that children perform better when they believe they ARE better, and I was certain that this was the case with my classes. However, I was, once again, asked to refrain from using my materals.

My belief was so strong that this was necessary to every child's education, that I eventually left the teaching profession rather than struggle with my dilemma.

After George's death, I began to realize that I had an opportunity to begin again. We all have that chance every day of our lives, but we are often so caught up with our jobs, family, home, etc., that we don't perceive it as such.

I began using my own system in earnest, applying it to things I had never thought of before. It became obvious to me that the Lord was through "hinting." I wasn't utilizing my talents to the fullest; I just hadn't been paying attention. This time through the tragedies in my life, he was making things perfectly clear, as only He can do.

Within the period of two years, I lost my business (due to city constuction), my father, my husband and my home. All I had left were my children and my teaching job, and that was even on rather shaky ground due to the pressures I had been undergoing. I was being called to a new land, a new family and a new life. With the help of my goal-setting and my "positive-thinking" training, I looked upon all of this as a challenge, and set out for Phoenix with great expectations.

Paradise Can Be Exactly What You Want It to Be

The Valley of the Sun was all that I had expected it to be...I was SURE I was in Paradise! Three and a half years later, I am more sure than ever.

Three years ago, I met and married the most wonderful man in the world. We began a real-estate investment adventure that led to his retirement after just twenty-two months on his new banking job. We literally went from bankruptcy to bliss in two years, and he soon discovered that it was my unique goal-setting system that made all the dif-ference. He began using it then, and we started publishing our far-fetched goals in our monthly investor newsletter. When our investments reached almost $4,000,000 in value, people began asking us

**Dottie Walters receives the
Certified Speaking Professional (CSP) designation
presented by Ty Boyd, past president of the
National Speakers Association.**

DOTTIE WALTERS, C.S.P.
Royal Publishing, Inc.
18825 Hicrest Road
P.O. Box 1120
Glendora, CA 91740
(818) 335-8069

HOW we did it, and the answers have grown from small meetings in our home to full-scale workshops and consulting.

Has My Whole Life Been Just a Dress Rehearsal?

The real growth of our present workshop came after I made a number of interesting discoveries about our clients.

1. They ALL wanted MORE out of life than they were presently getting.
2. None of them were ASKING life for more.
3. They ALL wanted to build a safer, surer retirement fund for themselves than they were currently building.
4. None of them had formulated a plan for achieving this.
5. They ALL lacked a definite purpose in life.
6. None of them BELIEVED they could have whatever they wanted in their life.
7. THEY HAD ALL GONE THROUGH THE PUBLIC SCHOOL SYSTEM IN THIS COUNTRY!
8. None of them had ever been taught how to do any of the things listed above.

That was the day I realized that I had a mission in life—that everything in my life up to this point had just been a dress rehearsal for the real performance. And that is just the beginning.

I am frequently asked, by people who haven't attended our workshop, "Don't you miss teaching?" I will spend the rest of my life teaching—and reaching out to people who are living a life similar to that of my first husband. I know that I can help them to change their lives before they fall too deeply into the pattern to pull themselves out.

If you feel that you are a part of the 95-98% of the people in this country who are NOT satisfied with your life, consider the following.

> *I believe that our society and our schools lead us to do what we don't necessarily enjoy doing.*
> *I believe that this causes many different kinds of stress in our lives—stress from job dissatisfaction as well as stress in competing with others whom we believe to be superior to us in some way.*
> *I believe that stress leads to disease, which is a state of Dis-EASE in our minds or bodies and can surface in the form of numerous ailments.*
> *I believe that this state of Dis-EASE in our bodies can result in death if we don't know how to combat it.*

Don't Get Comfortable— You're Not Done Yet!

Why not take just a fraction of that time that you now spend reading negative headline stories and

watching television's negative life si turn it into positive time? There hundreds of good self-help and self-i books on the market dealing with the stress and positive thinking. Reading bi successful people is a very inspiring w some of your free time. There are also seminars and workshops through whicl can become motivated and build self-confi

A human being is never through growing and developing. Just because you of school" doesn't mean that you should yourself finished. If my own experien taught me anything, it is that each and eve us, no matter who we are or how successfu should make self-improvement a personal, goal in our lives. Remember what hap sunlight when it is focused on a small area th magnifying glass. Depending upon the targ results can be either helpful or destructiv finding out WHAT you really want, setting goals properly, and then going after it, you can sure that you are focusing all of your attention consequently all of your energy, on SUC instead of STRESS.

> *"Be careful what you think about—you're surely going to get it."*
> **—Thomas Carlyle**

watching television's negative life situations, and turn it into positive time? There are literally hundreds of good self-help and self-improvement books on the market dealing with the subjects of stress and positive thinking. Reading biographies of successful people is a very inspiring way to spend some of your free time. There are also numerous seminars and workshops through which a person can become motivated and build self-confidence.

A human being is never through learning, growing and developing. Just because you are "out of school" doesn't mean that you should consider yourself finished. If my own experiences have taught me anything, it is that each and every one of us, no matter who we are or how successful we are, should make self-improvement a personal, on-going goal in our lives. Remember what happens to sunlight when it is focused on a small area through a magnifying glass. Depending upon the target, the results can be either helpful or destructive. By finding out WHAT you really want, setting your goals properly, and then going after it, you can make sure that you are focusing all of your attention, and consequently all of your energy, on SUCCESS instead of STRESS.

> *"Be careful what you think about—you're surely going to get it."*
>
> **—Thomas Carlyle**

**Dottie Walters receives the
Certified Speaking Professional (CSP) designation
presented by Ty Boyd, past president of the
National Speakers Association.**

DOTTIE WALTERS, C.S.P.
Royal Publishing, Inc.
18825 Hicrest Road
P.O. Box 1120
Glendora, CA 91740
(818) 335-8069

Dorothy M. Walters, C.S.P.

Dottie Walters is unique. She began her long and illustrious career with no car, one rickety stroller, two babies, a borrowed typewriter and a high school education. There were no jobs. The country was in a recession when Dottie started down the long road. She put cardboard in her shoes and kicked the wheel back on the stroller each time it came off.

Today Dottie is a World Class Speaker, President of her International Speakers Bureau and Publisher of the largest newsmagazine in the world of Speakers. She has been honored three times by the National Speakers Association, with the Certified Speaking Professional designation, one of the first four United States women to receive it. She is a founding member of N.S.A., as well as the founding member and officer of the Greater Los Angeles N.S.A. Chapter. She has initiated and sold several businesses, all based on advertising and publishing. She is Executive Director of International Group of Agents and Bureaus.

She is president of four corporations, author, speaker, seminar leader, publisher (anthologies featuring outstanding speakers), poet, featured in many TV radio shows, newspaper and magazine articles, books and cassettes worldwide. Her first book, Never Underestimate the Selling Power of a Woman *is in its 14th edition.*

Dottie and Bob Walters have three children, an attorney, a drama teacher and the manager of their International Speakers Bureau. Dottie and Bob live in Glendora, California.

Epilog

The Ancient Chinese Secret
by Dottie Walters, C.S.P.

In the Chinese Language whole words are written with a symbol. Often two completely unlike symbols when put together, have a meaning different than either of their two separate components.

An example is the symbol for "Man," and that for "Woman." When combined, they mean "Good." How wise are the Chinese.

These two symbols above stand for "Trouble," and "Gathering Crisis." When brought together, as they are here, they mean "Opportunity."

As the answers always lie in the questions, so the opportunities of life lie directly in our problems. Thomas Edison said, "There is much more Opportunity than there are people to see it."

All great leaders emerge when a crisis occurs. In the life of people of achievement we read repeatedly of terrible trouble which forced them to rise above the commonplace. Not only did they find the answers but they discovered a tremendous power within themselves. Like a ground swell far out in the ocean, this force within explodes into a mighty wave when we overcome. Then out steps the athlete, the author, the statesman, the scientist, the businessperson creating jobs for many people. David Sarnoff said, "There is plenty of security in the cemetery, I long only for opportunity."

People of achievement know this secret. The winds of adversity cannot shake them. As Charles Lummis said:

"I am bigger than anything that can happen to me.

"All these things—sorrow, misfortune and suffering—are outside my door.

"I am in the house, and I *have the key!*"

Here is the secret of the ancient Chinese:

"Hidden in trouble lies the key,
our own magnificent opportunity."

ORDER FORM

ROYAL PUBLISHING, INC.
18825 Hicrest Road, P.O. Box 1120
Glendora, California 91740
(818) 335-8069 or call toll-free (800) 438-1242

Name _____

Organization_____ Title _____

Address _____

City_____ State _____ Zip _____

Phone (day) _____ (evening) _____

☐ *I have enclosed a check/money order for $* _____

☐ *MasterCard*   ☐ *Visa account #* _____

Exp. date _____ *Signature* _____

Include $3.00 shipping and handling. California residents add 6½% sales tax.

TOTAL ORDER: $ _____